LOVE

JESSE REKLAW

FANTAGRAPHICS BOOKS INC
7563 LAKE CITY WAY NE
SEATTLE, WASHINGTON, 98115
EDITOR AND ASSOCIATE PUBLISHER:
  ERIC REYNOLDS
BOOK DESIGN: MICHAEL HECK
PRODUCTION: PAUL BARESH
PUBLISHER: GARY GROTH

ISBN 978-1-60699-937-0
LIBRARY OF CONGRESS CONTROL NUMBER:
  2016933586

FIRST PRINTING: JUNE 2016
PRINTED IN SOUTH KOREA

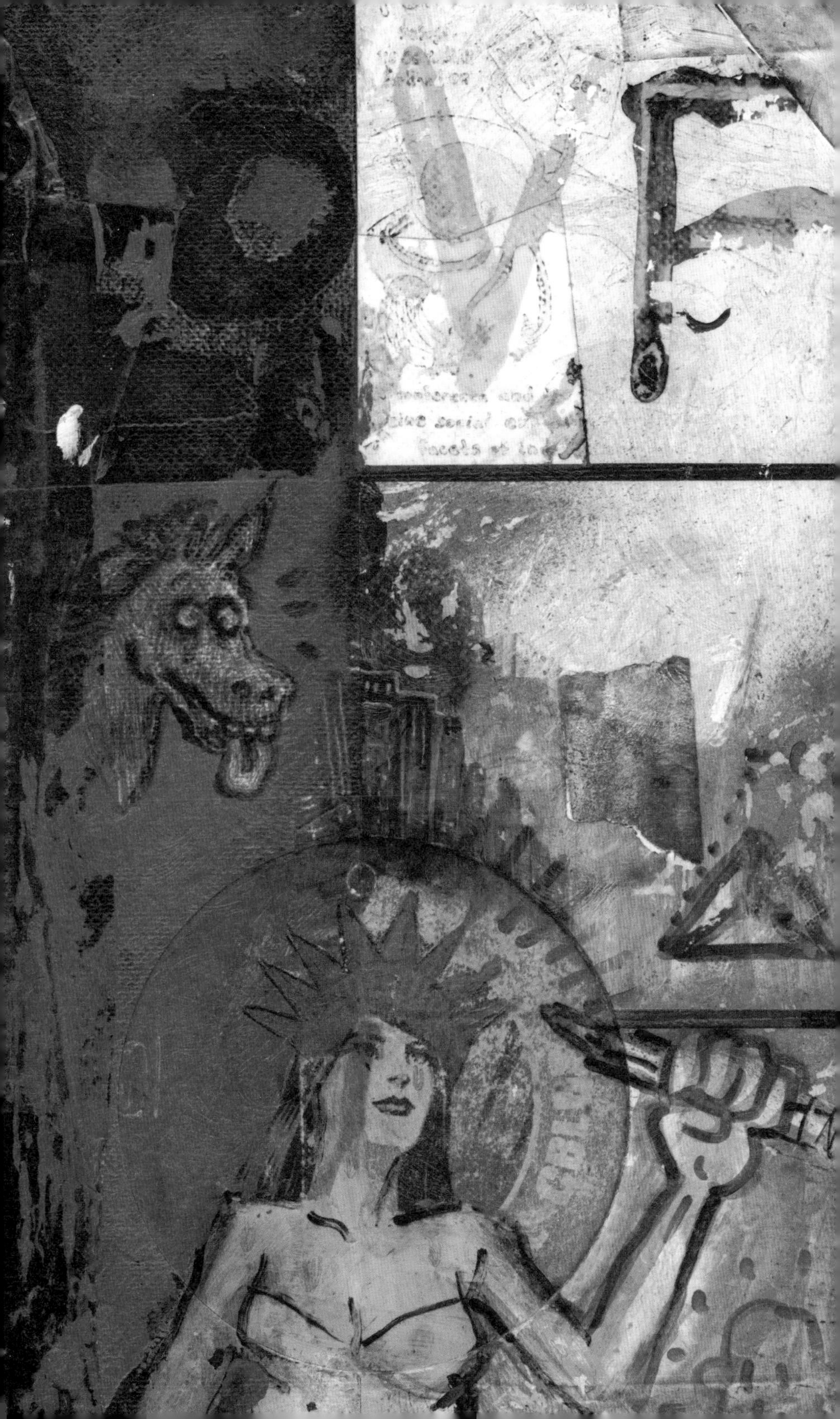

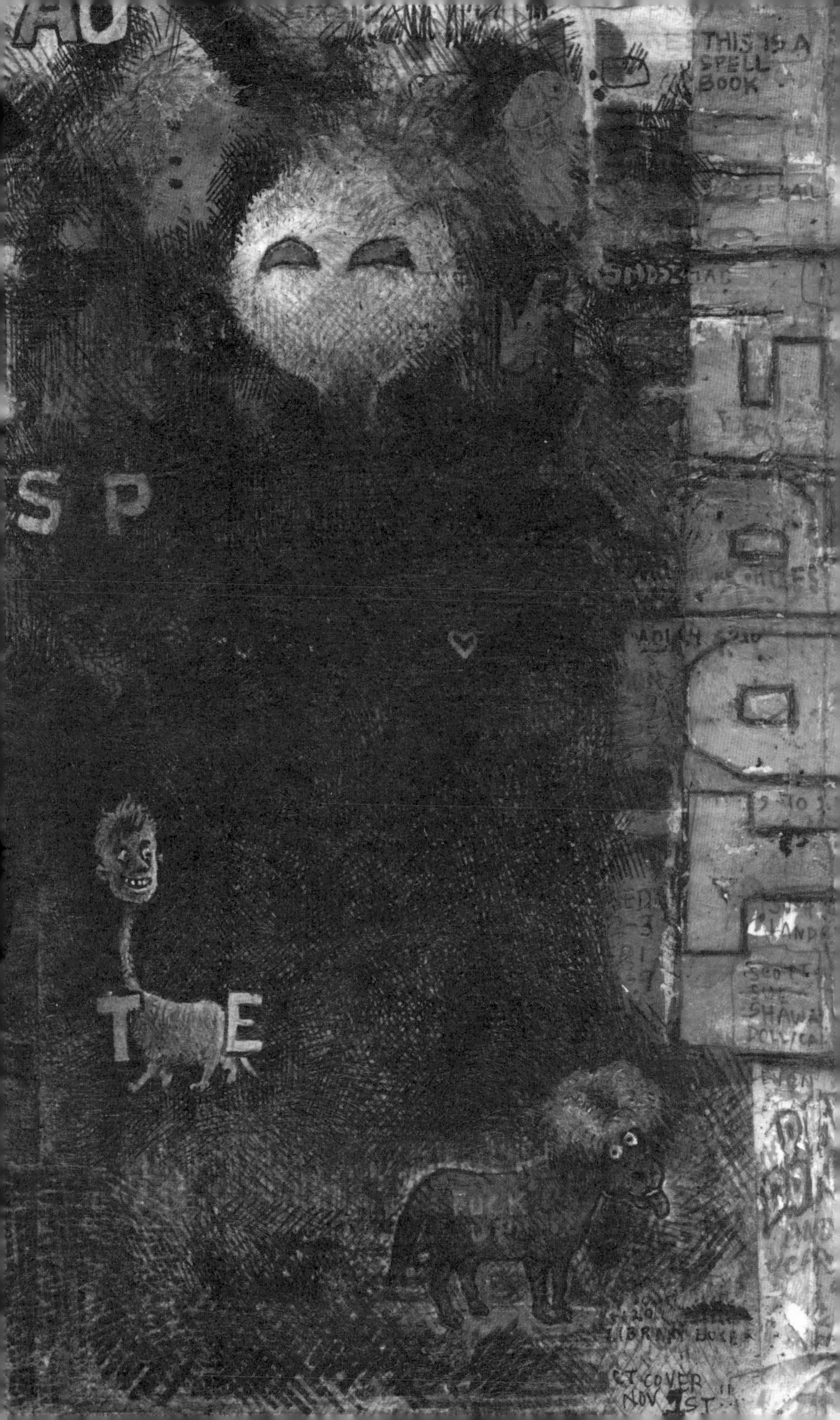
AU
THIS IS A SPELL BOOK
S P
T E
CT COVER NOV 1ST

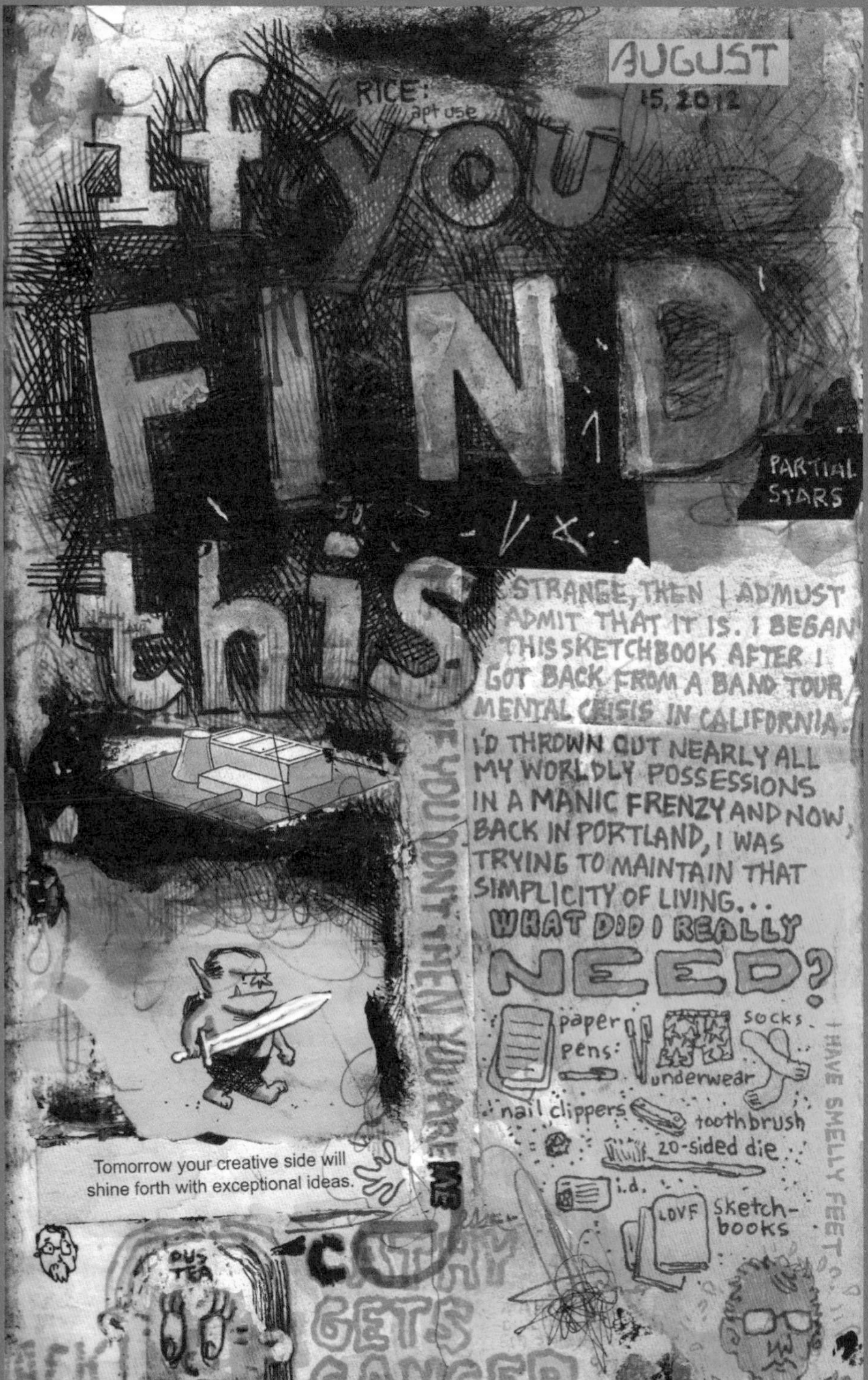
AUGUST
15, 2012
RICE:
apt use
if YOU FIND this
PARTIAL STARS
STRANGE, THEN I AD MUST ADMIT THAT IT IS. I BEGAN THIS SKETCHBOOK AFTER I GOT BACK FROM A BAND TOUR / MENTAL CRISIS IN CALIFORNIA.
I'D THROWN OUT NEARLY ALL MY WORLDLY POSSESSIONS IN A MANIC FRENZY AND NOW, BACK IN PORTLAND, I WAS TRYING TO MAINTAIN THAT SIMPLICITY OF LIVING...
WHAT DID I REALLY NEED?
paper
pens
underwear
socks
nail clippers
toothbrush
20-sided die
i.d.
sketch-books
LOVF
I HAVE SMELLY FEET
IF YOU DON'T THEN YOU ARE ME
Tomorrow your creative side will shine forth with exceptional ideas.
DUS TEA
GETS CANCER

PENTEL SES 15
Pentel
SIGN PEN
ABCDEF
GHIJKL
MNOPQR
STUVWXYZ
123456789
LUCY
MUFFIN
STOP

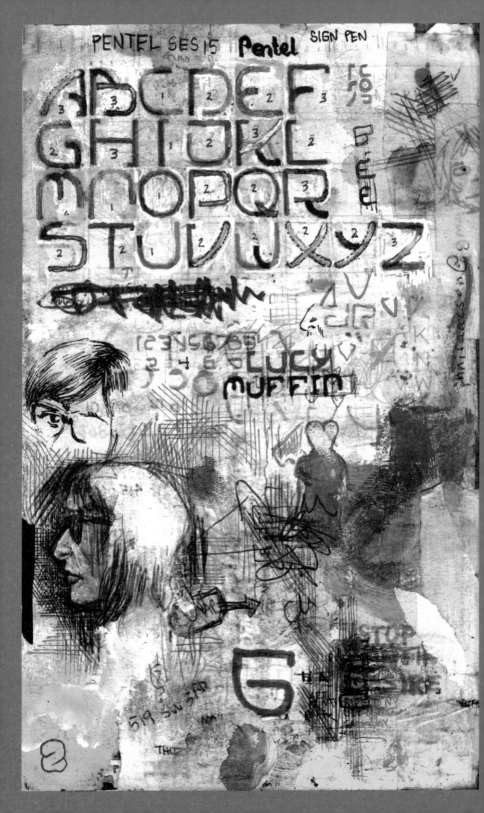

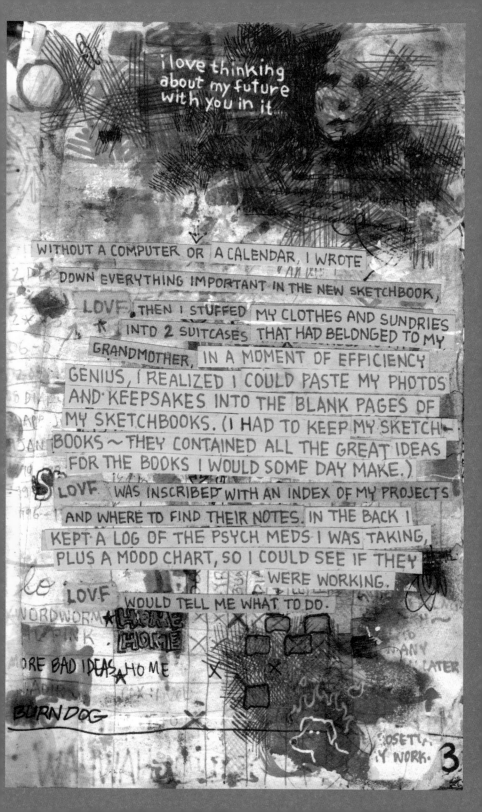

i love thinking
about my future
with you in it

WITHOUT A COMPUTER OR A CALENDAR, I WROTE
DOWN EVERYTHING IMPORTANT IN THE NEW SKETCHBOOK,
LOVE, THEN I STUFFED MY CLOTHES AND SUNDRIES
INTO 2 SUITCASES THAT HAD BELONGED TO MY
GRANDMOTHER, IN A MOMENT OF EFFICIENCY
GENIUS, I REALIZED I COULD PASTE MY PHOTOS
AND KEEPSAKES INTO THE BLANK PAGES OF
MY SKETCHBOOKS. (I HAD TO KEEP MY SKETCH-
BOOKS ~ THEY CONTAINED ALL THE GREAT IDEAS
FOR THE BOOKS I WOULD SOME DAY MAKE.)
LOVE WAS INSCRIBED WITH AN INDEX OF MY PROJECTS
AND WHERE TO FIND THEIR NOTES. IN THE BACK I
KEPT A LOG OF THE PSYCH MEDS I WAS TAKING,
PLUS A MOOD CHART, SO I COULD SEE IF THEY
WERE WORKING.
LOVE WOULD TELL ME WHAT TO DO.

NORDWORM
PINK
HOME
HOME
MORE BAD IDEAS HOME

BURN DOG

Y WORK 3

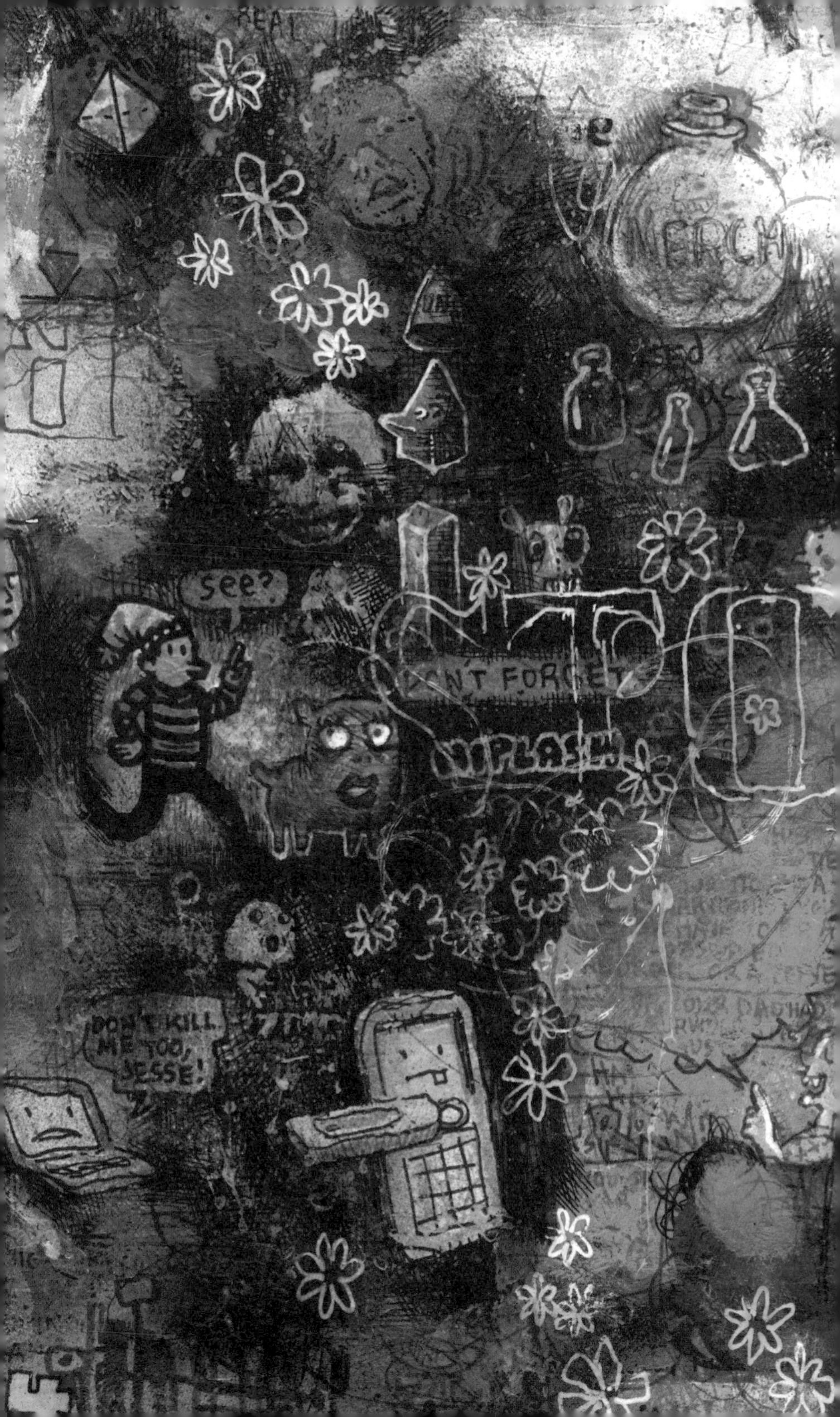
MERCH
see?
DON'T FORGET
DON'T KILL ME TOO, JESSE!

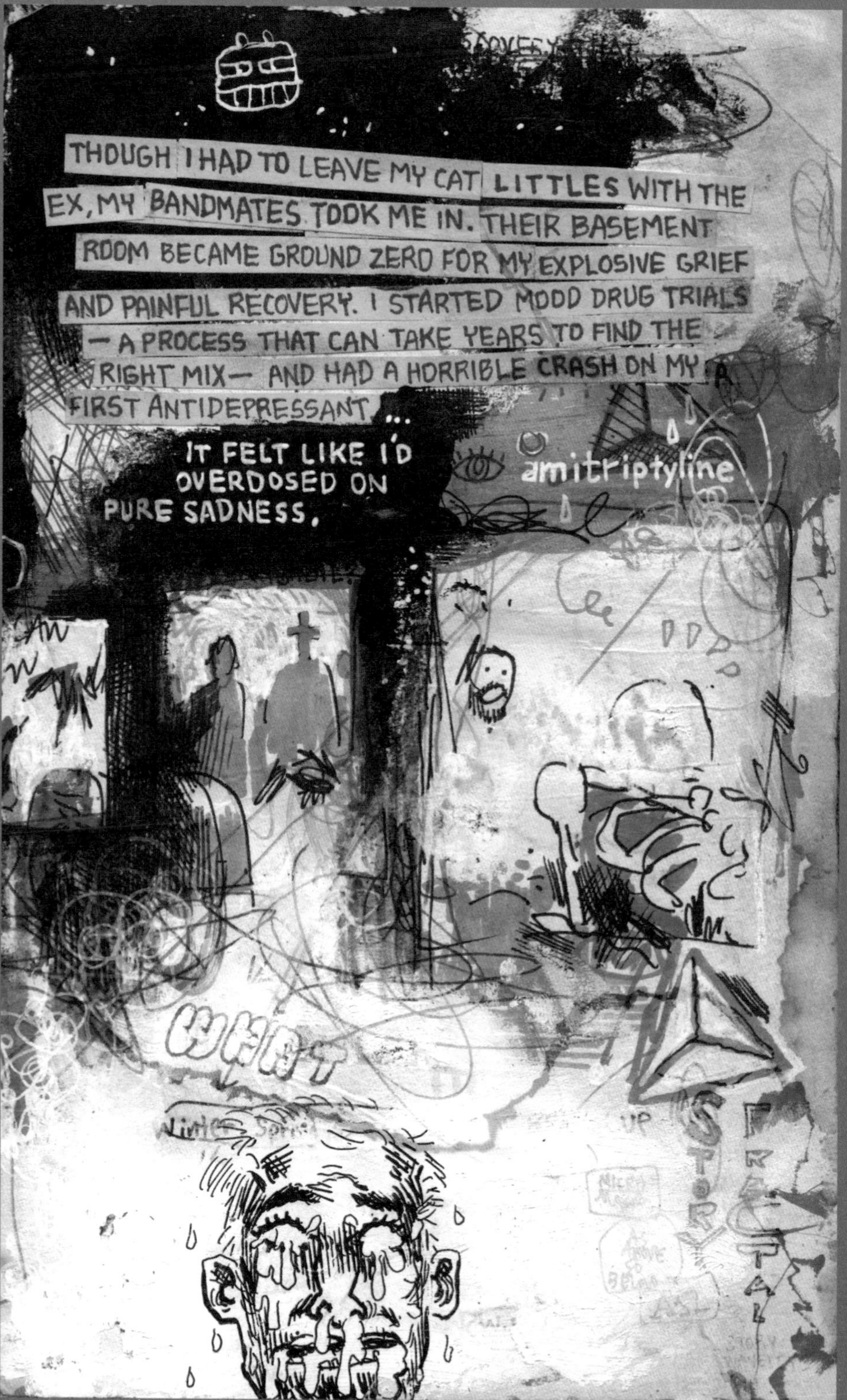
THOUGH I HAD TO LEAVE MY CAT LITTLES WITH THE EX, MY BANDMATES TOOK ME IN. THEIR BASEMENT ROOM BECAME GROUND ZERO FOR MY EXPLOSIVE GRIEF AND PAINFUL RECOVERY. I STARTED MOOD DRUG TRIALS — A PROCESS THAT CAN TAKE YEARS TO FIND THE RIGHT MIX— AND HAD A HORRIBLE CRASH ON MY FIRST ANTIDEPRESSANT...
IT FELT LIKE I'D OVERDOSED ON PURE SADNESS.
amitriptyline
WHAT
STORY
FRACTAL

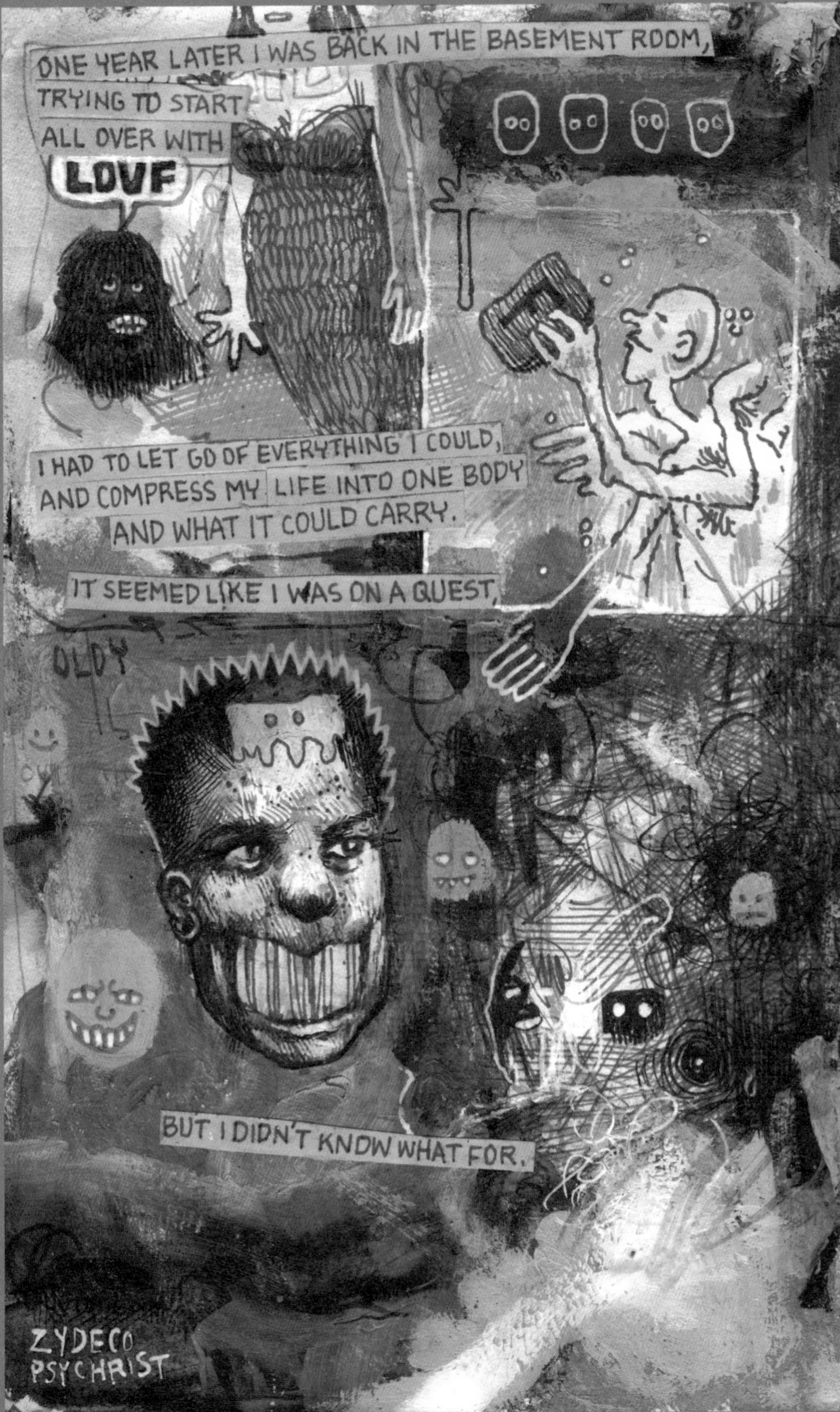

ONE YEAR LATER I WAS BACK IN THE BASEMENT ROOM,
TRYING TO START
ALL OVER WITH
LOVF
I HAD TO LET GO OF EVERYTHING I COULD,
AND COMPRESS MY LIFE INTO ONE BODY
AND WHAT IT COULD CARRY.
IT SEEMED LIKE I WAS ON A QUEST,
OLDY
BUT I DIDN'T KNOW WHAT FOR.
ZYDECO
PSYCHRIST

THE ITALIAN NAVIGATOR HAS JUST LANDED IN THE NEW WORLD.
RALPH EINSTEIN
WOW, THAT'S CREEPY
STAR PUBES
JULES FERMI
TRITOSIS
HALLUCINATION
FOOD
PSYCHEDELIC
GUILID FERMI
ARCHITECTURAL BUILDING
FERMI ROD

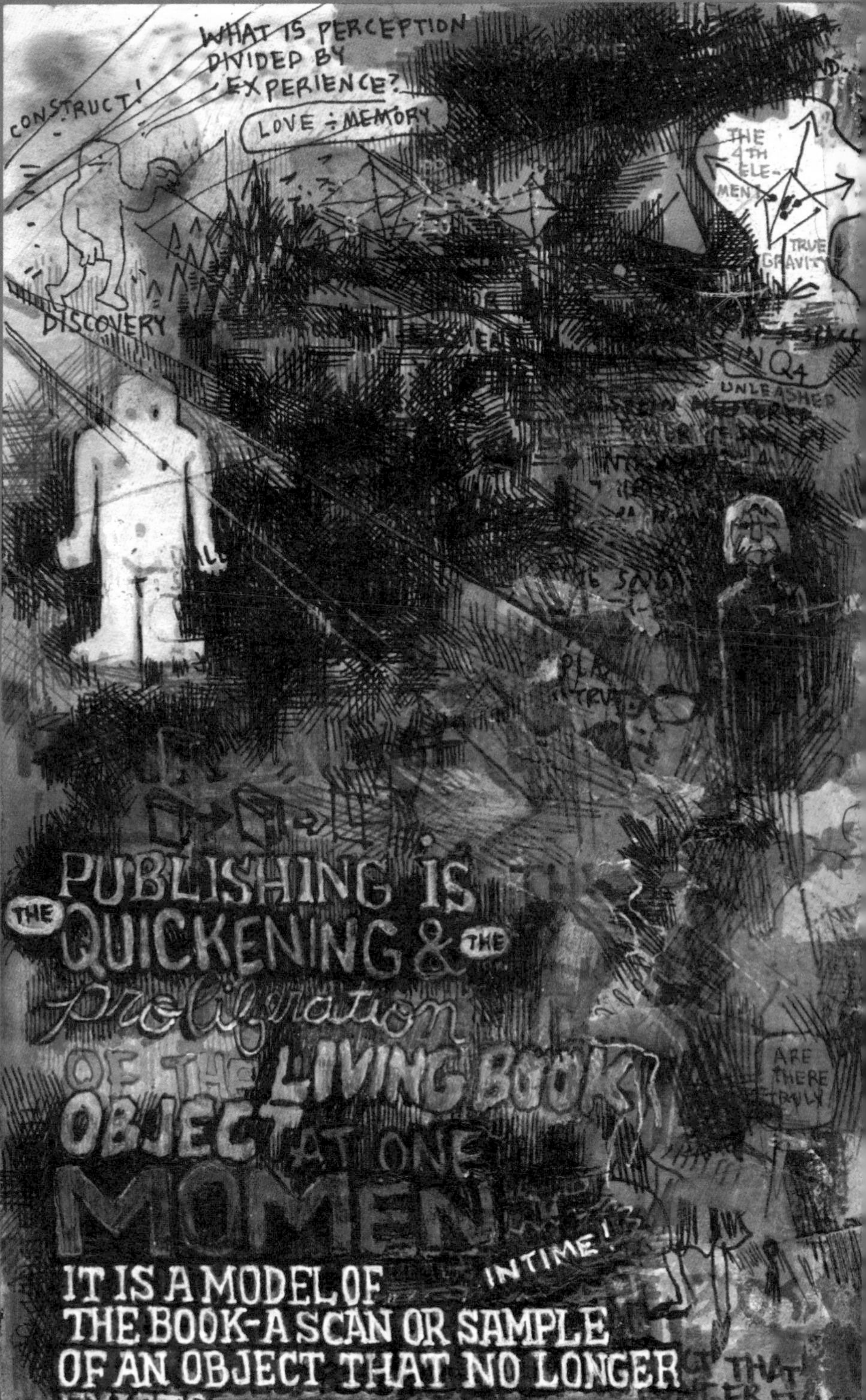
WHAT IS PERCEPTION DIVIDED BY EXPERIENCE?
CONSTRUCT!
LOVE ÷ MEMORY
THE 4TH ELE-MENT
TRUE GRAVITY
DISCOVERY
Q4
UNLEASHED
ARE THERE TRULY
PUBLISHING IS THE QUICKENING & THE proliferation OF THE LIVING BOOK OBJECT AT ONE MOMEN
IN TIME!
IT IS A MODEL OF THE BOOK-A SCAN OR SAMPLE OF AN OBJECT THAT NO LONGER EXISTS
THE PUBLISHED BOOK IS NOT THE BOOK!

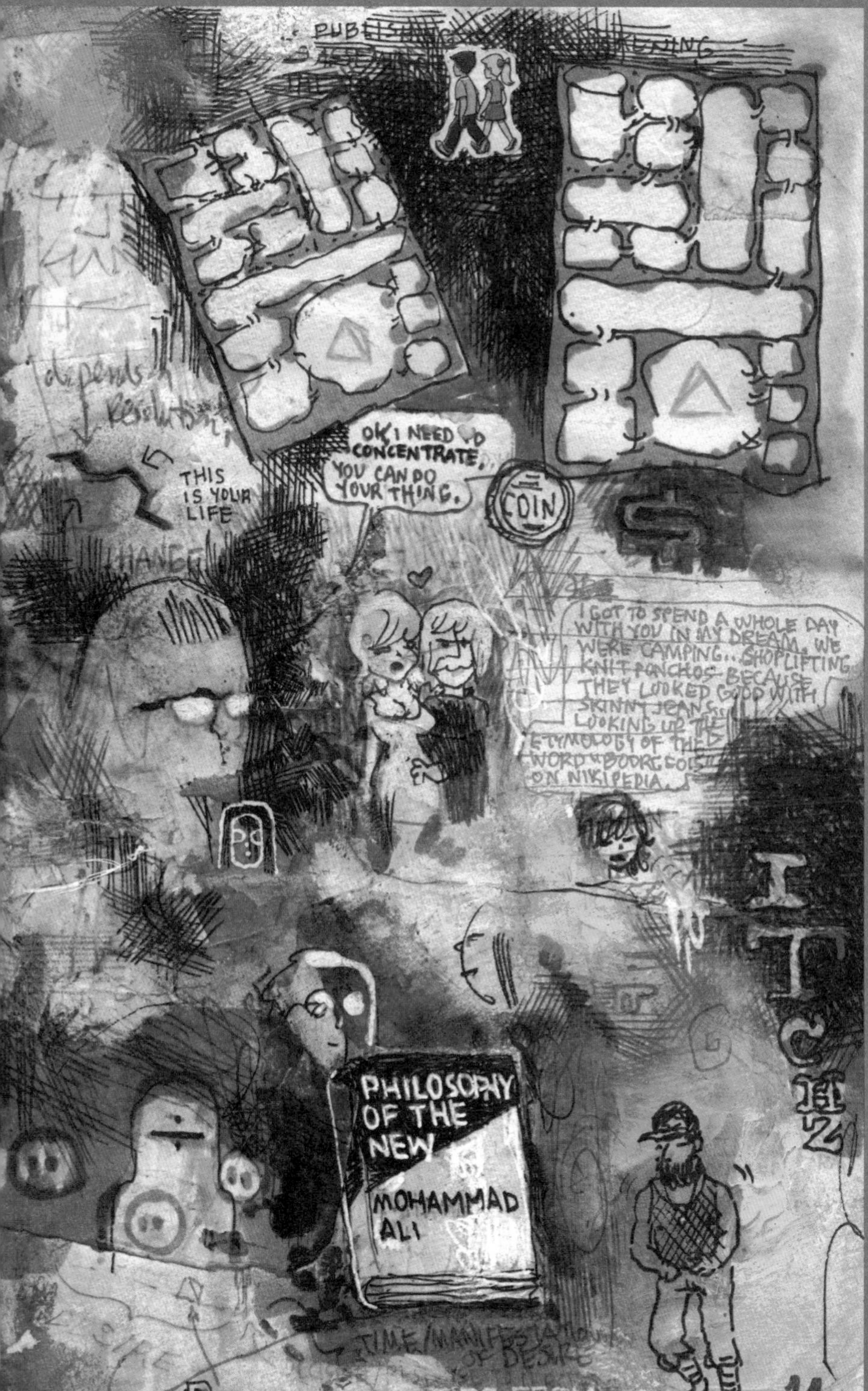

OK, I NEED TO CONCENTRATE. YOU CAN DO YOUR THING.
THIS IS YOUR LIFE
COIN
I GOT TO SPEND A WHOLE DAY WITH YOU IN MY DREAM. WE WERE CAMPING... SHOPLIFTING KNIT PONCHOS BECAUSE THEY LOOKED GOOD WITH SKINNY JEANS... LOOKING UP THE ETYMOLOGY OF THE WORD "BOURGEOIS" ON WIKIPEDIA.
PHILOSOPHY OF THE NEW
MOHAMMAD ALI
TIME/MANIFESTATION OF DESIRE
RESOLUTION

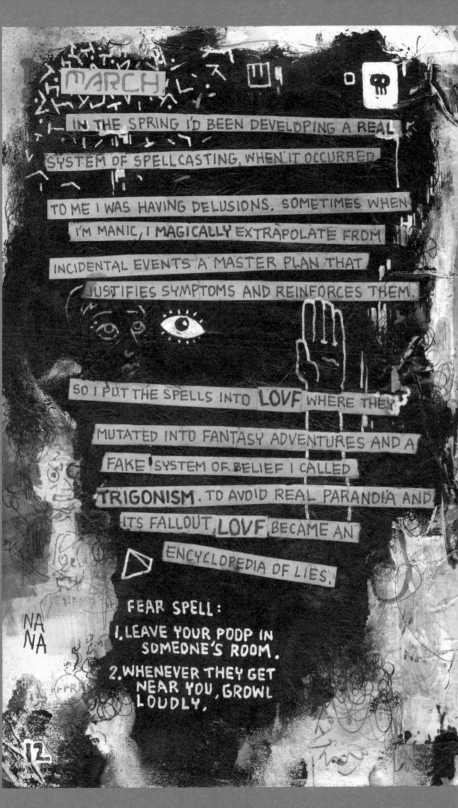

MARCH.

IN THE SPRING I'D BEEN DEVELOPING A REAL SYSTEM OF SPELLCASTING, WHEN IT OCCURRED TO ME I WAS HAVING DELUSIONS. SOMETIMES WHEN I'M MANIC, I MAGICALLY EXTRAPOLATE FROM INCIDENTAL EVENTS A MASTER PLAN THAT JUSTIFIES SYMPTOMS AND REINFORCES THEM.

SO I PUT THE SPELLS INTO LOVF WHERE THEY MUTATED INTO FANTASY ADVENTURES AND A FAKE SYSTEM OF BELIEF I CALLED TRIGONISM. TO AVOID REAL PARANOIA AND ITS FALLOUT, LOVF BECAME AN ENCYCLOPEDIA OF LIES.

FEAR SPELL:
1. LEAVE YOUR POOP IN SOMEONE'S ROOM.
2. WHENEVER THEY GET NEAR YOU, GROWL LOUDLY.

NA NA

12

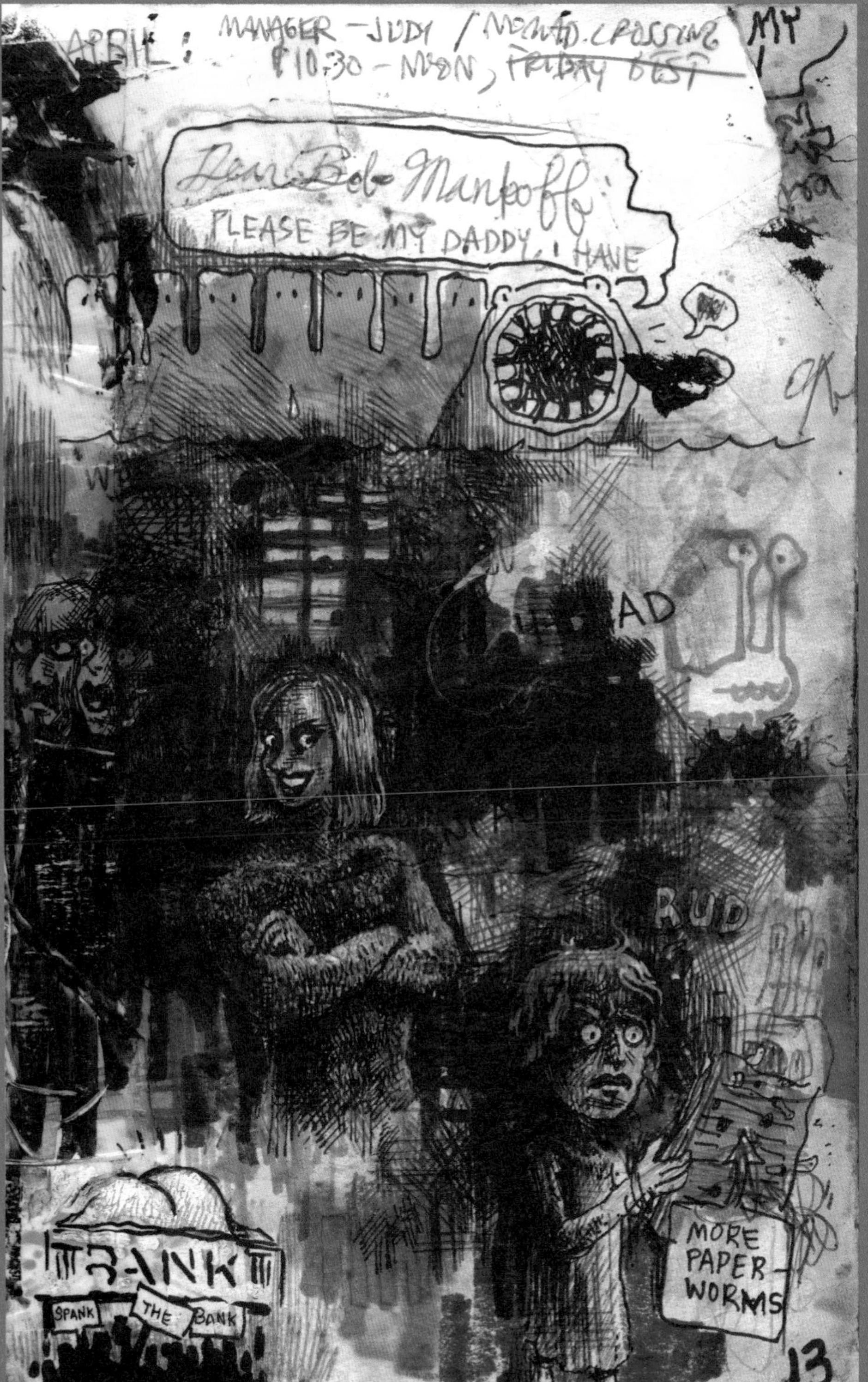

MANAGER - JUDY
Dear Bob Mankoff
PLEASE BE MY DADDY, I HAVE
RUD
MORE PAPER - WORMS
BANK
SPANK THE BANK

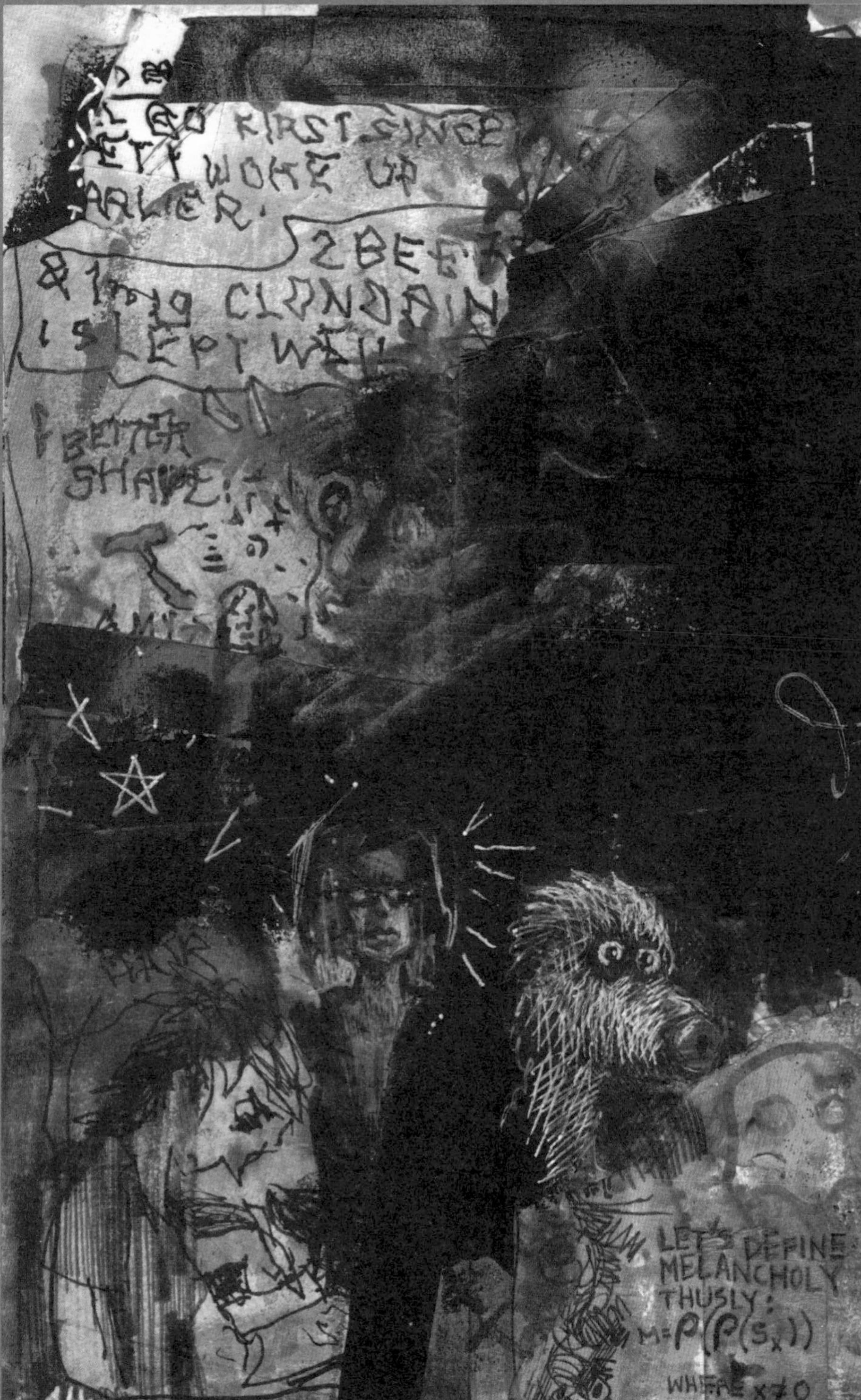
L GO FIRST SINCE
I WOKE UP
ARLIER.
2 BEE
& 1
I SLEPT WELL
BETTER SHAVE!
LET'S DEFINE MELANCHOLY THUSLY:
M=P(P(Sx))
WHERE x≠0

DRAWN WITH MY LEFT HAND ON THE BUS
AND THEN NOT
LITTLES
TRASH CAN MAN
live by my wills
steal

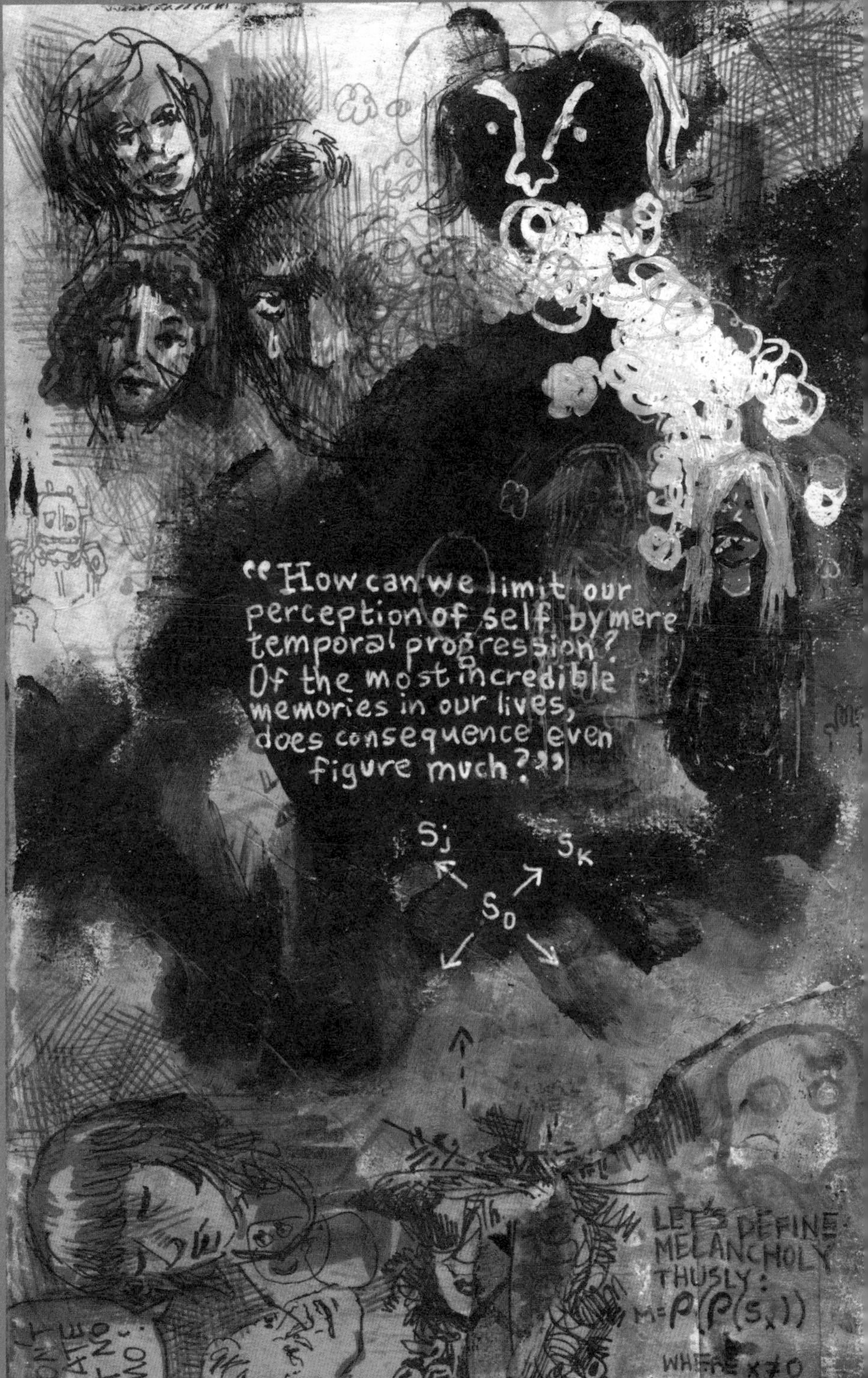
"How can we limit our perception of self by mere temporal progression? Of the most incredible memories in our lives, does consequence even figure much?"
S_j
S_k
S_0
LET'S DEFINE MELANCHOLY THUSLY:
M=P(P(S,1))
WHERE x>0
DON'T HATE ON IT MO.

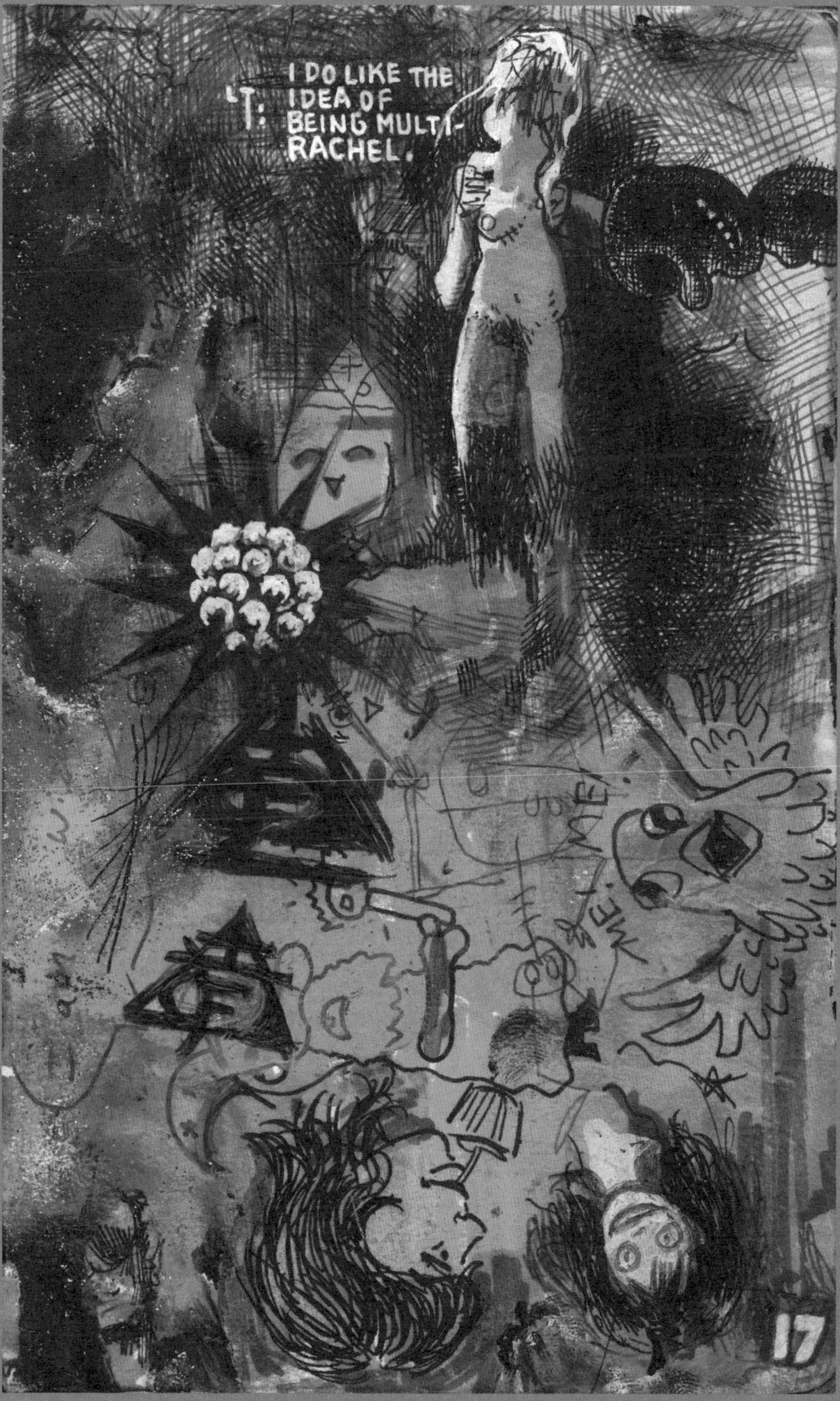
T: I DO LIKE THE IDEA OF BEING MULTI-RACHEL.
ME!
ME.

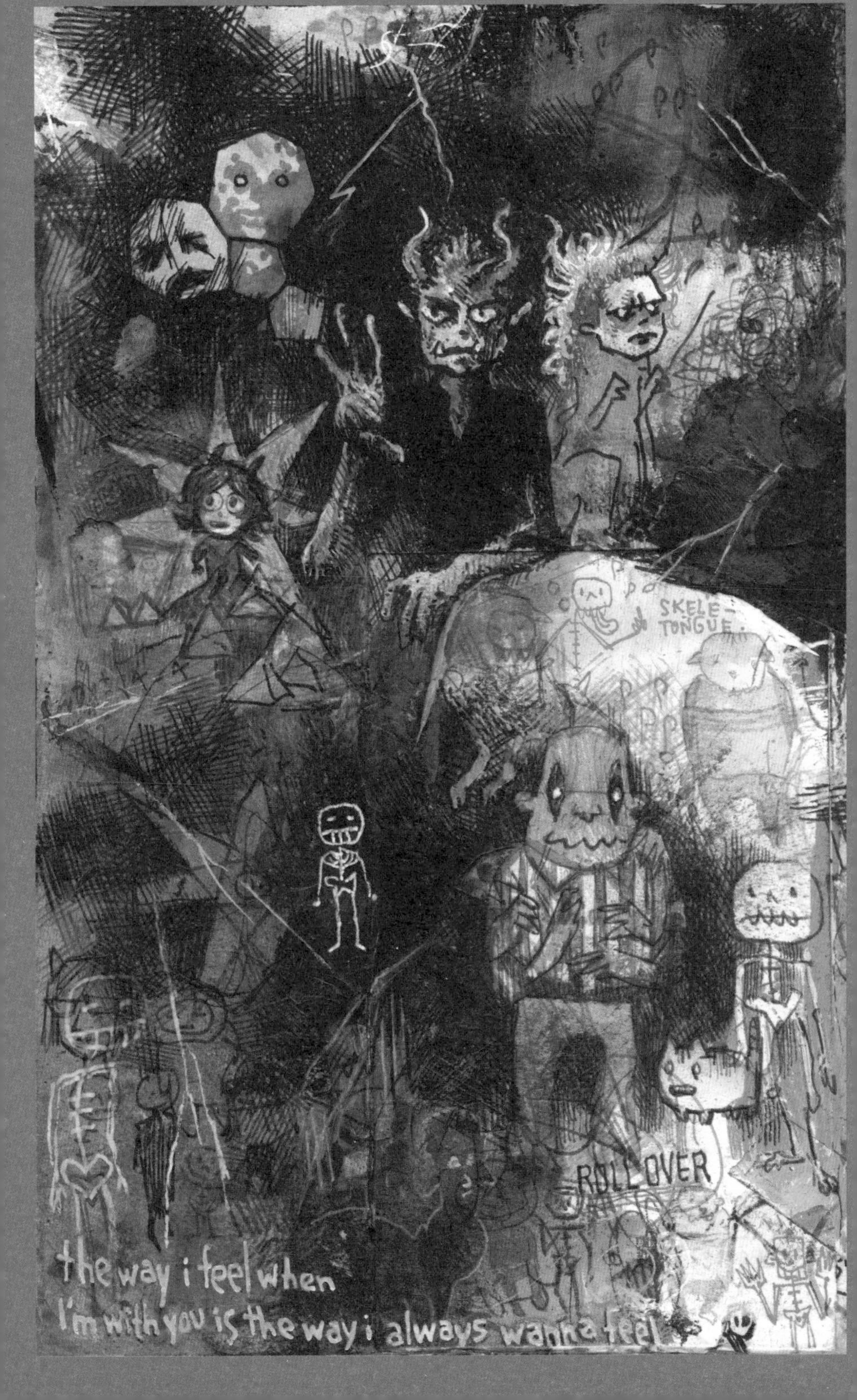
SKELE-
TONGUE.
ROLL OVER
the way i feel when
I'm with you is the way i always wanna feel

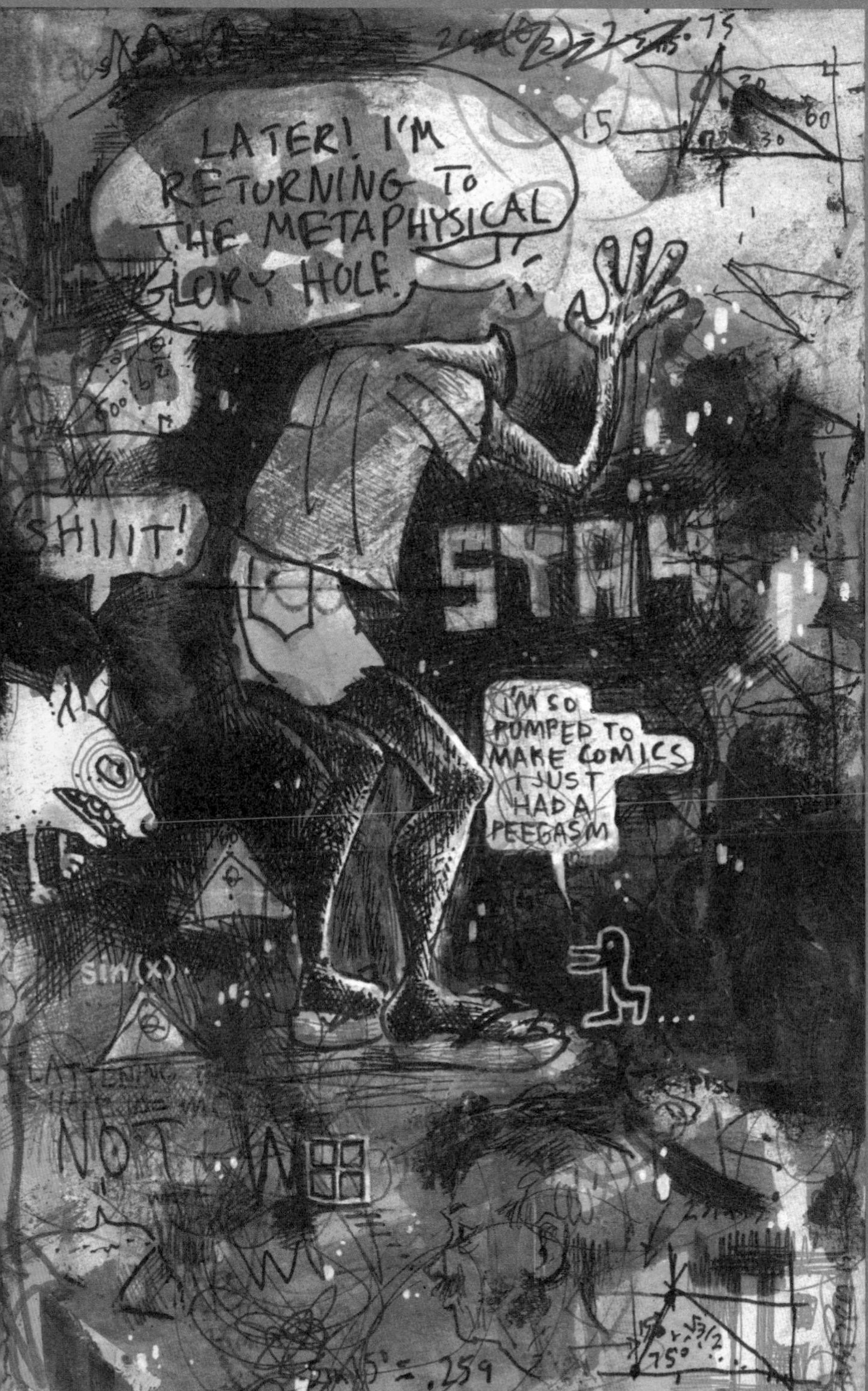

LATER! I'M RETURNING TO THE METAPHYSICAL GLORY HOLE.
SHIIIT!
I'M SO PUMPED TO MAKE COMICS I JUST HAD A PEEGASM
sin(x)
NOT
.259
.966

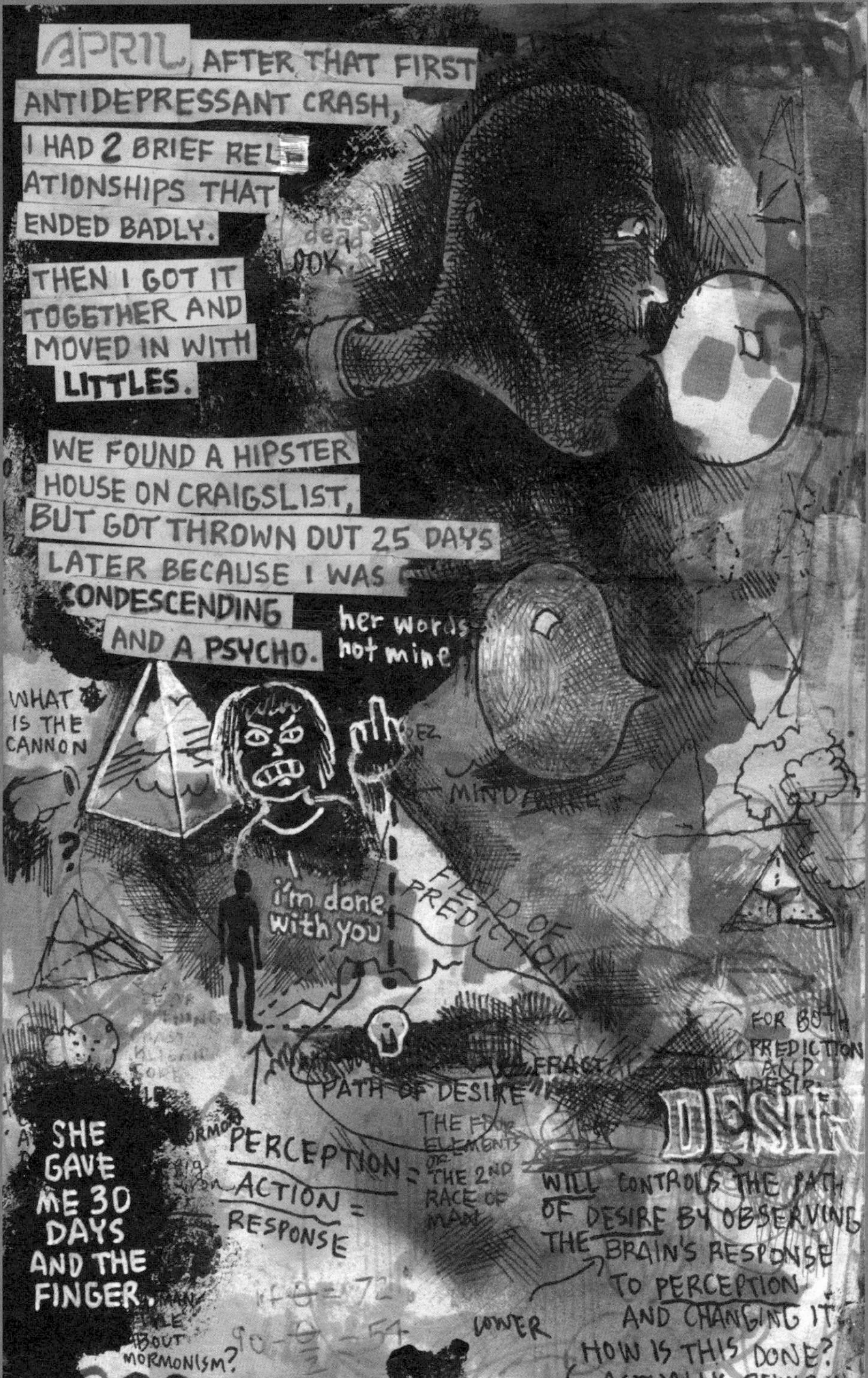
APRIL, AFTER THAT FIRST ANTIDEPRESSANT CRASH, I HAD 2 BRIEF RELATIONSHIPS THAT ENDED BADLY.
she's dead LOOK
THEN I GOT IT TOGETHER AND MOVED IN WITH LITTLES.
WE FOUND A HIPSTER HOUSE ON CRAIGSLIST, BUT GOT THROWN OUT 25 DAYS LATER BECAUSE I WAS CONDESCENDING AND A PSYCHO.
her words not mine
WHAT IS THE CANNON
?
MIND
FIELD OF PREDICTION
i'm done with you
PATH OF DESIRE
FRACT
FOR BOTH PREDICTION AND DESIRE
DESIR
SHE GAVE ME 30 DAYS AND THE FINGER.
PERCEPTION = ACTION = RESPONSE
THE FOUR ELEMENTS OF THE 2ND RACE OF MAN
WILL CONTROLS THE PATH OF DESIRE BY OBSERVING THE BRAIN'S RESPONSE TO PERCEPTION AND CHANGING IT.
LOWER
HOW IS THIS DONE?
ACTUALLY REWIRIN
MORMONISM?
20

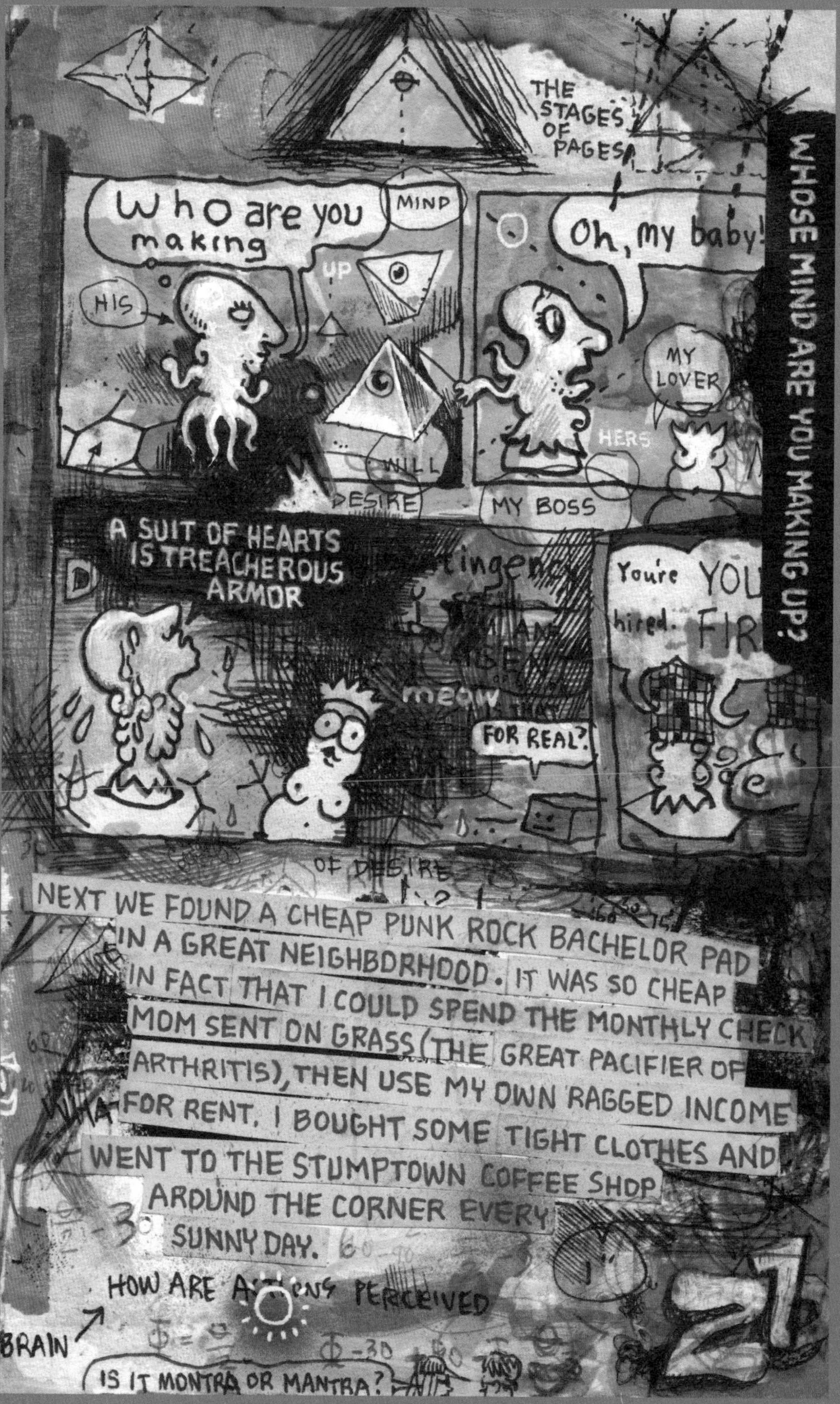
THE STAGES OF PAGES
WHOSE MIND ARE YOU MAKING UP?
Who are you making
MIND
UP
HIS
Oh, my baby!
MY LOVER
HERS
WILL
DESIRE
MY BOSS
A SUIT OF HEARTS IS TREACHEROUS ARMOR
meow
FOR REAL?
You're hired.
YOU FIR
OF DESIRE
NEXT WE FOUND A CHEAP PUNK ROCK BACHELOR PAD IN A GREAT NEIGHBORHOOD. IT WAS SO CHEAP IN FACT THAT I COULD SPEND THE MONTHLY CHECK MOM SENT ON GRASS (THE GREAT PACIFIER OF ARTHRITIS), THEN USE MY OWN RAGGED INCOME FOR RENT. I BOUGHT SOME TIGHT CLOTHES AND WENT TO THE STUMPTOWN COFFEE SHOP AROUND THE CORNER EVERY SUNNY DAY.
HOW ARE ACTIONS PERCEIVED
BRAIN
IS IT MONTRA OR MANTRA?
27

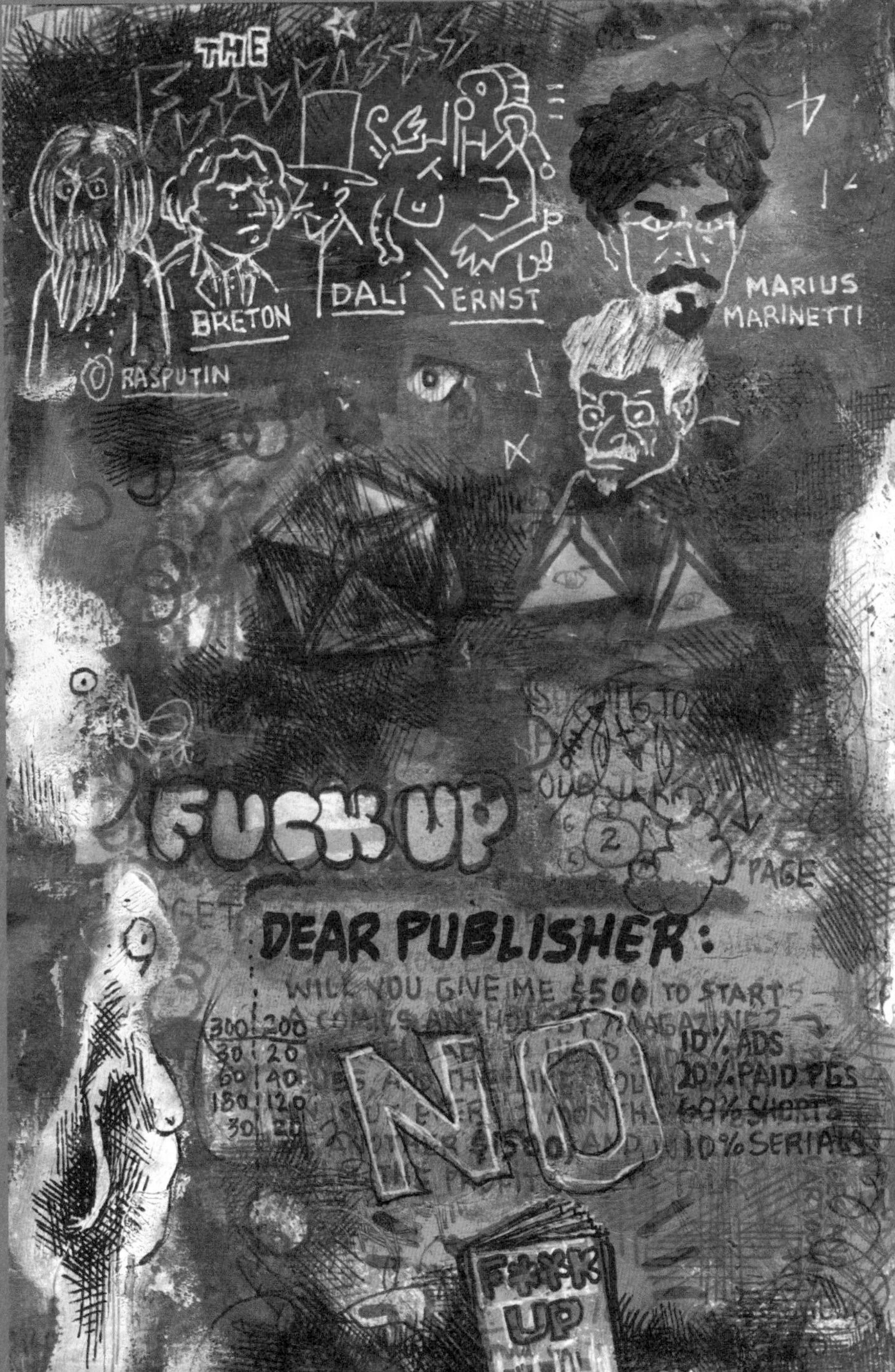
THE
BRETON
DALÍ
ERNST
RASPUTIN
MARIUS
MARINETTI
FUCK UP
PAGE
DEAR PUBLISHER:
WILL YOU GIVE ME $500 TO START
300 200
30 20
60 40
180 120
30 20
10% ADS
20% PAID PGS
60% SHORTS
10% SERIALS
NO
F**K UP
OUR LORD
& FAILURE

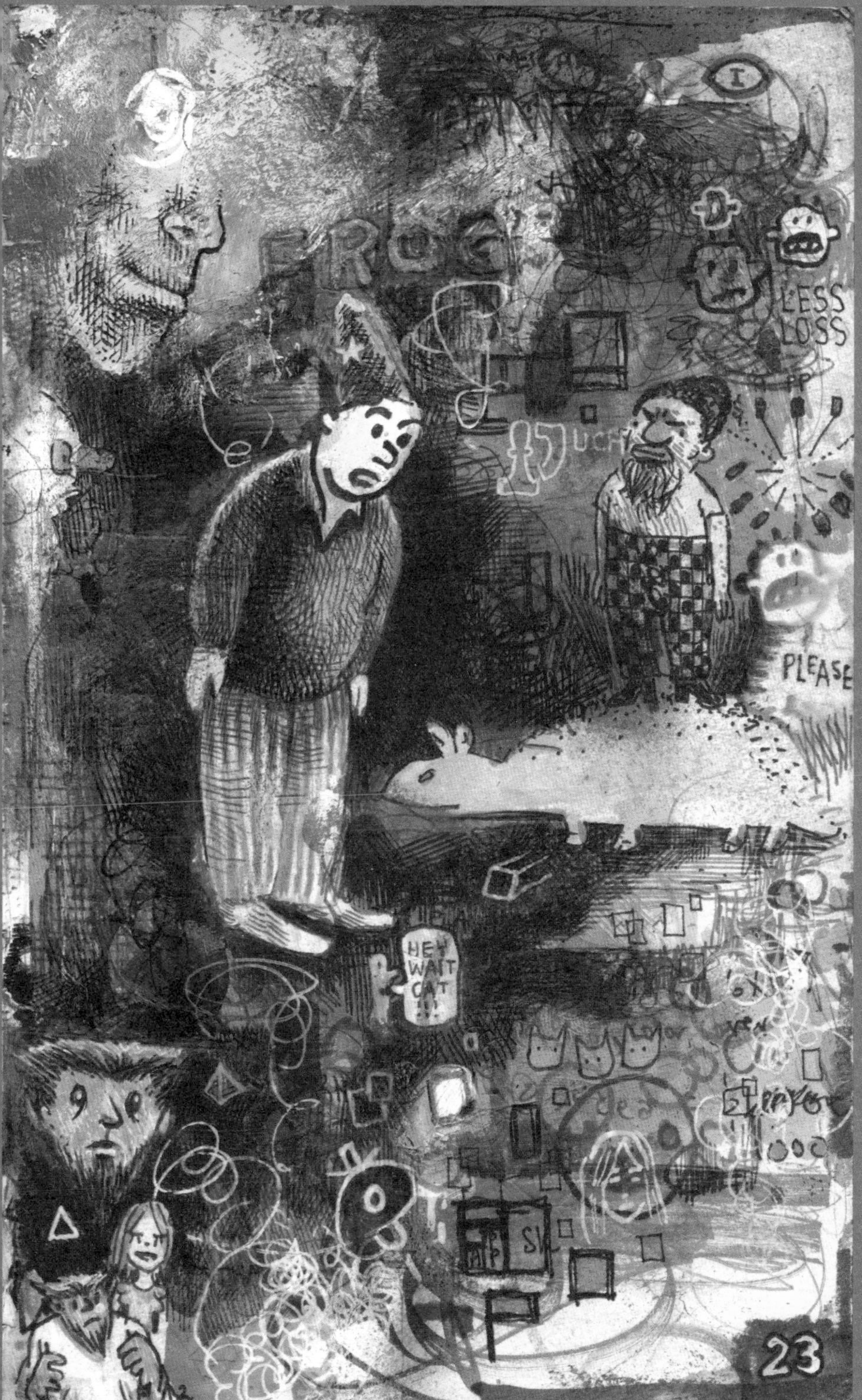
LESS
LOSS
PLEASE
HEY WAIT CAT

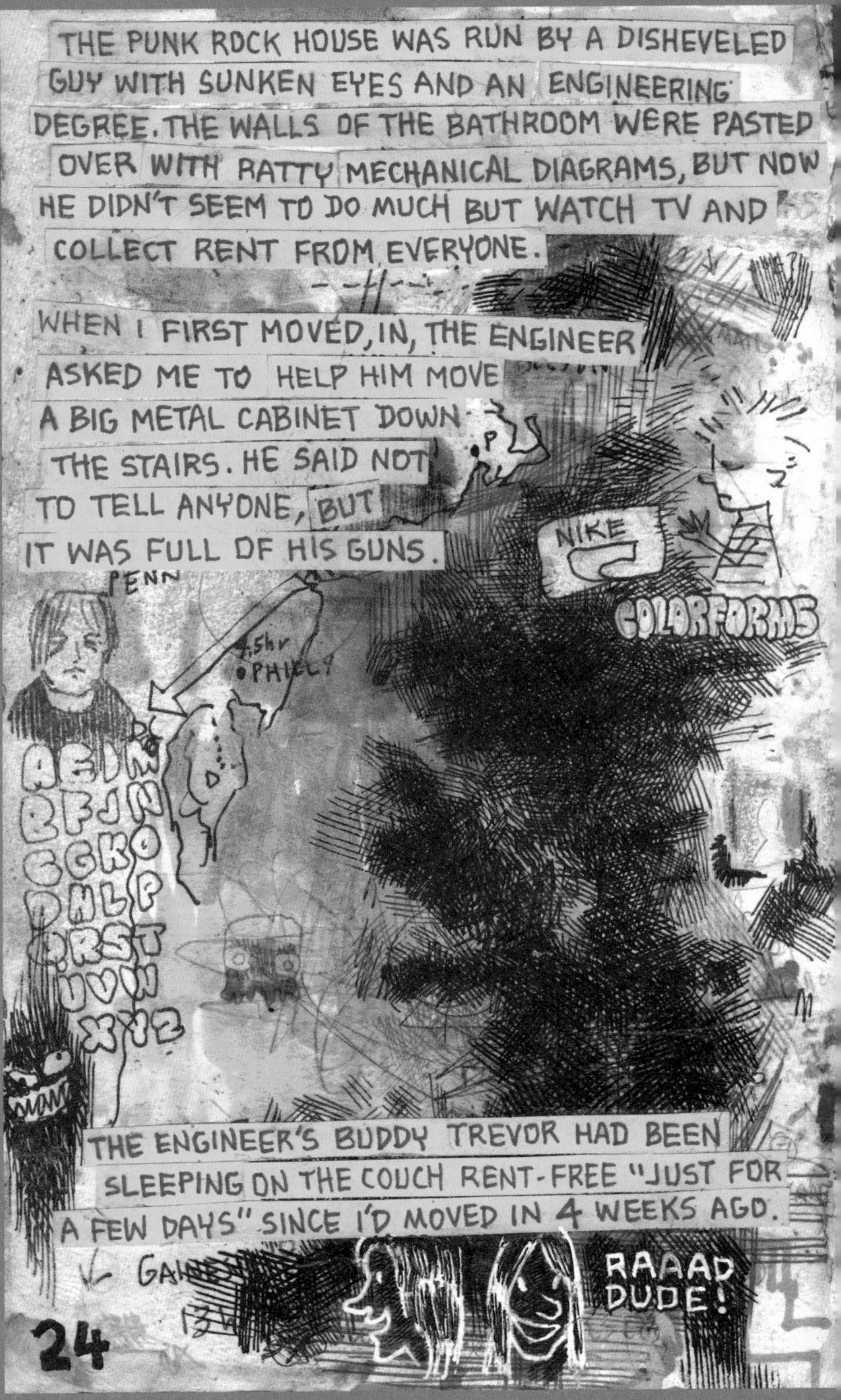
THE PUNK ROCK HOUSE WAS RUN BY A DISHEVELED GUY WITH SUNKEN EYES AND AN ENGINEERING DEGREE. THE WALLS OF THE BATHROOM WERE PASTED OVER WITH RATTY MECHANICAL DIAGRAMS, BUT NOW HE DIDN'T SEEM TO DO MUCH BUT WATCH TV AND COLLECT RENT FROM EVERYONE.
WHEN I FIRST MOVED IN, THE ENGINEER ASKED ME TO HELP HIM MOVE A BIG METAL CABINET DOWN THE STAIRS. HE SAID NOT TO TELL ANYONE, BUT IT WAS FULL OF HIS GUNS.
NIKE
COLORFORMS
4.5hr
PHILLY
THE ENGINEER'S BUDDY TREVOR HAD BEEN SLEEPING ON THE COUCH RENT-FREE "JUST FOR A FEW DAYS" SINCE I'D MOVED IN 4 WEEKS AGO.
RAAAD DUDE!

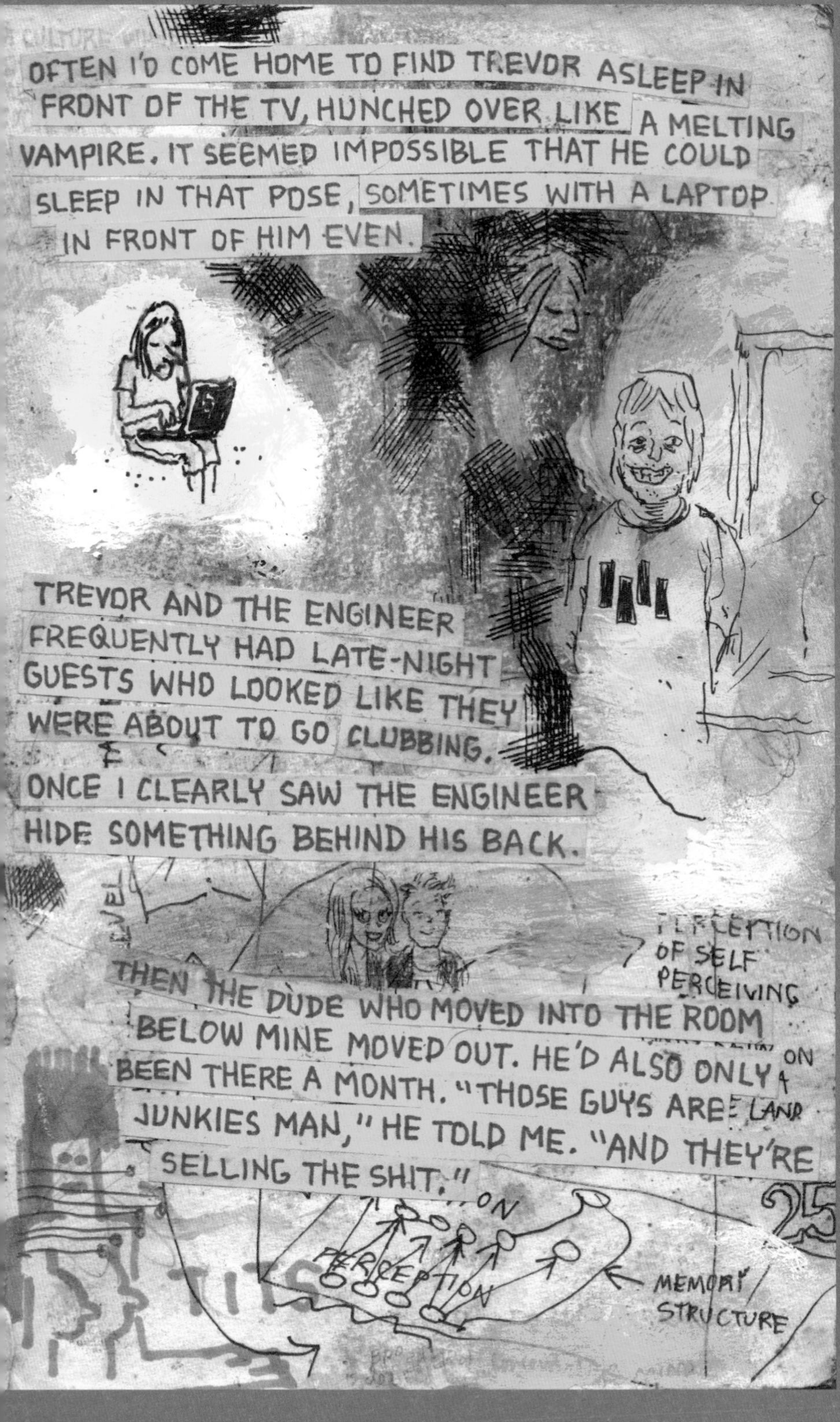
OFTEN I'D COME HOME TO FIND TREVOR ASLEEP IN FRONT OF THE TV, HUNCHED OVER LIKE A MELTING VAMPIRE. IT SEEMED IMPOSSIBLE THAT HE COULD SLEEP IN THAT POSE, SOMETIMES WITH A LAPTOP IN FRONT OF HIM EVEN.
TREVOR AND THE ENGINEER FREQUENTLY HAD LATE-NIGHT GUESTS WHO LOOKED LIKE THEY WERE ABOUT TO GO CLUBBING.
ONCE I CLEARLY SAW THE ENGINEER HIDE SOMETHING BEHIND HIS BACK.
PERCEPTION OF SELF PERCEIVING
THEN THE DUDE WHO MOVED INTO THE ROOM BELOW MINE MOVED OUT. HE'D ALSO ONLY BEEN THERE A MONTH. "THOSE GUYS ARE JUNKIES MAN," HE TOLD ME. "AND THEY'RE SELLING THE SHIT."
PERCEPTION
TITS
MEMORY/
STRUCTURE

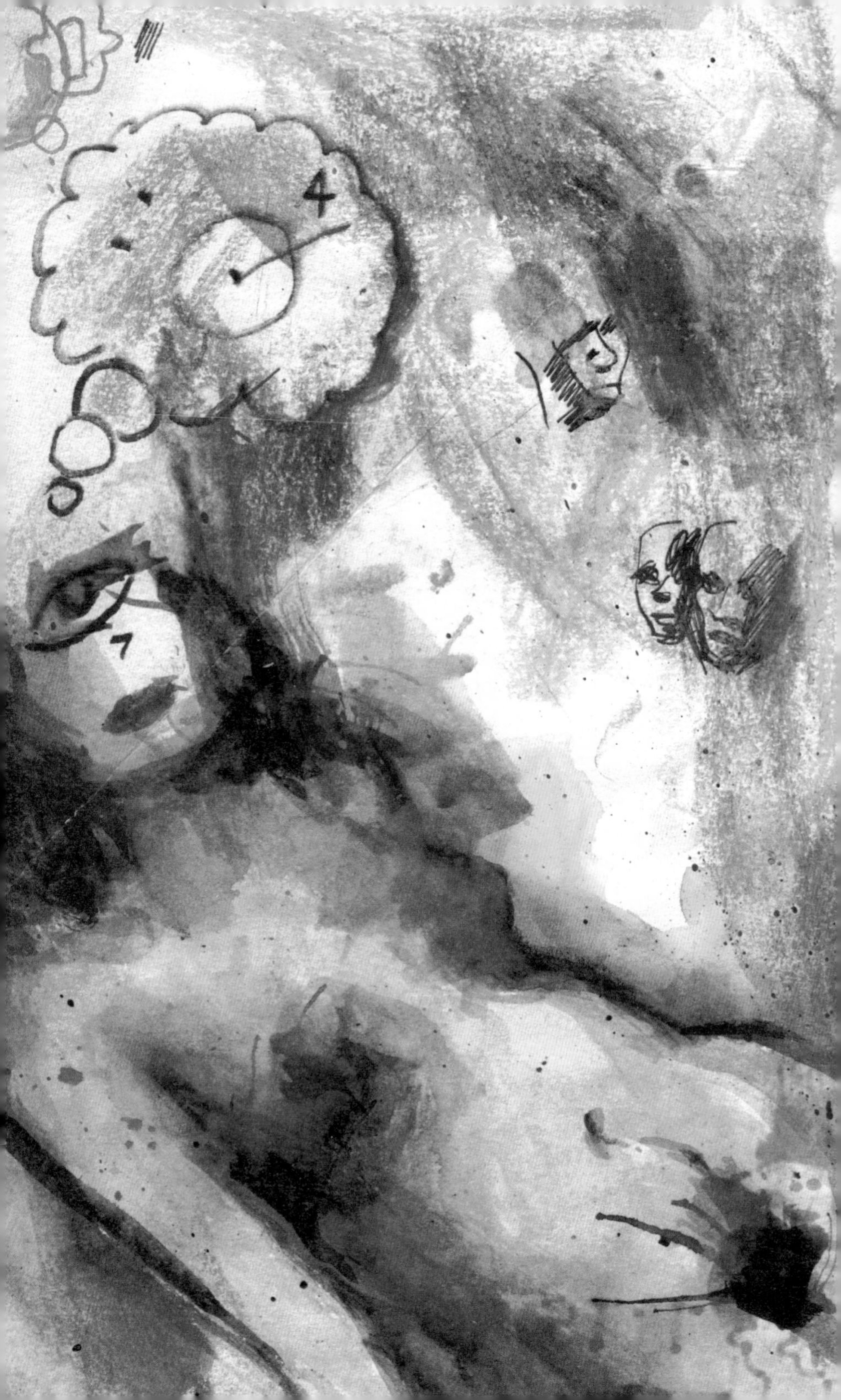
4

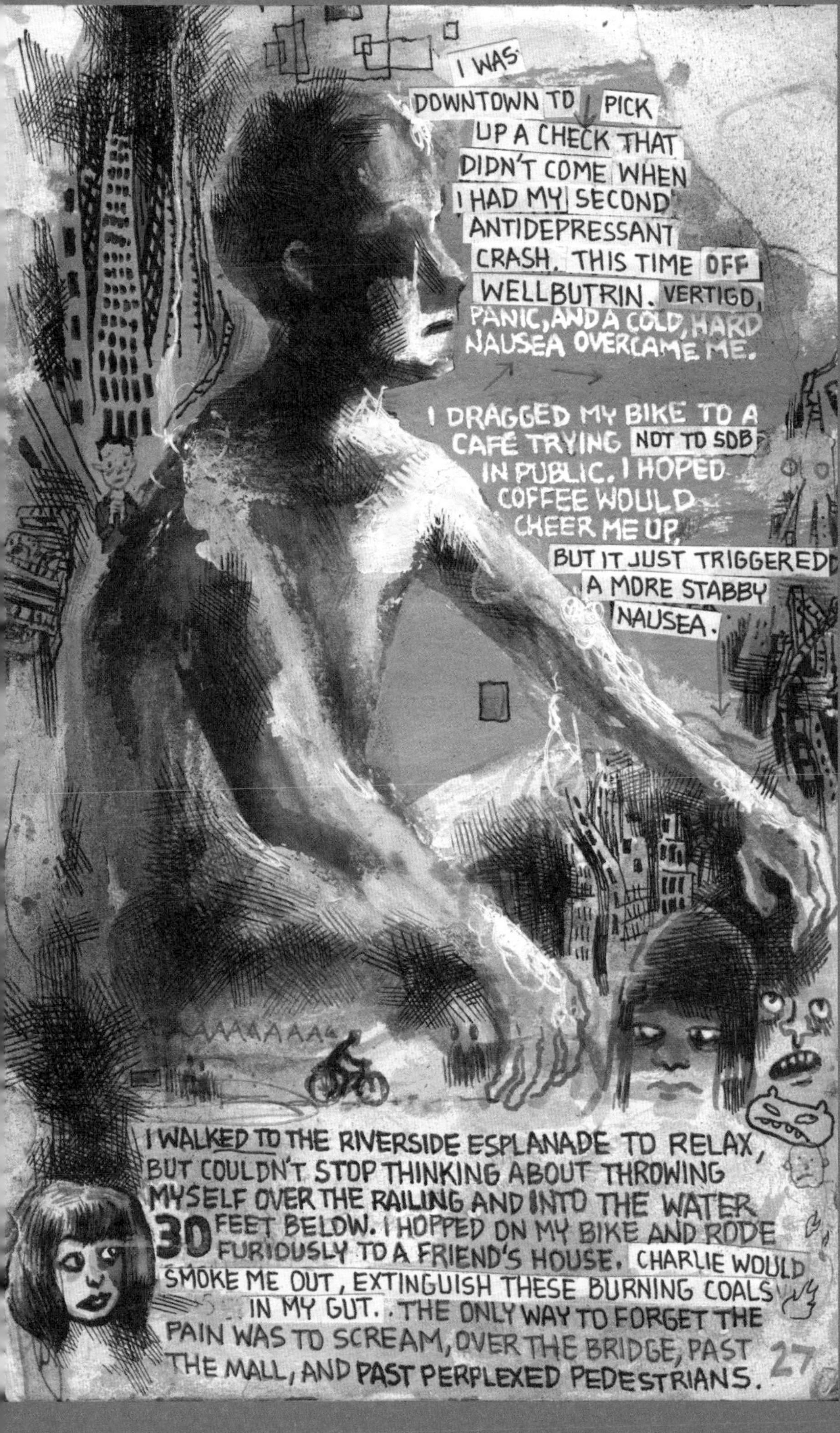
I WAS DOWNTOWN TO PICK UP A CHECK THAT DIDN'T COME WHEN I HAD MY SECOND ANTIDEPRESSANT CRASH. THIS TIME OFF WELLBUTRIN. VERTIGO, PANIC, AND A COLD, HARD NAUSEA OVERCAME ME.
I DRAGGED MY BIKE TO A CAFE TRYING NOT TO SOB IN PUBLIC. I HOPED COFFEE WOULD CHEER ME UP,
BUT IT JUST TRIGGERED A MORE STABBY NAUSEA.
AAAAAAAA
I WALKED TO THE RIVERSIDE ESPLANADE TO RELAX, BUT COULDN'T STOP THINKING ABOUT THROWING MYSELF OVER THE RAILING AND INTO THE WATER 30 FEET BELOW. I HOPPED ON MY BIKE AND RODE FURIOUSLY TO A FRIEND'S HOUSE. CHARLIE WOULD SMOKE ME OUT, EXTINGUISH THESE BURNING COALS IN MY GUT. THE ONLY WAY TO FORGET THE PAIN WAS TO SCREAM, OVER THE BRIDGE, PAST THE MALL, AND PAST PERPLEXED PEDESTRIANS.

ONE SUNNY AFTERNOON I CAME HOME TO FIND THE LANDLORD DIGGING AROUND IN THE BACKYARD. HE WAS BRUSQUE AND IRRITABLE, BUT I WON HIM OVER BY AGREEING WITH EVERYTHING HE SAID. I COULDN'T UNDERSTAND MUCH OF IT THROUGH HIS HEAVY **ACCENT**, BUT HE CLEARLY DIDN'T LIKE THE OTHER TENANTS. **"BULLSHIT ENGINEER"** HE SAID. HE ASKED WHAT I PAID IN RENT, AND IT TURNED OUT THE ENGINEER **WAS LIVING RENT-FREE, PLUS** MAKING $100 OFF US THREE TENANTS. "HE'S RIPPING YOU OFF," THE LANDLORD SAID, AND INSISTED THAT "**IF ANYTHING HAPPENS**" I SHOULD STAY IN THE HOUSE. PLUS HE WAS GOING TO PUT THE LEASE IN MY NAME.

WHAT THE FUCK IS GOING ON
BLOW 'IM AWAY MAN

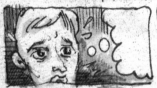

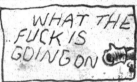

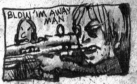

A COUPLE HOURS LATER THE ENGINEER CAME HOME, HAVING GOTTEN A CALL FROM THE LANDLORD. I ASSURED HIM THAT I DID **NOT WANT** THE LEASE IN MY NAME, AND THAT THE LANDLORD SEEMED **VERY** CONFUSED. WE HAD TO GO OVER IT SEVERAL TIMES, ESPECIALLY THE PART WHERE I SAID **IT WASN'T MY IDEA** TO GET THE LEASE.

BACK IN MY ROOM I FOUND LITTLES IN THE ATTIC STORAGE, SITTING NEXT TO A CASE OF BULLETS.

IF ANYTHING
HAPPENS

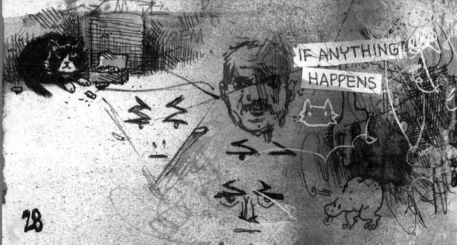

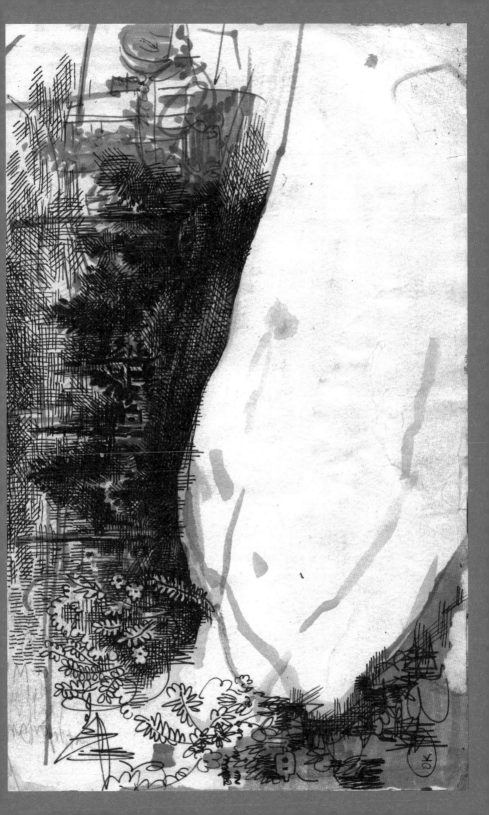

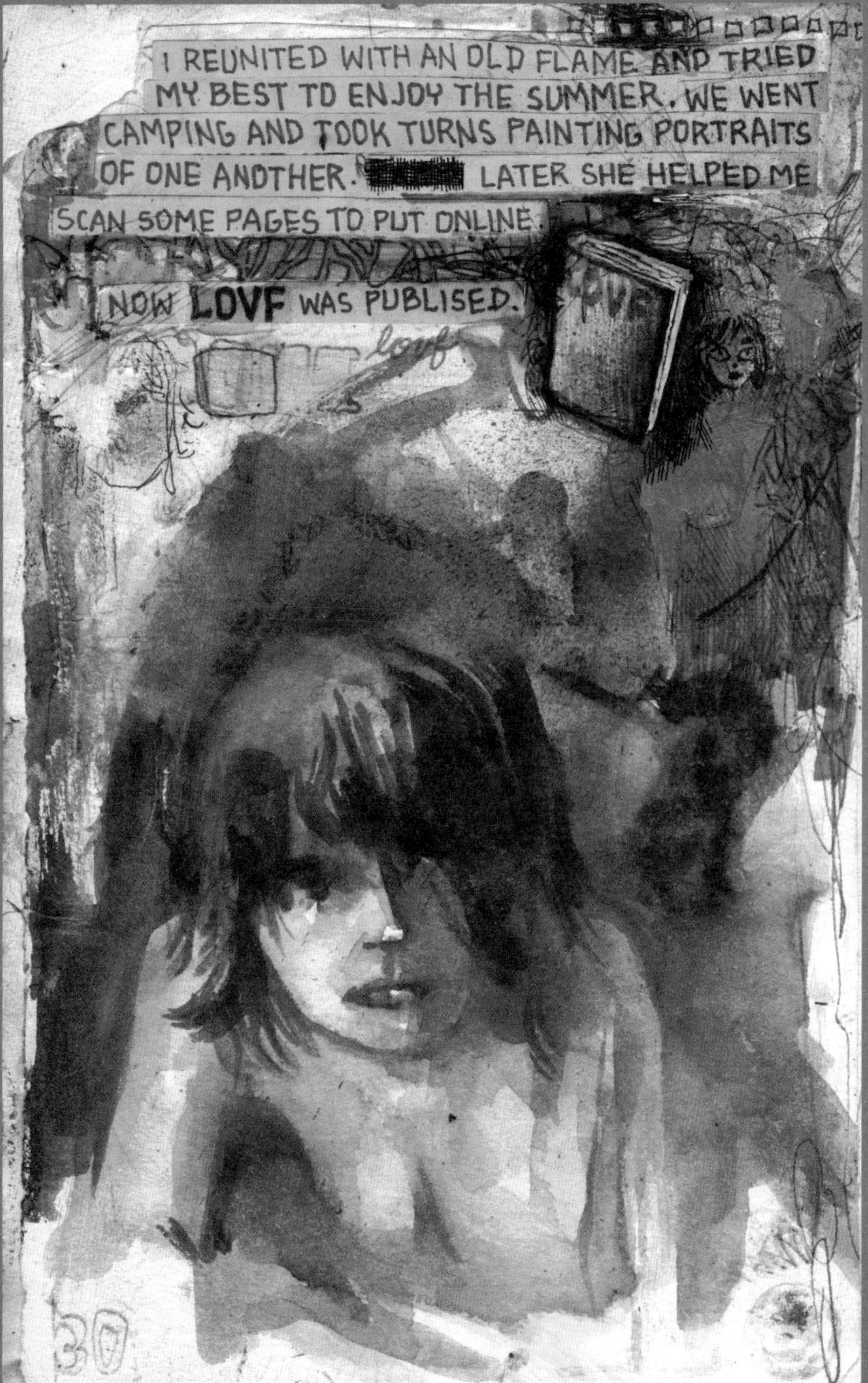
I REUNITED WITH AN OLD FLAME AND TRIED MY BEST TO ENJOY THE SUMMER. WE WENT CAMPING AND TOOK TURNS PAINTING PORTRAITS OF ONE ANOTHER. [redacted] LATER SHE HELPED ME SCAN SOME PAGES TO PUT ONLINE.
NOW LOVF WAS PUBLISED.
lovf

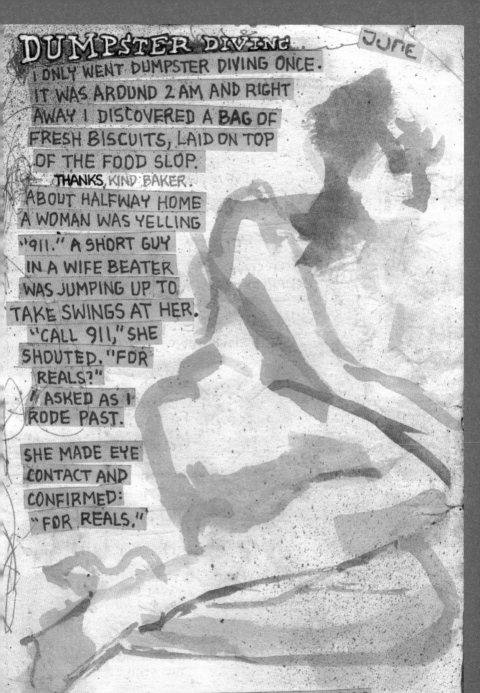

DUMPSTER DIVING

I ONLY WENT DUMPSTER DIVING ONCE.
IT WAS AROUND 2 AM AND RIGHT
AWAY I DISCOVERED A **BAG** OF
FRESH BISCUITS, LAID ON TOP
OF THE FOOD SLOP.
THANKS, KIND BAKER.

ABOUT HALFWAY HOME
A WOMAN WAS YELLING
"911." A SHORT GUY
IN A WIFE BEATER
WAS JUMPING UP TO
TAKE SWINGS AT HER.
"CALL 911," SHE
SHOUTED. "FOR
REALS?"
I ASKED AS I
RODE PAST.

SHE MADE EYE
CONTACT AND
CONFIRMED:
"FOR REALS."

I PARKED MY BIKE TO CALL, BUT
DIDN'T STOP FAR ENOUGH AWAY.

FOR REALS

31

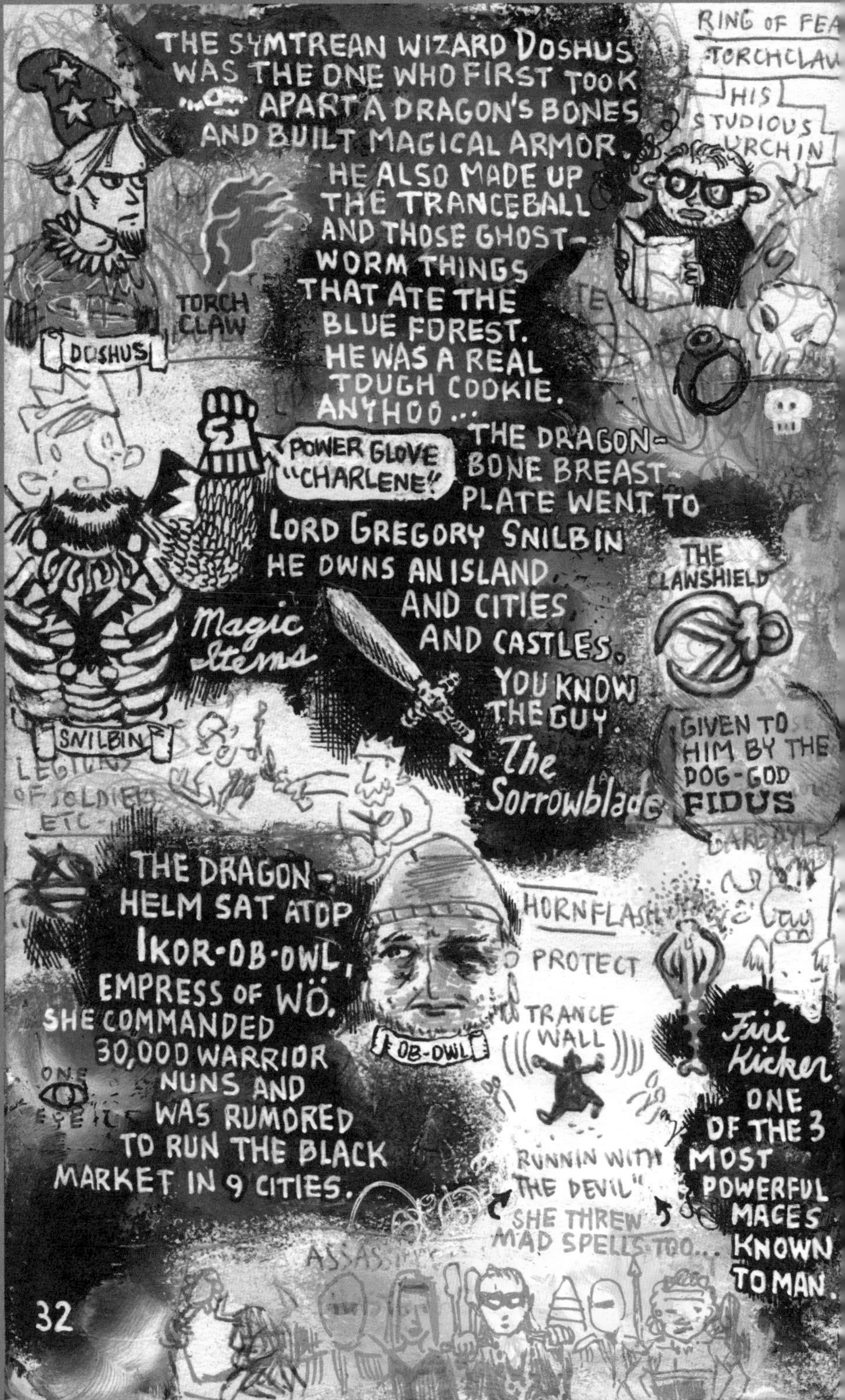
THE SYMTREAN WIZARD DOSHUS WAS THE ONE WHO FIRST TOOK APART A DRAGON'S BONES AND BUILT MAGICAL ARMOR.
HE ALSO MADE UP THE TRANCEBALL AND THOSE GHOST-WORM THINGS THAT ATE THE BLUE FOREST.
HE WAS A REAL TOUGH COOKIE.
ANYHOO...
DOSHUS
TORCH CLAW
RING OF FEA
TORCHCLAW
HIS STUDIOUS URCHIN
POWER GLOVE "CHARLENE"
THE DRAGON-BONE BREAST-PLATE WENT TO LORD GREGORY SNILBIN
HE OWNS AN ISLAND AND CITIES AND CASTLES.
YOU KNOW THE GUY.
Magic Items
SNILBIN
The Sorrowblade
THE CLAWSHIELD
GIVEN TO HIM BY THE DOG-GOD FIDUS
THE DRAGON-HELM SAT ATOP IKOR-OB-OWL, EMPRESS OF WÖ.
SHE COMMANDED 30,000 WARRIOR NUNS AND WAS RUMORED TO RUN THE BLACK MARKET IN 9 CITIES.
OB-OWL
HORNFLASH
TRANCE WALL
"RUNNIN WITH THE DEVIL"
SHE THREW MAD SPELLS TOO...
Fire Kicker
ONE OF THE 3 MOST POWERFUL MACES KNOWN TO MAN.
ONE EYE
32

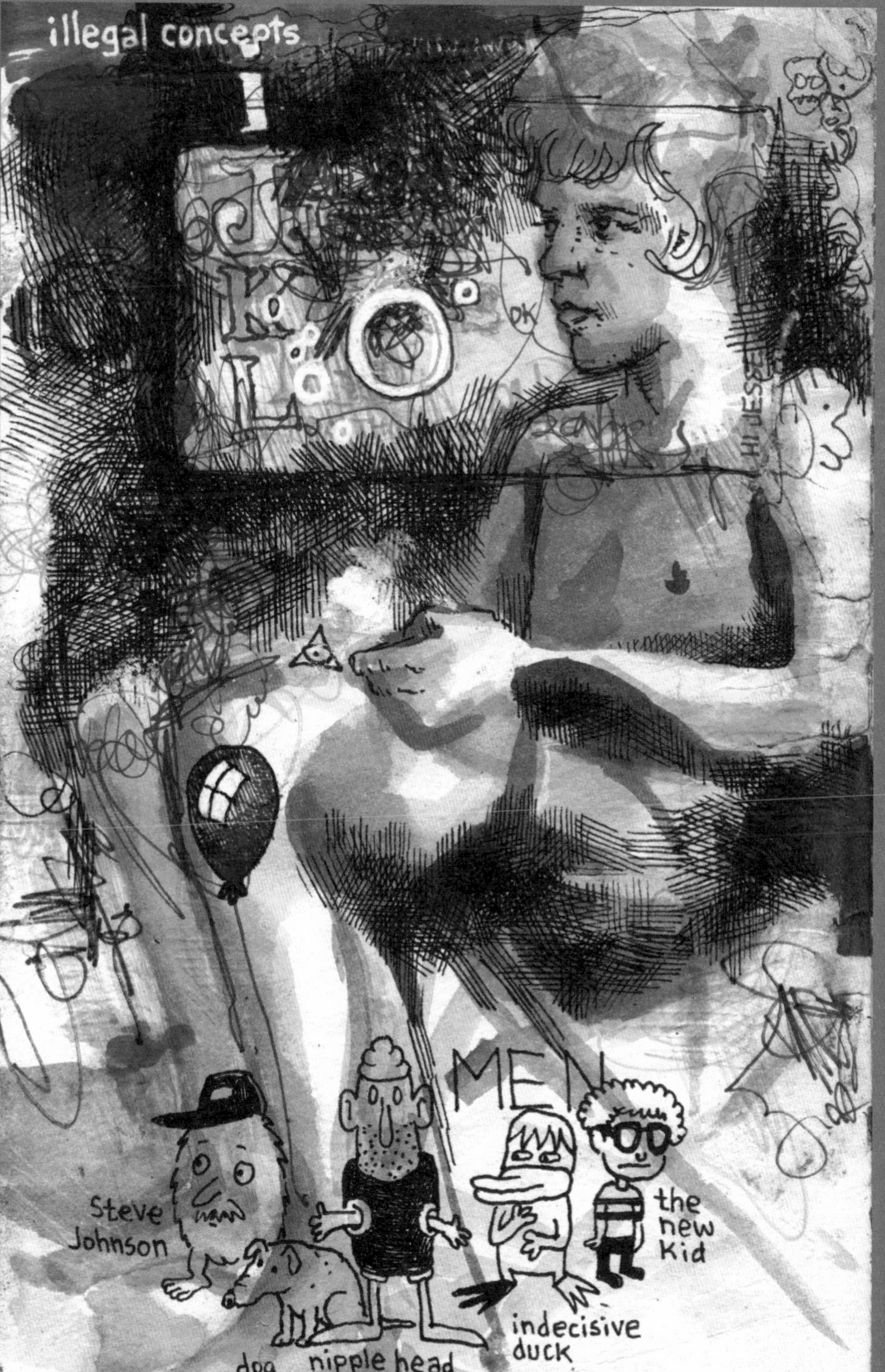
illegal concepts
OK
HI JESSE
MEN
Steve Johnson
dog
nipple head
indecisive duck
the new kid

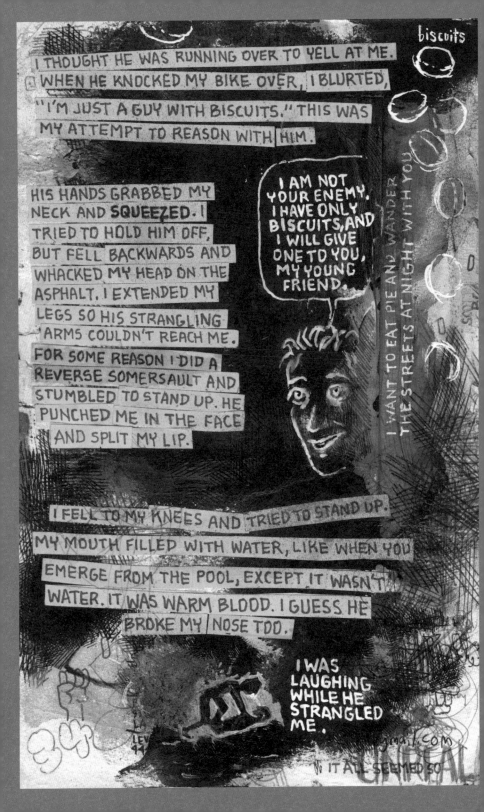

biscuits

I THOUGHT HE WAS RUNNING OVER TO YELL AT ME. WHEN HE KNOCKED MY BIKE OVER, I BLURTED, "I'M JUST A GUY WITH BISCUITS." THIS WAS MY ATTEMPT TO REASON WITH HIM.

HIS HANDS GRABBED MY NECK AND **SQUEEZED**. I TRIED TO HOLD HIM OFF, BUT FELL BACKWARDS AND WHACKED MY HEAD ON THE ASPHALT. I EXTENDED MY LEGS SO HIS STRANGLING ARMS COULDN'T REACH ME. FOR SOME REASON I DID A REVERSE SOMERSAULT AND STUMBLED TO STAND UP. HE PUNCHED ME IN THE FACE AND SPLIT MY LIP.

I AM NOT YOUR ENEMY. I HAVE ONLY BISCUITS, AND I WILL GIVE ONE TO YOU, MY YOUNG FRIEND.

I WANT TO EAT PIE AND WANDER THE STREETS AT NIGHT WITH YOU.

I FELL TO MY KNEES AND TRIED TO STAND UP. MY MOUTH FILLED WITH WATER, LIKE WHEN YOU EMERGE FROM THE POOL, EXCEPT IT WASN'T WATER. IT WAS WARM BLOOD. I GUESS HE BROKE MY NOSE TOO.

I WAS LAUGHING WHILE HE STRANGLED ME.

IT ALL SEEMED SO

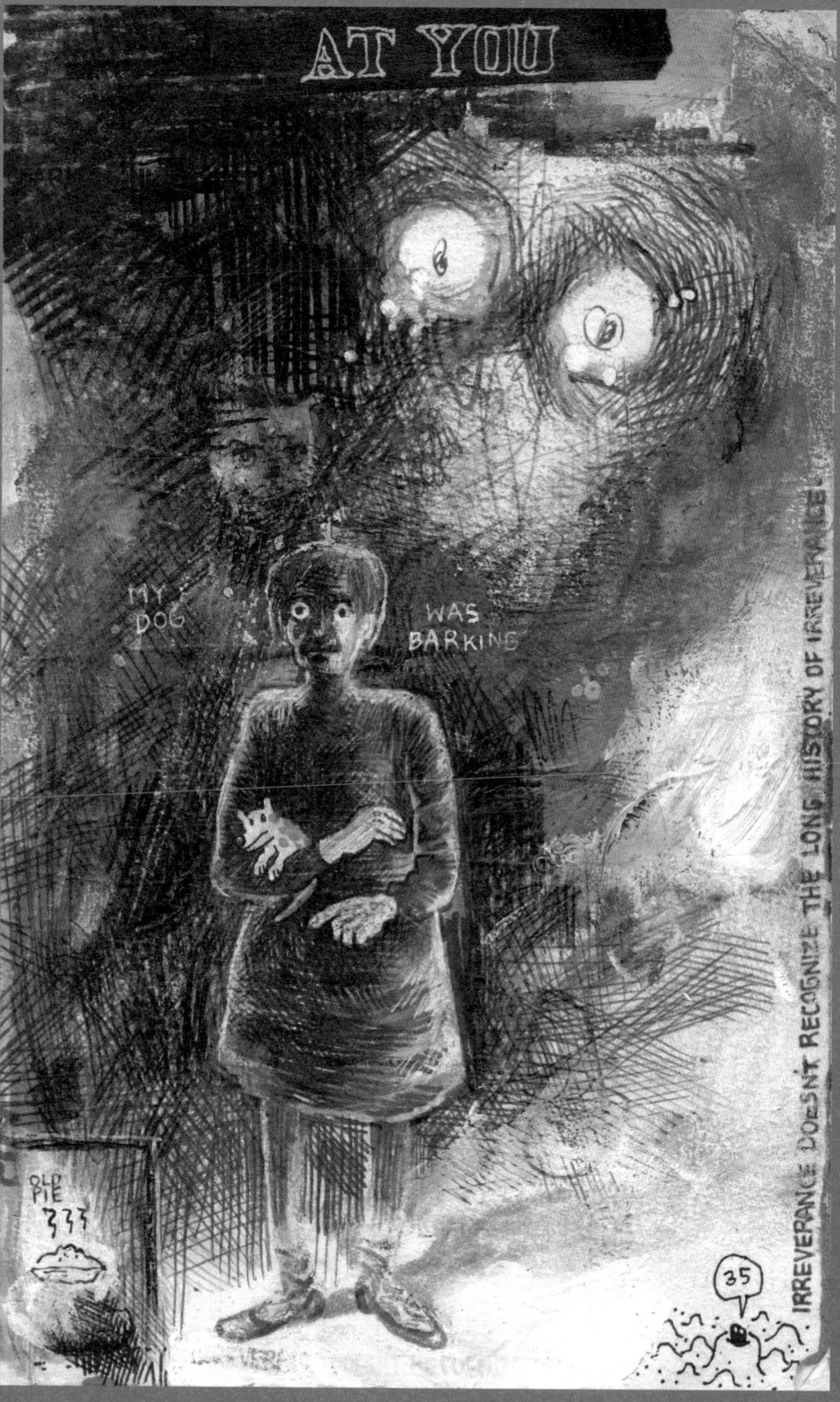
AT YOU
MY DOG
WAS BARKING
OLD PIE
IRREVERANCE DOESN'T RECOGNIZE THE LONG HISTORY OF IRREVERANCE
35

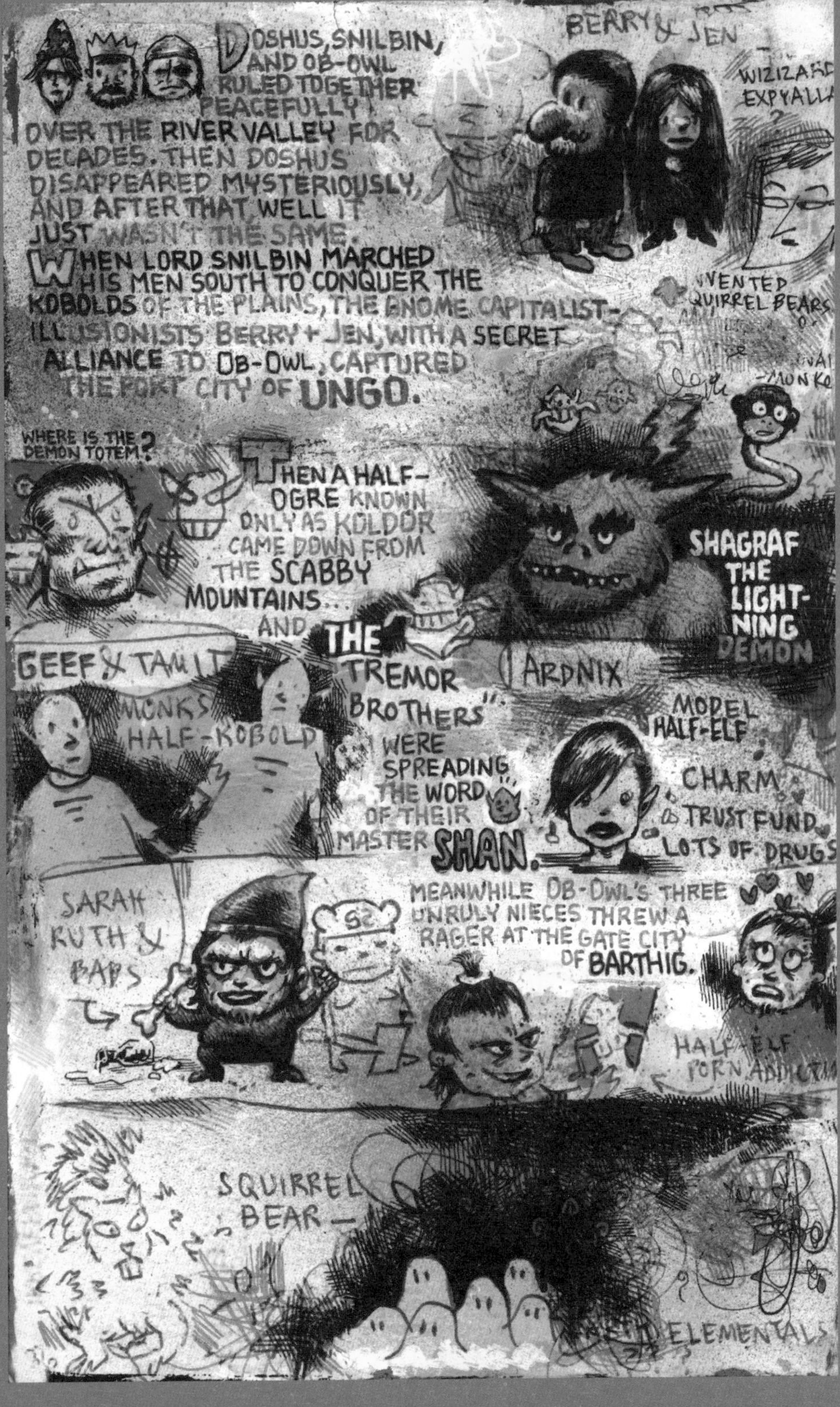

DOSHUS, SNILBIN, AND OB-OWL RULED TOGETHER PEACEFULLY OVER THE RIVER VALLEY FOR DECADES. THEN DOSHUS DISAPPEARED MYSTERIOUSLY, AND AFTER THAT WELL IT JUST WASN'T THE SAME.
BERRY & JEN
WIZIZARD EXPYALLA ?
WHEN LORD SNILBIN MARCHED HIS MEN SOUTH TO CONQUER THE KOBOLDS OF THE PLAINS, THE GNOME CAPITALIST-ILLUSIONISTS BERRY + JEN, WITH A SECRET ALLIANCE TO OB-OWL, CAPTURED THE PORT CITY OF UNGO.
INVENTED SQUIRREL BEARS
MONKO
WHERE IS THE DEMON TOTEM?
THEN A HALF-OGRE KNOWN ONLY AS KOLDOR CAME DOWN FROM THE SCABBY MOUNTAINS... AND
SHAGRAF THE LIGHTNING DEMON
GEEF & TAMIT
MONKS HALF-KOBOLD
"THE TREMOR BROTHERS" WERE SPREADING THE WORD OF THEIR MASTER SHAN.
ARDNIX
MODEL HALF-ELF
CHARM
TRUST FUND
LOTS OF DRUGS
SARAH RUTH & BABS
MEANWHILE OB-OWL'S THREE UNRULY NIECES THREW A RAGER AT THE GATE CITY OF BARTHIG.
HALF-ELF PORN ADDICTION
SQUIRREL BEAR—
ELEMENTALS

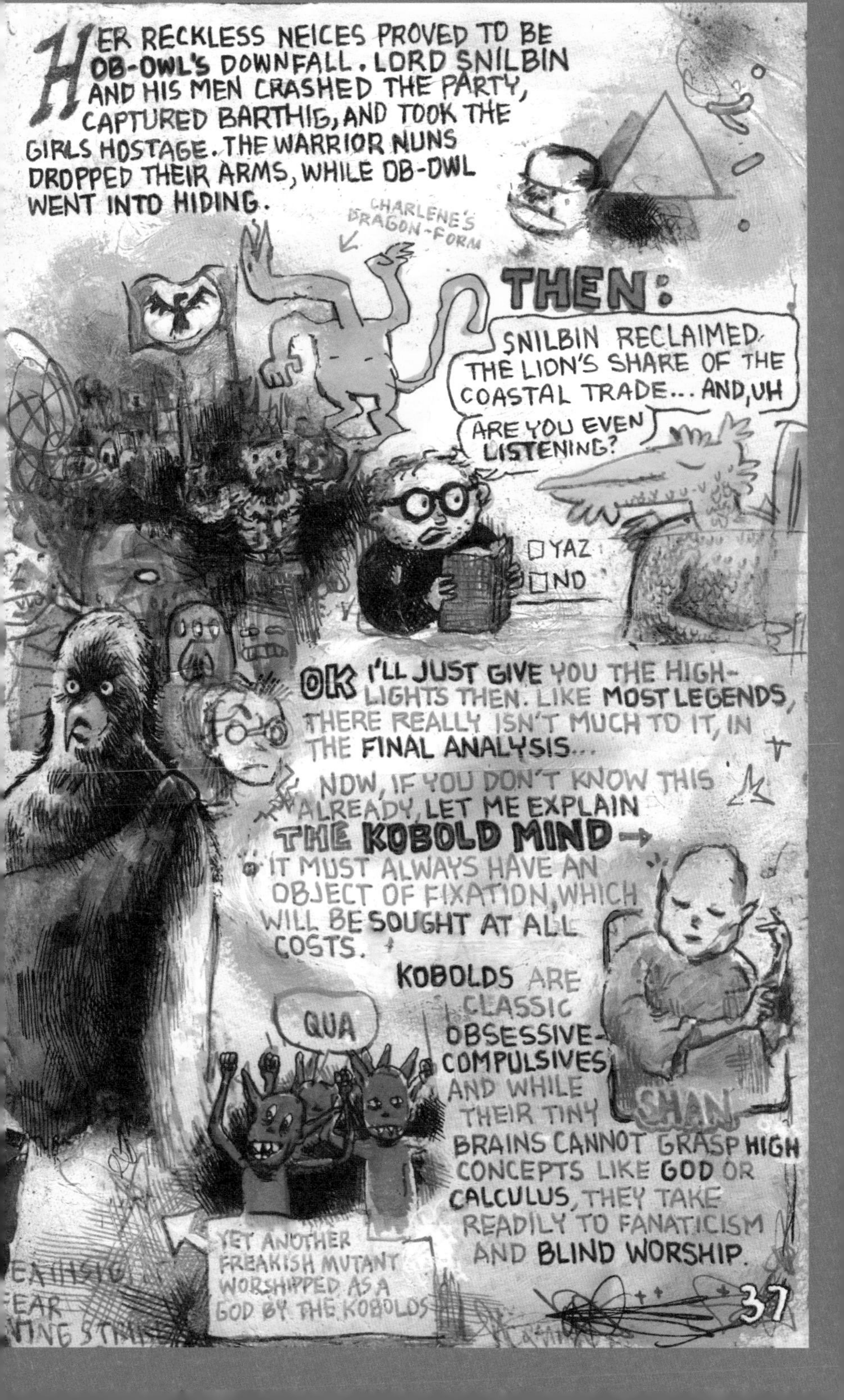
HER RECKLESS NEICES PROVED TO BE HOB-OWL'S DOWNFALL. LORD SNILBIN AND HIS MEN CRASHED THE PARTY, CAPTURED BARTHIG, AND TOOK THE GIRLS HOSTAGE. THE WARRIOR NUNS DROPPED THEIR ARMS, WHILE OB-OWL WENT INTO HIDING.
CHARLENE'S DRAGON-FORM
THEN:
SNILBIN RECLAIMED THE LION'S SHARE OF THE COASTAL TRADE... AND, UH
ARE YOU EVEN LISTENING?
☐ YAZ
☐ ND
OK I'LL JUST GIVE YOU THE HIGH-LIGHTS THEN. LIKE MOST LEGENDS, THERE REALLY ISN'T MUCH TO IT, IN THE FINAL ANALYSIS...
NOW, IF YOU DON'T KNOW THIS ALREADY, LET ME EXPLAIN
THE KOBOLD MIND →
IT MUST ALWAYS HAVE AN OBJECT OF FIXATION, WHICH WILL BE SOUGHT AT ALL COSTS.
KOBOLDS ARE CLASSIC OBSESSIVE-COMPULSIVES AND WHILE THEIR TINY BRAINS CANNOT GRASP HIGH CONCEPTS LIKE GOD OR CALCULUS, THEY TAKE READILY TO FANATICISM AND BLIND WORSHIP.
QUA
SHAN
YET ANOTHER FREAKISH MUTANT WORSHIPPED AS A GOD BY THE KOBOLDS

I DECIDED TO GIVE UP THE STRUGGLE, BUT WHEN
I LOOKED UP
HE HIT ME SO HARD IT KNOCKED THE
CONTACT LENS OUT OF MY EYE.
OW!
HE WANTED MY PHONE, EVEN THOUGH I NEVER COMPLETED THE CALL.
WHAT'S YOUR PROBLEM?
I THREW IT OVER THERE.
THEN IT HIT ME: PORTLAND DON'T WANT ME AROUND NO MO
AFTER I POINTED OUT WHERE I'D TOSSED THE PHONE, HE GRABBED IT AND RAN OFF.
BISCUITS ROLLED IN THE STREET. I USED ONE TO SOAK UP THE BLOOD LEAKING OUT OF MY NOSE.
FUCKIN PUSSY

SPARKPLUG ORDERS

HIS OFFICE BUYING MORE MESKIN PAGES ON EBAY WHILE PACKING

AND PERIODICALLY RUNNING INTO HIS... FUNK!

A REPORTER WITH A UNIBALL... OR ENTER THE DRAGON AGAIN

WHOSE ROBE... WHILE WATCHING A... WEARING THE HOTEL

IN BED AT THE HOLIDAY INN WHERE HE'S ORG...

AUTHOR DYLAN WILL PUBLISH IN 3 YEARS

A NEIGHBORHOOD TOMCAT AND MAKING THE

AFTER HE SUGGESTS SHE DO SOME PENCILLING

ORGANIZED A ROOM FOR ALL HIS

THINK YOU'RE COMING UP WITH THE MOST SUBTLE SHIT

THAT YOU ALMOST THINK YOU'RE COMING UP WITH

WHERE FRIENDS CAN STAY

HE'S AMAZINGLY TALENTED AND UNIQUE

ON WHAT HE'S BEEN TELLING ME ABOUT THIS COLORIST

NOTICES & MIRACLES &

WOW THAT HE APPRECIATED THE THINGS IS

AND PAY HIM LATER. HE'S

RIST NAMED GEORGE SOMETHING

ME THAT I WANT EVERYONE TO KNOW ABOUT ME

A MONTH BEFORE HE DIED

BULLDOZER. LOVED THAT WOODEN BOX WITH DIRT. I DIDN'T WANT TO HANG ANY MEMORIES OF THAT. DYLAN IS SITTING IN

DYLAN IS LAYING ON... HIMALAYAN RUG LIKE A 10- OR 11-YR-OLD DRAWING. THE NEXT IMAGE

ESQUE ACETATE SCREENS FOR SILVER AGE COMICS. DYLAN IS WEARING THE

LAUGHING OUT LOUD OVER A NEW MINICOMIC HE DISCOVERED AT A SHOW.

CODE THE WAY YOU'RE DOING IT. WOW. PLAY STORE. DYLAN IS STROKING

IN PDFS, I FELT THIS WAS A KIND OF OLIVE BRANCH OFFERING. I FORGOT

TO TELL HIM I LOVED HIM. I DIDN'T WANT TO SEE HIM SICK OR SEE TH...

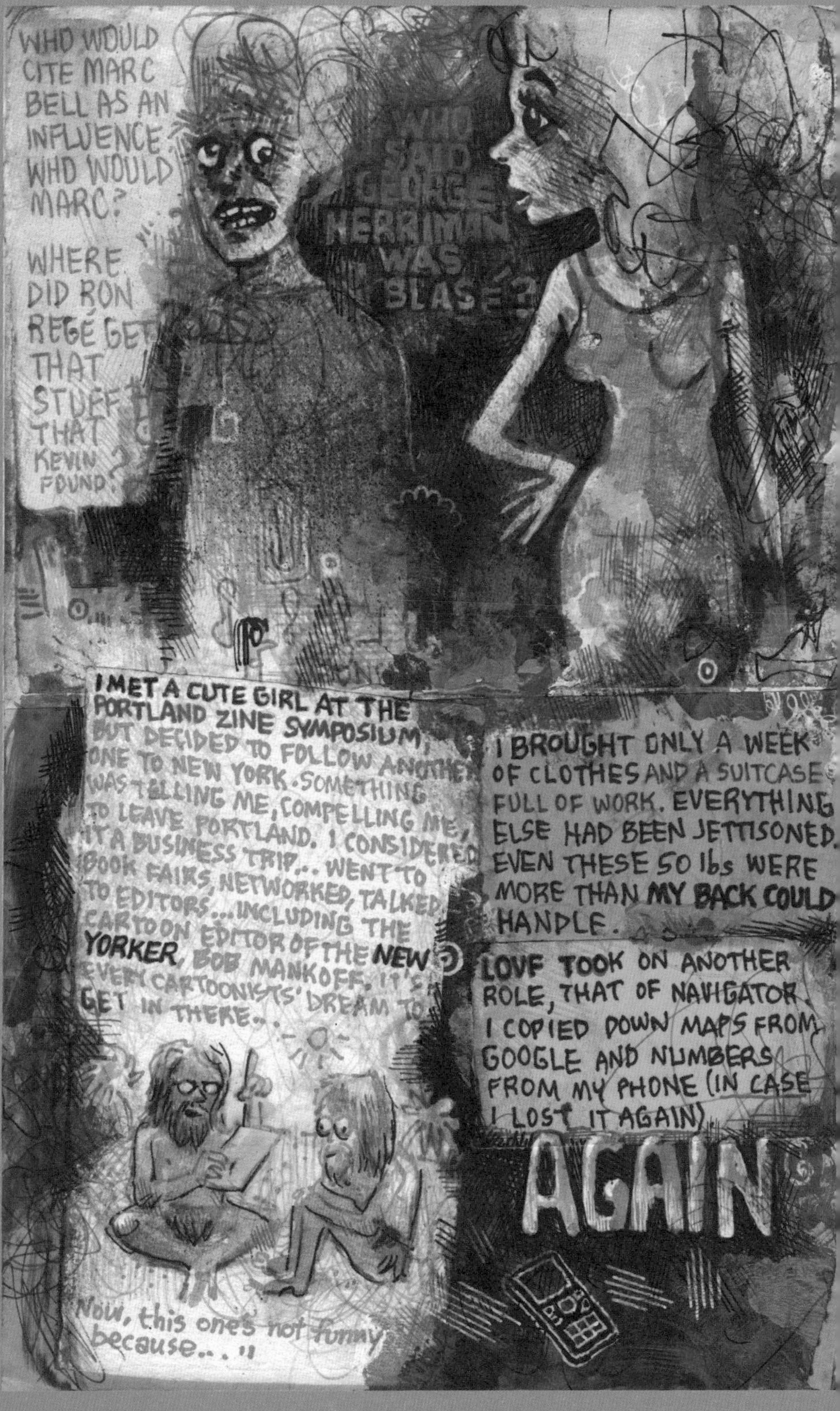

WHO WOULD CITE MARC BELL AS AN INFLUENCE. WHO WOULD MARC?
WHERE DID RON REGÉ GET THAT STUFF THAT KEVIN FOUND?
WHO SAID GEORGE HERRIMAN WAS BLASÉ?
I MET A CUTE GIRL AT THE PORTLAND ZINE SYMPOSIUM, BUT DECIDED TO FOLLOW ANOTHER ONE TO NEW YORK. SOMETHING WAS TELLING ME, COMPELLING ME, TO LEAVE PORTLAND. I CONSIDERED IT A BUSINESS TRIP... WENT TO BOOK FAIRS, NETWORKED, TALKED TO EDITORS... INCLUDING THE CARTOON EDITOR OF THE NEW YORKER, BOB MANKOFF. IT'S EVERY CARTOONISTS' DREAM TO GET IN THERE...
"Now, this one's not funny because..."
I BROUGHT ONLY A WEEK OF CLOTHES AND A SUITCASE FULL OF WORK. EVERYTHING ELSE HAD BEEN JETTISONED. EVEN THESE 50 lbs WERE MORE THAN MY BACK COULD HANDLE.
LOVE TOOK ON ANOTHER ROLE, THAT OF NAVIGATOR. I COPIED DOWN MAPS FROM GOOGLE AND NUMBERS FROM MY PHONE (IN CASE I LOST IT AGAIN)
AGAIN

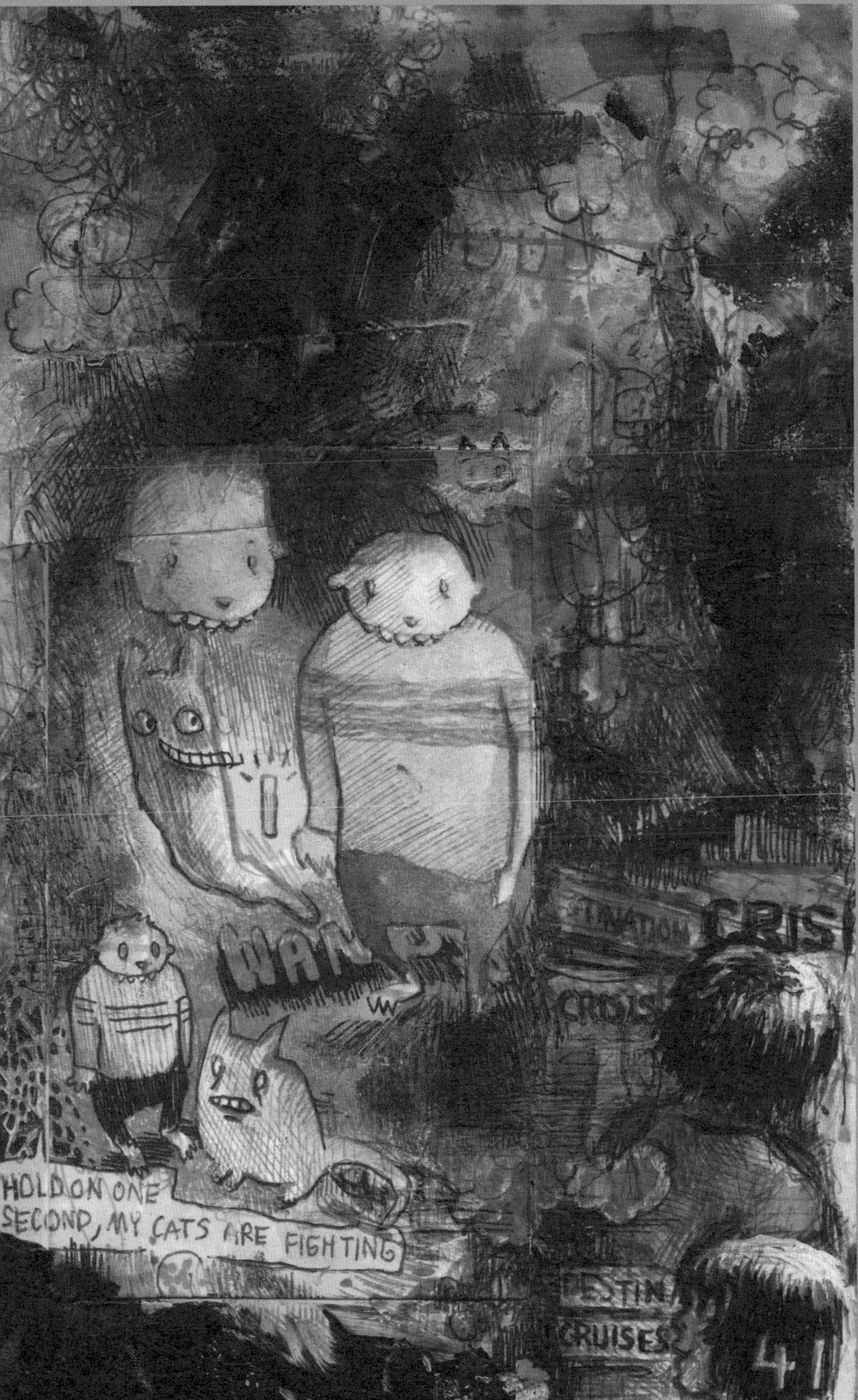

HOLD ON ONE SECOND, MY CATS ARE FIGHTING
CRIS
CRUISES
41

I'D BUY THAT IF IT WAS A
LAMP.
YOU DON'T SEEM LIKE AN UNMANAGEABLE PART OF MY LIFE
YOGA

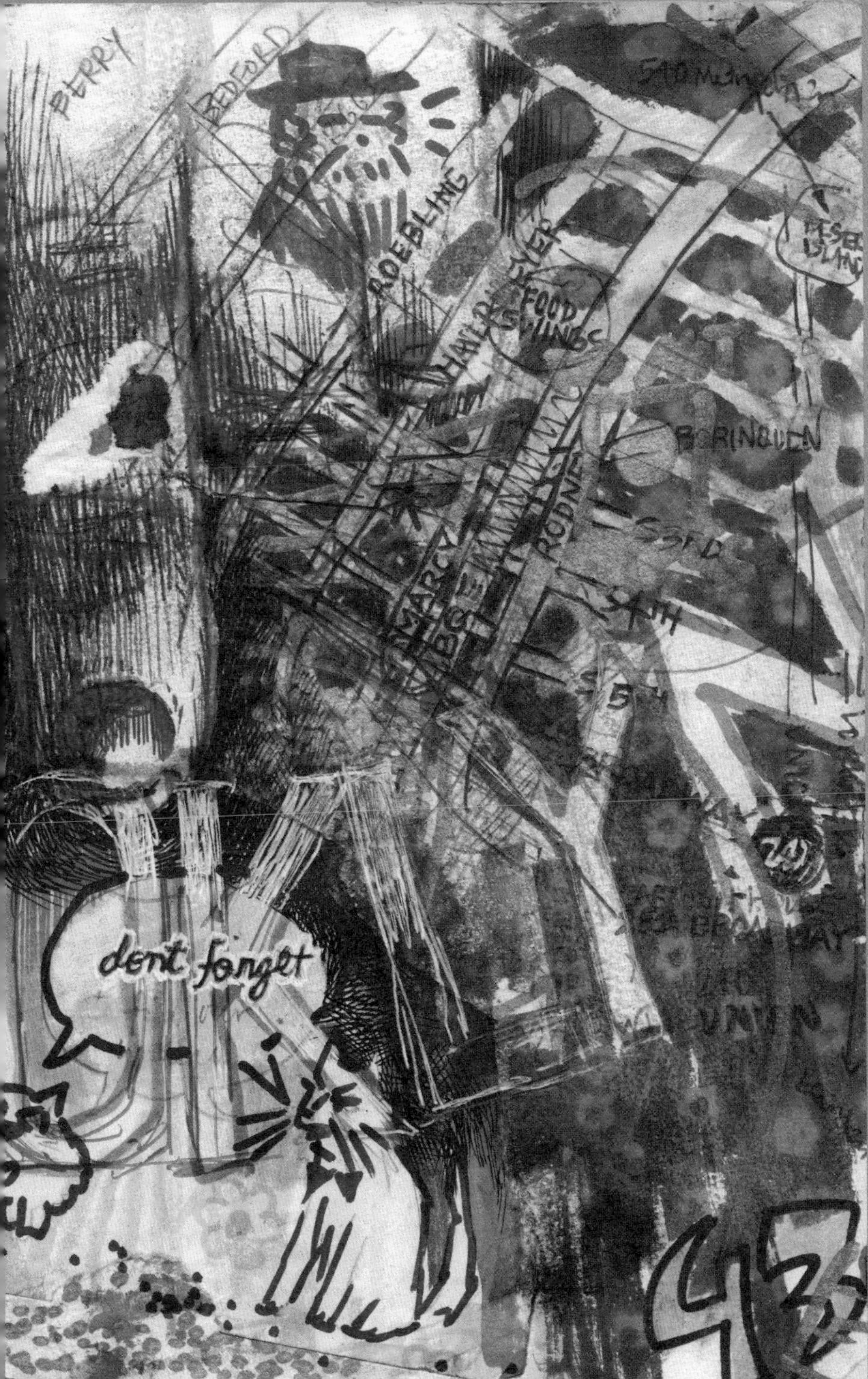
BERRY
BEDFORD
ROEBLING
HAVEMEYER
RODNEY
MARCY
BORINQUEN
dont forget
ST
PENN STATION 7TH AVE & 30TH ST

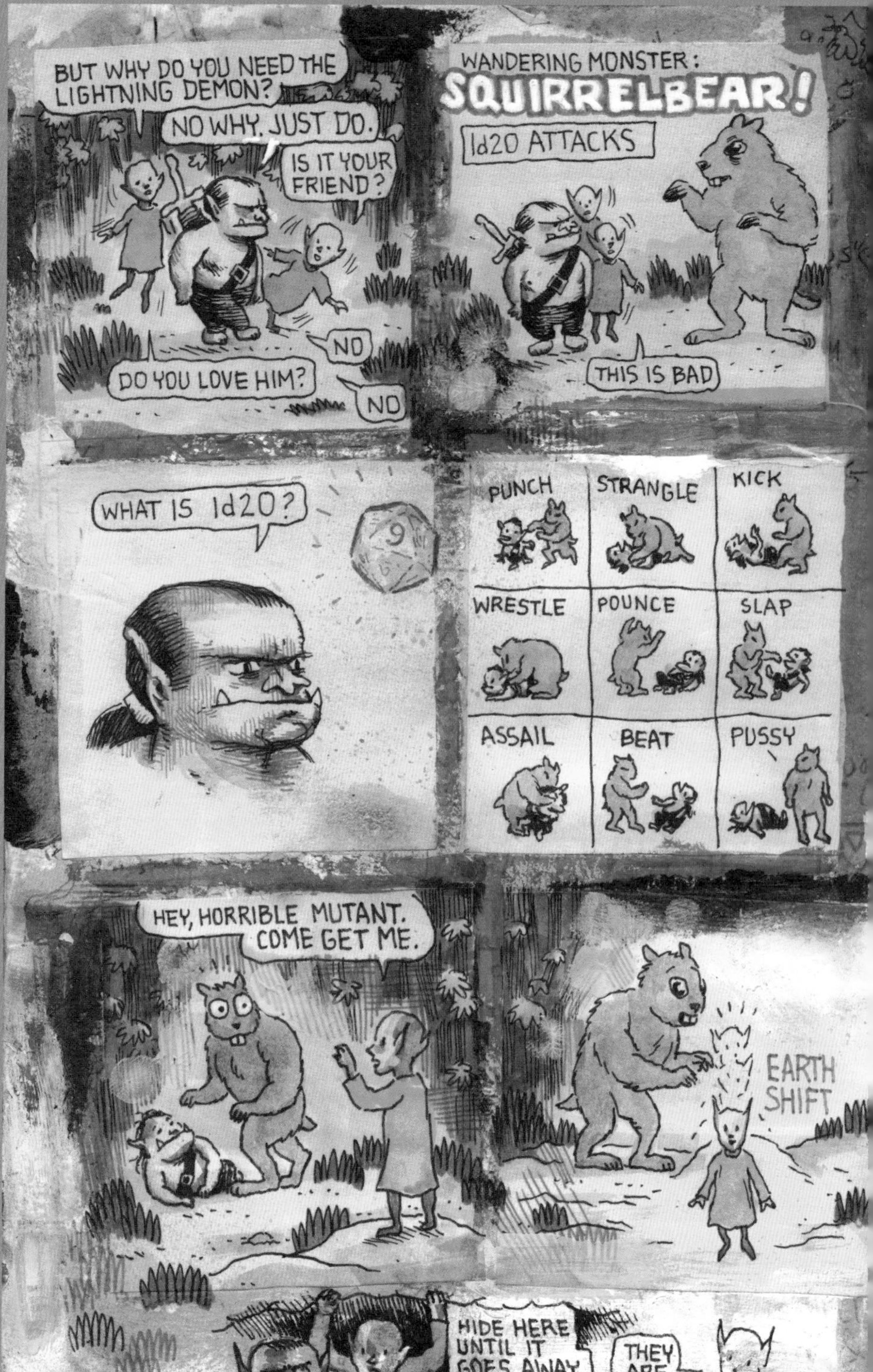
BUT WHY DO YOU NEED THE LIGHTNING DEMON?
NO WHY. JUST DO.
IS IT YOUR FRIEND?
DO YOU LOVE HIM?
NO
NO
WANDERING MONSTER:
SQUIRRELBEAR!
1d20 ATTACKS
THIS IS BAD
WHAT IS 1d20?
9
PUNCH
STRANGLE
KICK
WRESTLE
POUNCE
SLAP
ASSAIL
BEAT
PUSSY
HEY, HORRIBLE MUTANT. COME GET ME.
EARTH SHIFT
HIDE HERE UNTIL IT GOES AWAY.
THEY ARE DIS-TRACTABLE.

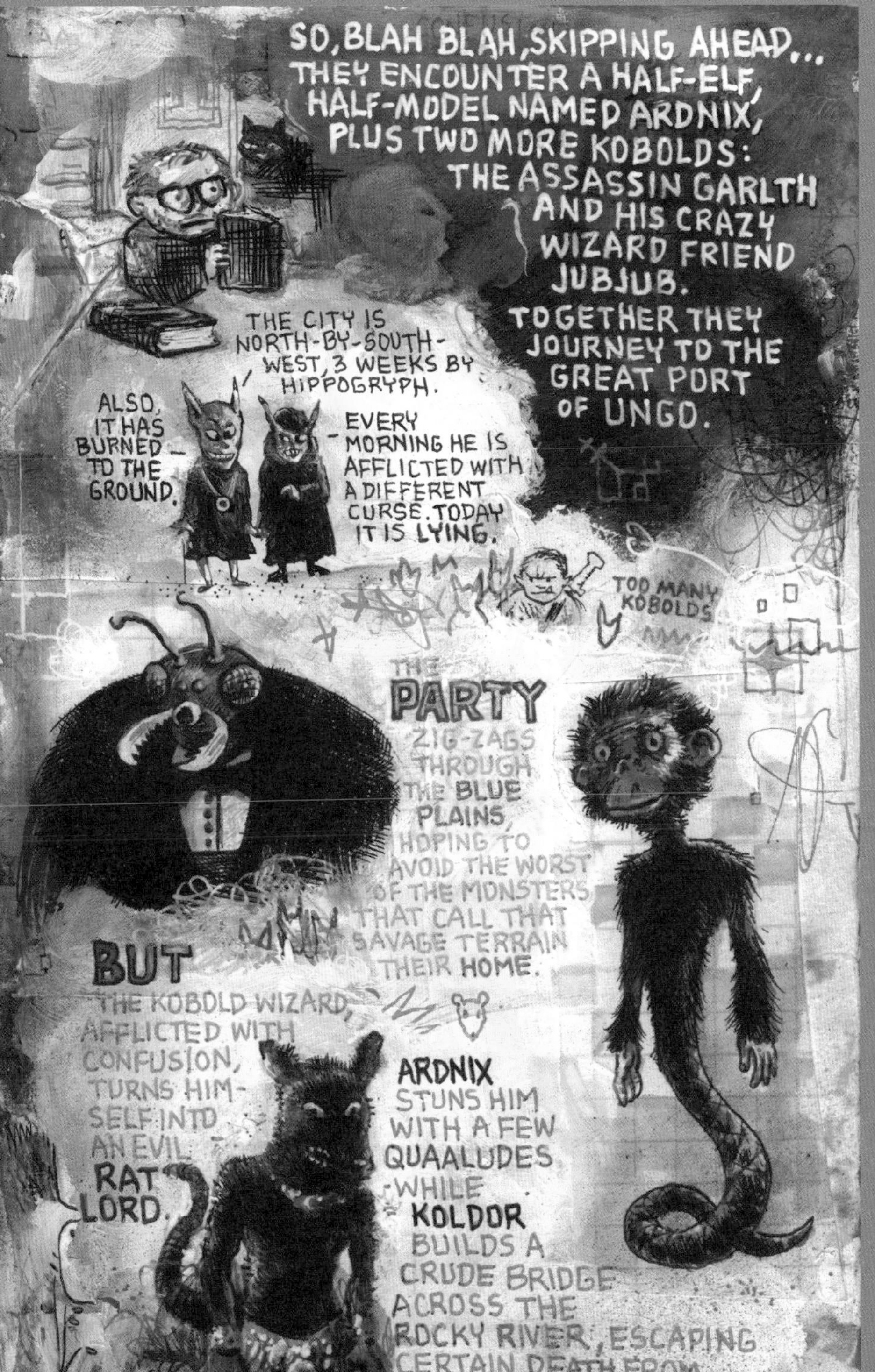

SO, BLAH BLAH, SKIPPING AHEAD... THEY ENCOUNTER A HALF-ELF, HALF-MODEL NAMED ARDNIX, PLUS TWO MORE KOBOLDS: THE ASSASSIN GARLTH AND HIS CRAZY WIZARD FRIEND JUBJUB.
TOGETHER THEY JOURNEY TO THE GREAT PORT OF UNGO.
THE CITY IS NORTH-BY-SOUTH-WEST, 3 WEEKS BY HIPPOGRYPH.
ALSO, IT HAS BURNED TO THE GROUND.
EVERY MORNING HE IS AFFLICTED WITH A DIFFERENT CURSE. TODAY IT IS LYING.
TOO MANY KOBOLDS
THE PARTY ZIG-ZAGS THROUGH THE BLUE PLAINS, HOPING TO AVOID THE WORST OF THE MONSTERS THAT CALL THAT SAVAGE TERRAIN THEIR HOME.
BUT THE KOBOLD WIZARD, AFFLICTED WITH CONFUSION, TURNS HIMSELF INTO AN EVIL RAT LORD.
ARDNIX STUNS HIM WITH A FEW QUAALUDES WHILE KOLDOR BUILDS A CRUDE BRIDGE ACROSS THE ROCKY RIVER, ESCAPING CERTAIN DEATH FROM THE LORD'S RAT ARMY.

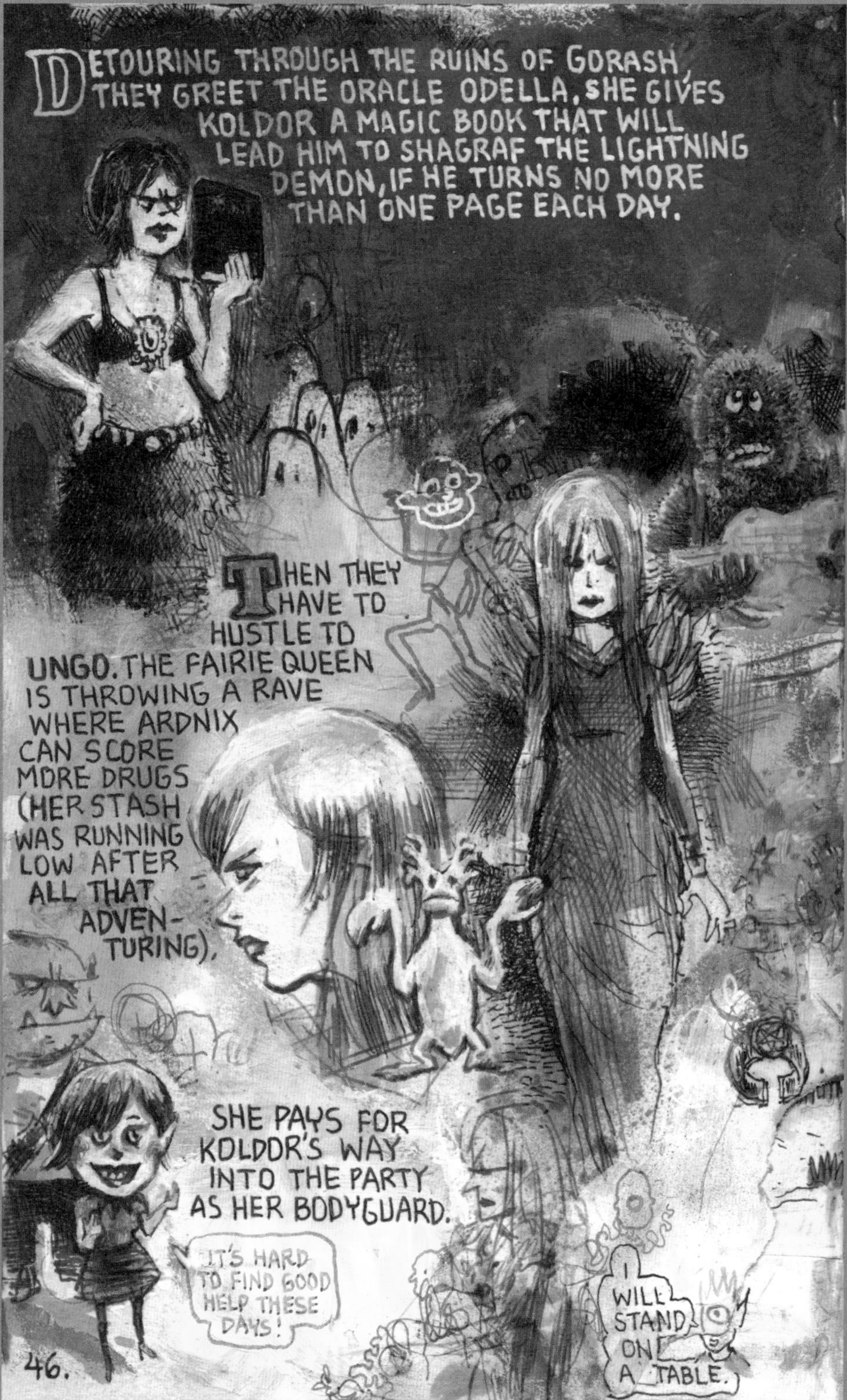
DETOURING THROUGH THE RUINS OF GORASH, THEY GREET THE ORACLE ODELLA, SHE GIVES KOLDOR A MAGIC BOOK THAT WILL LEAD HIM TO SHAGRAF THE LIGHTNING DEMON, IF HE TURNS NO MORE THAN ONE PAGE EACH DAY.
THEN THEY HAVE TO HUSTLE TO UNGO. THE FAIRIE QUEEN IS THROWING A RAVE WHERE ARDNIX CAN SCORE MORE DRUGS (HER STASH WAS RUNNING LOW AFTER ALL THAT ADVEN-TURING).
SHE PAYS FOR KOLDOR'S WAY INTO THE PARTY AS HER BODYGUARD.
IT'S HARD TO FIND GOOD HELP THESE DAYS!
I WILL STAND ON A TABLE.

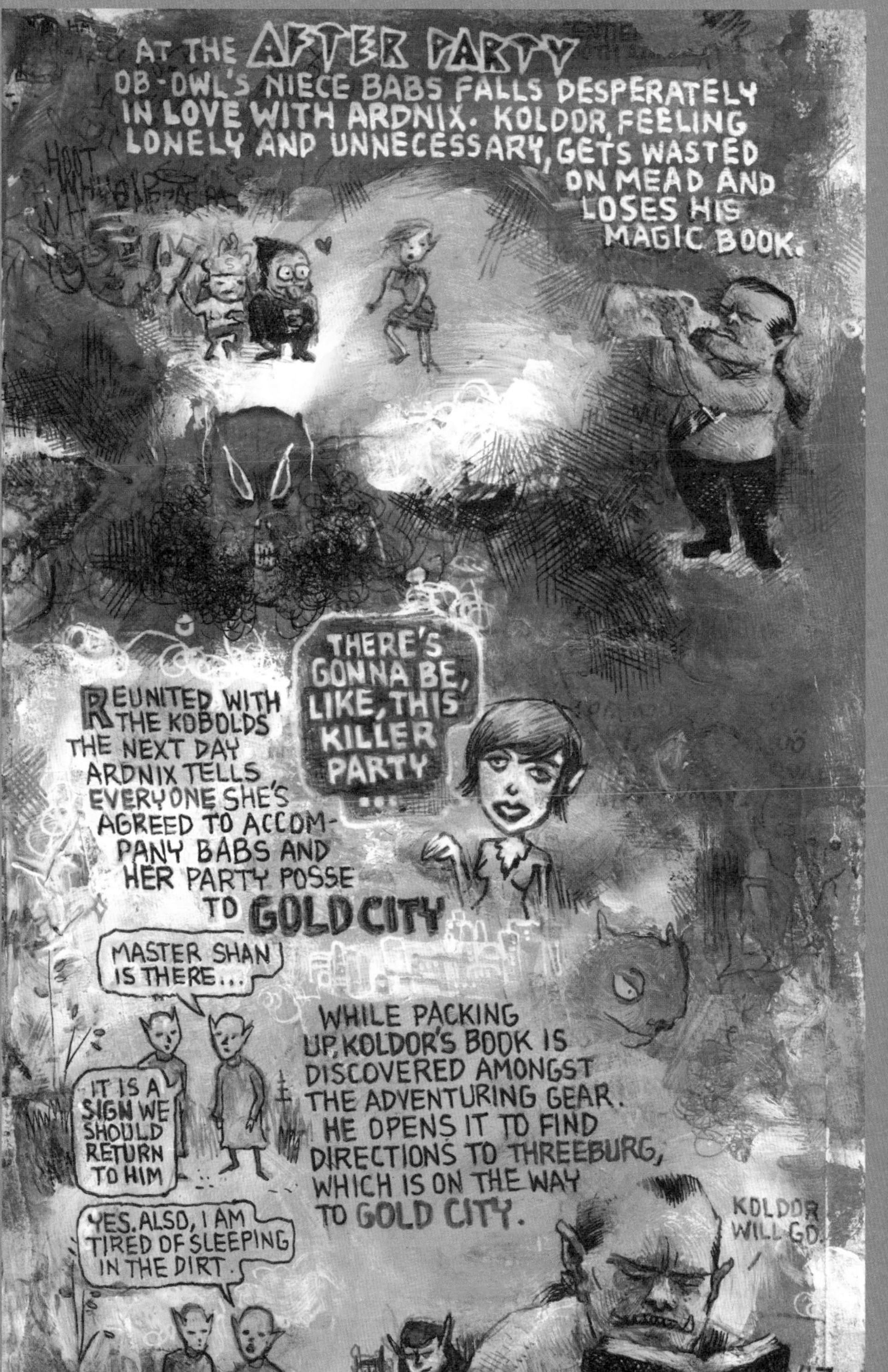

AT THE AFTER PARTY
OB-OWL'S NIECE BABS FALLS DESPERATELY IN LOVE WITH ARDNIX. KOLDOR, FEELING LONELY AND UNNECESSARY, GETS WASTED ON MEAD AND LOSES HIS MAGIC BOOK.
THERE'S GONNA BE, LIKE, THIS KILLER PARTY ...
REUNITED WITH THE KOBOLDS THE NEXT DAY ARDNIX TELLS EVERYONE SHE'S AGREED TO ACCOMPANY BABS AND HER PARTY POSSE TO GOLD CITY
MASTER SHAN IS THERE...
IT IS A SIGN WE SHOULD RETURN TO HIM
YES. ALSO, I AM TIRED OF SLEEPING IN THE DIRT.
WHILE PACKING UP, KOLDOR'S BOOK IS DISCOVERED AMONGST THE ADVENTURING GEAR. HE OPENS IT TO FIND DIRECTIONS TO THREEBURG, WHICH IS ON THE WAY TO GOLD CITY.
KOLDOR WILL GO.
47.

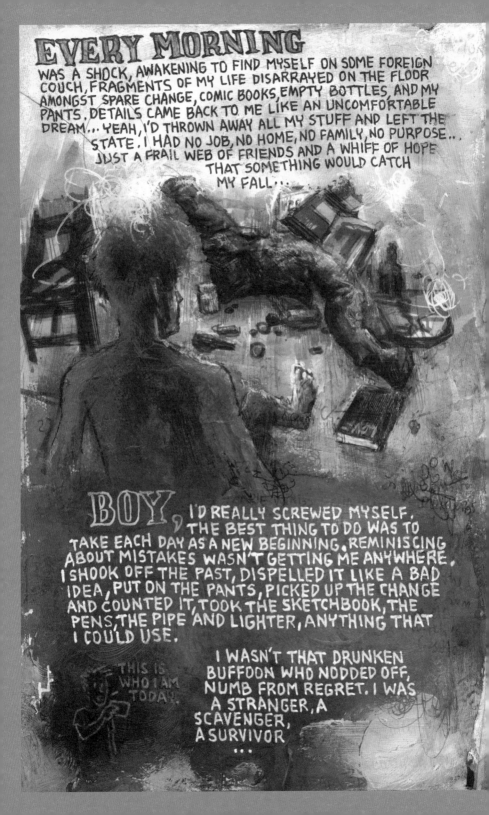

EVERY MORNING

WAS A SHOCK, AWAKENING TO FIND MYSELF ON SOME FOREIGN COUCH, FRAGMENTS OF MY LIFE DISARRAYED ON THE FLOOR AMONGST SPARE CHANGE, COMIC BOOKS, EMPTY BOTTLES, AND MY PANTS. DETAILS CAME BACK TO ME LIKE AN UNCOMFORTABLE DREAM... YEAH, I'D THROWN AWAY ALL MY STUFF AND LEFT THE STATE. I HAD NO JOB, NO HOME, NO FAMILY, NO PURPOSE... JUST A FRAIL WEB OF FRIENDS AND A WHIFF OF HOPE THAT SOMETHING WOULD CATCH MY FALL...

BOY, I'D REALLY SCREWED MYSELF. THE BEST THING TO DO WAS TO TAKE EACH DAY AS A NEW BEGINNING. REMINISCING ABOUT MISTAKES WASN'T GETTING ME ANYWHERE. I SHOOK OFF THE PAST, DISPELLED IT LIKE A BAD IDEA, PUT ON THE PANTS, PICKED UP THE CHANGE AND COUNTED IT, TOOK THE SKETCHBOOK, THE PENS, THE PIPE AND LIGHTER, ANYTHING THAT I COULD USE.

THIS IS WHO I AM TODAY.

I WASN'T THAT DRUNKEN BUFFOON WHO NODDED OFF, NUMB FROM REGRET. I WAS A STRANGER, A SCAVENGER, A SURVIVOR
...

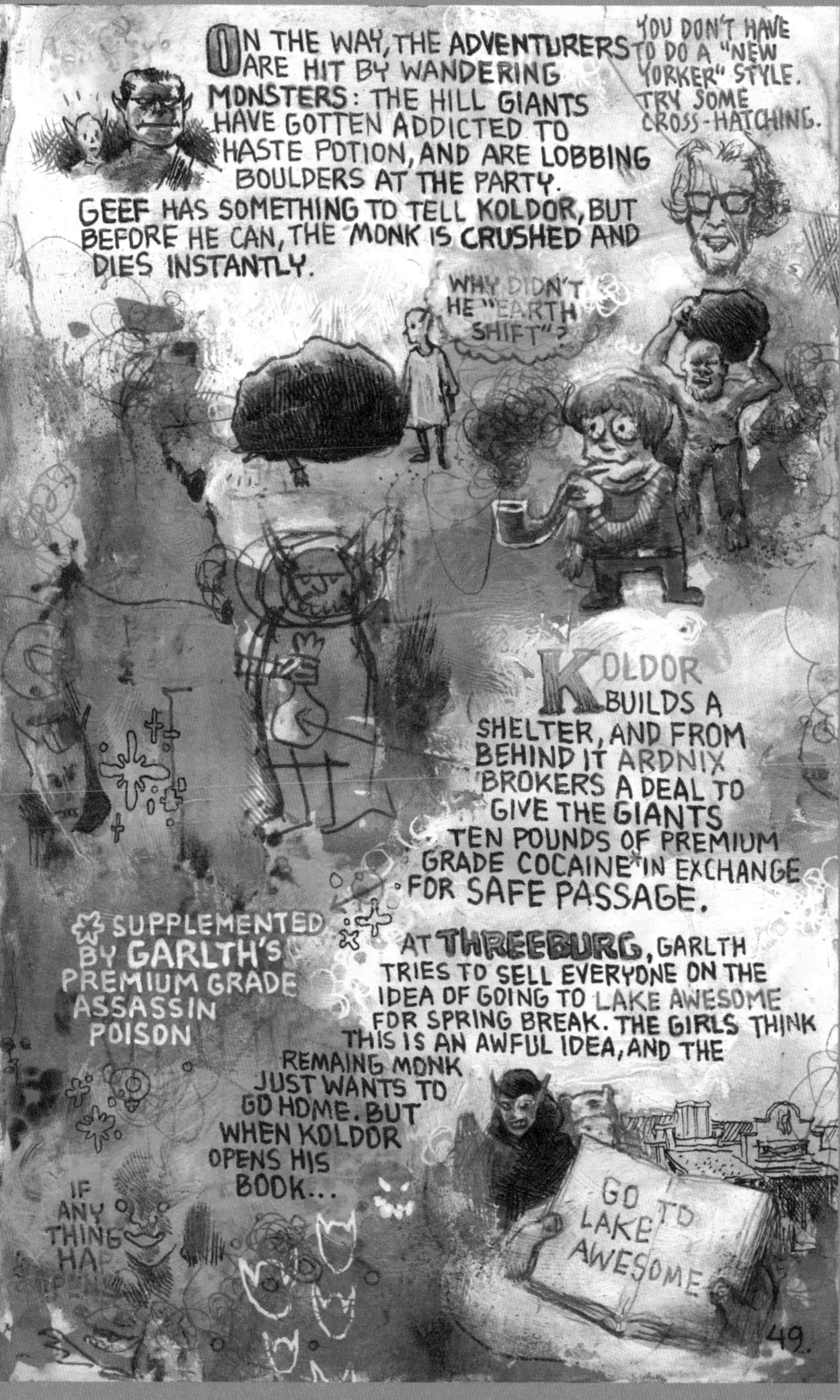

ON THE WAY, THE ADVENTURERS ARE HIT BY WANDERING MONSTERS: THE HILL GIANTS HAVE GOTTEN ADDICTED TO HASTE POTION, AND ARE LOBBING BOULDERS AT THE PARTY.
YOU DON'T HAVE TO DO A "NEW YORKER" STYLE. TRY SOME CROSS-HATCHING.
GEEF HAS SOMETHING TO TELL KOLDOR, BUT BEFORE HE CAN, THE MONK IS CRUSHED AND DIES INSTANTLY.
WHY DIDN'T HE "EARTH SHIFT"?
KOLDOR BUILDS A SHELTER, AND FROM BEHIND IT ARDNIX BROKERS A DEAL TO GIVE THE GIANTS TEN POUNDS OF PREMIUM GRADE COCAINE* IN EXCHANGE FOR SAFE PASSAGE.
* SUPPLEMENTED BY GARLTH'S PREMIUM GRADE ASSASSIN POISON
AT THREEBURG, GARLTH TRIES TO SELL EVERYONE ON THE IDEA OF GOING TO LAKE AWESOME FOR SPRING BREAK. THE GIRLS THINK THIS IS AN AWFUL IDEA, AND THE REMAING MONK JUST WANTS TO GO HOME. BUT WHEN KOLDOR OPENS HIS BOOK...
IF ANY THING HA
GO TO LAKE AWESOME
49.

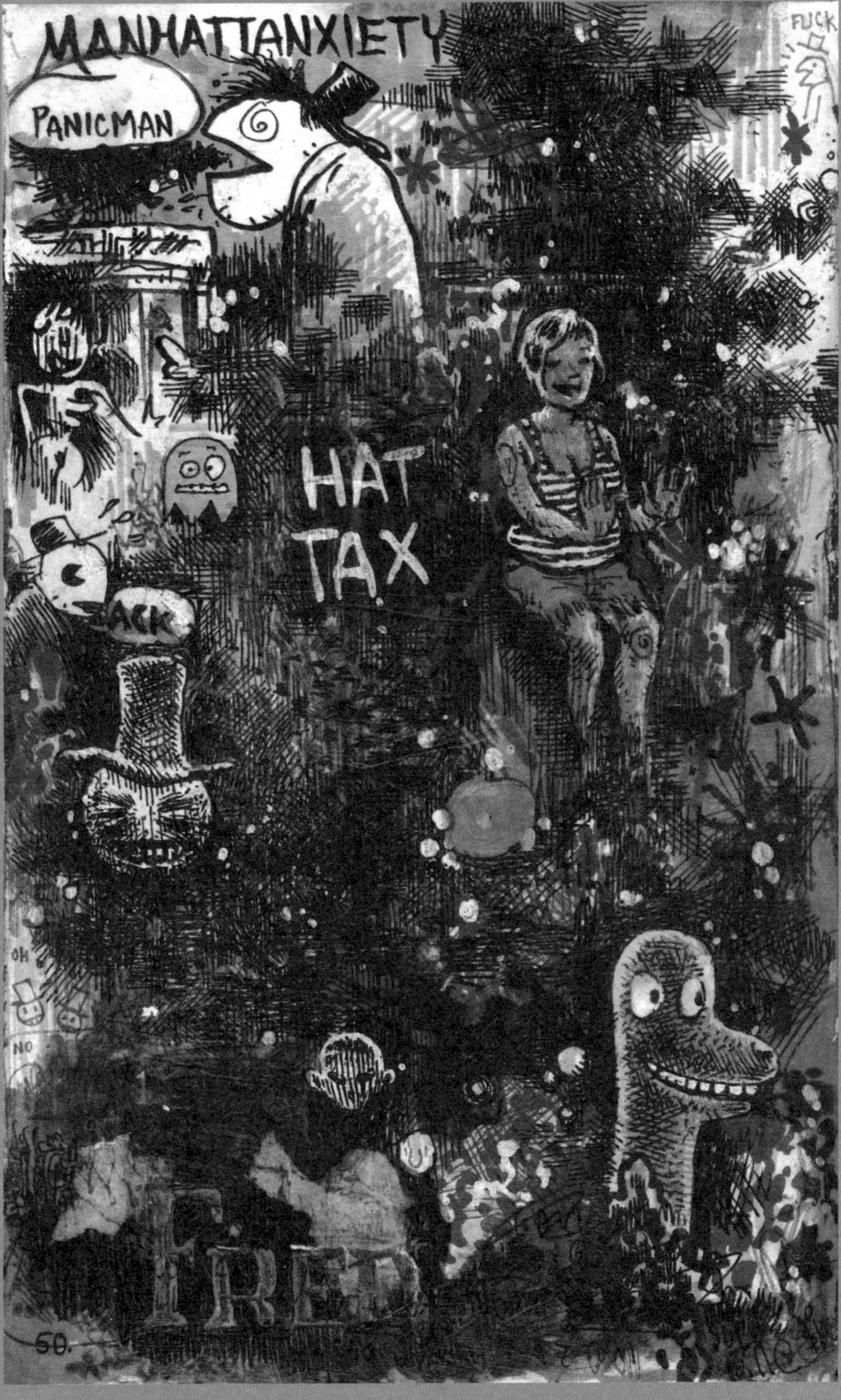
MANHATTANXIETY
PANICMAN
FUCK
HAT TAX
ACK
OH
NO
50.

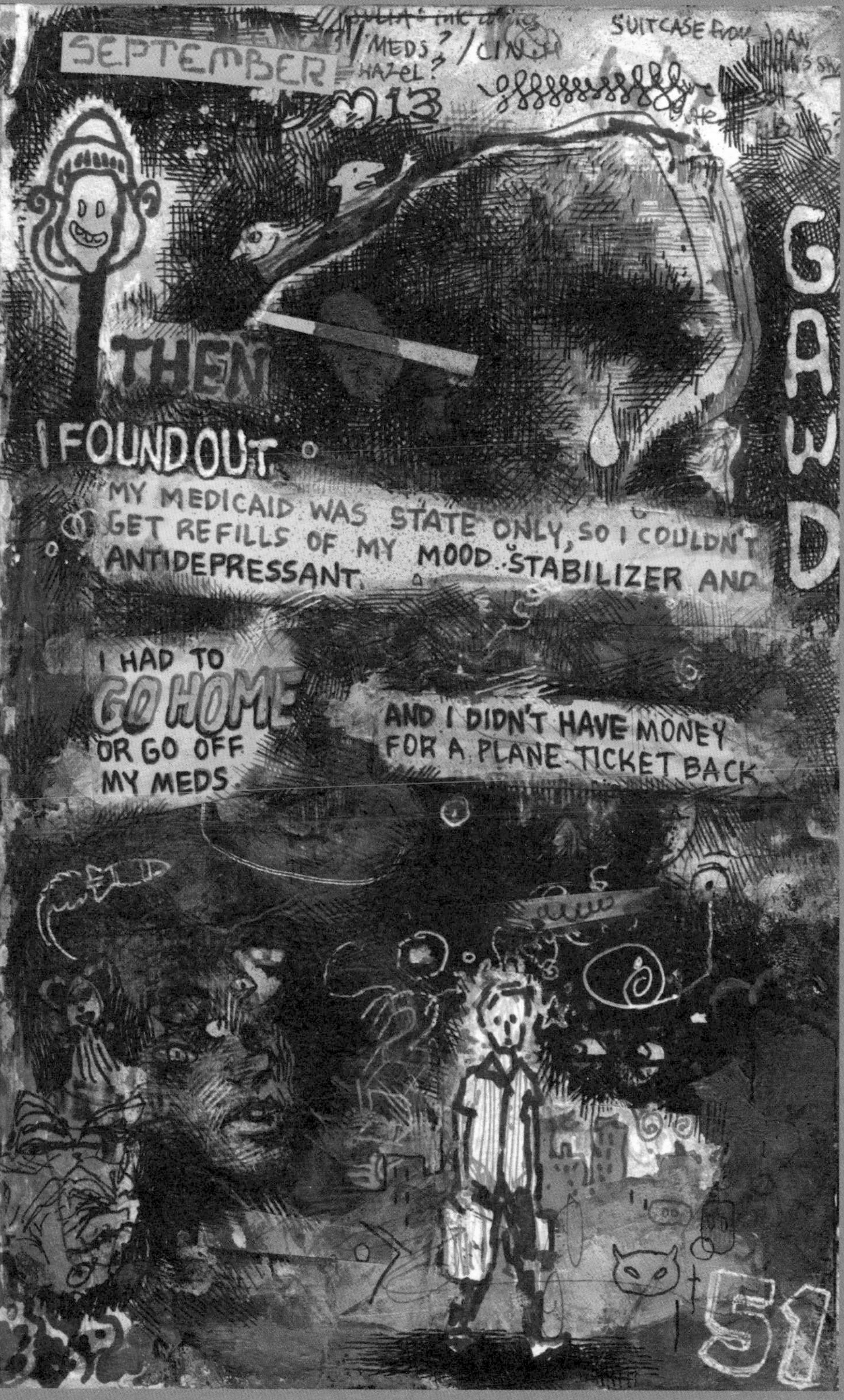

SEPTEMBER
MEDS? HAZEL?
13
SUITCASE FROM JOAN
THEN
I FOUND OUT
MY MEDICAID WAS STATE ONLY, SO I COULDN'T GET REFILLS OF MY MOOD STABILIZER AND ANTIDEPRESSANT.
GAWD
I HAD TO GO HOME OR GO OFF MY MEDS
AND I DIDN'T HAVE MONEY FOR A PLANE TICKET BACK
51

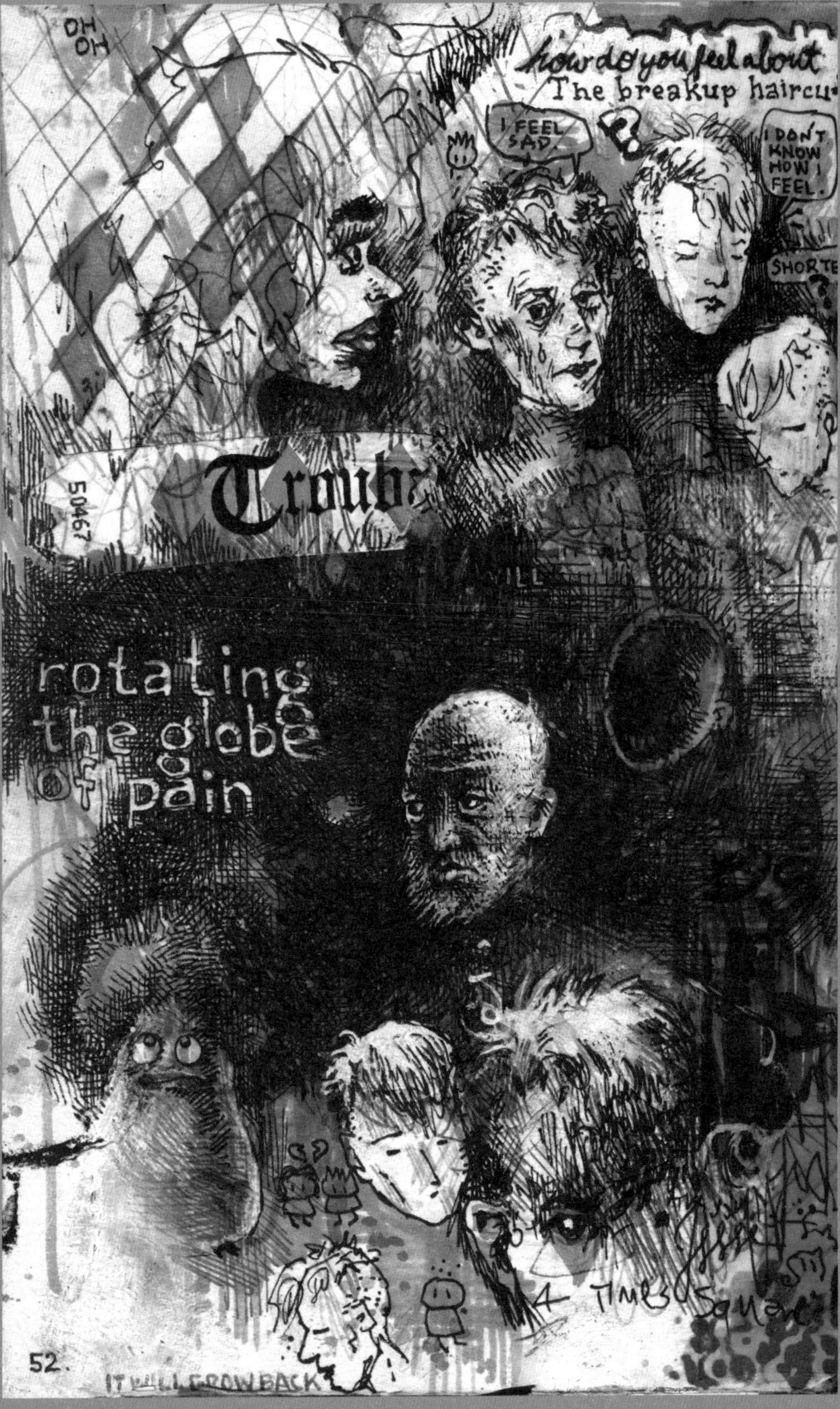
OH OH
how do you feel about
The breakup haircu
I FEEL SAD.
I DON'T KNOW HOW I FEEL.
SHORTE
Troub
50467
rotating the globe of pain
TIMES Square
IT WILL GROW BACK

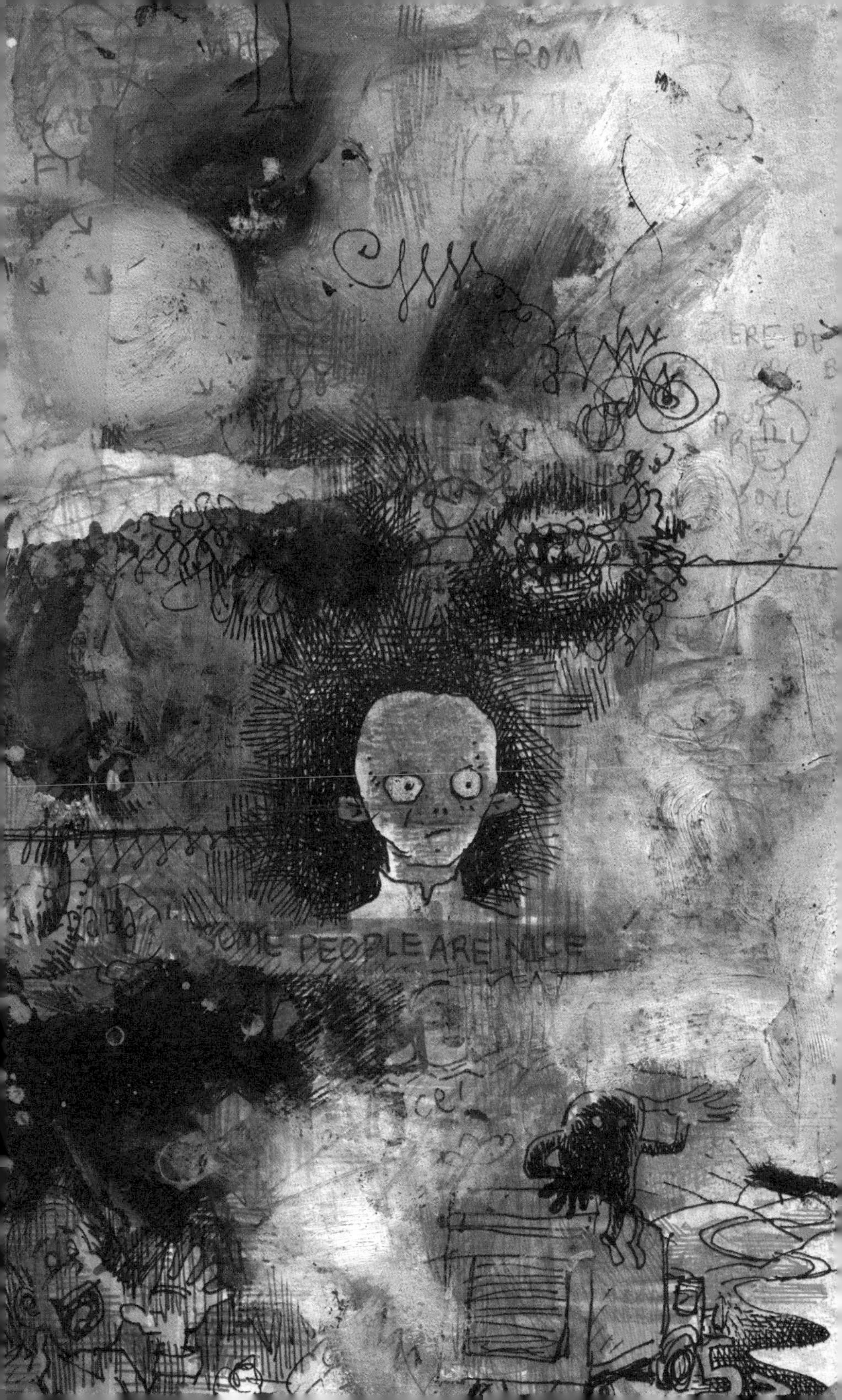
SOME PEOPLE ARE NICE

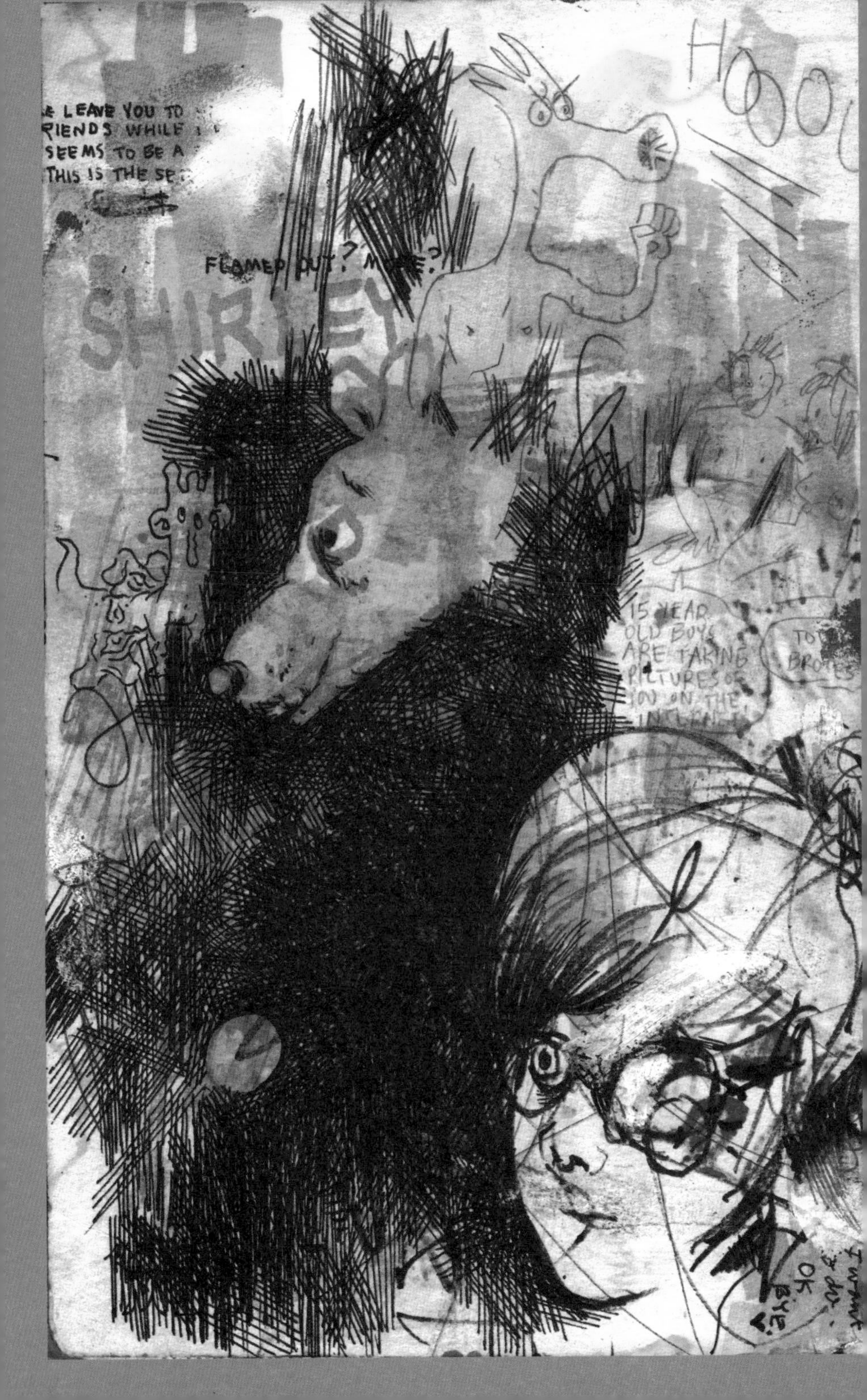
LEAVE YOU TO
RIENDS WHILE
SEEMS TO BE A
THIS IS THE SE
FLAMED OUT?
HOOO
15 YEAR OLD BOYS ARE TAKING PICTURES OF YOU ON THE
OK BYE

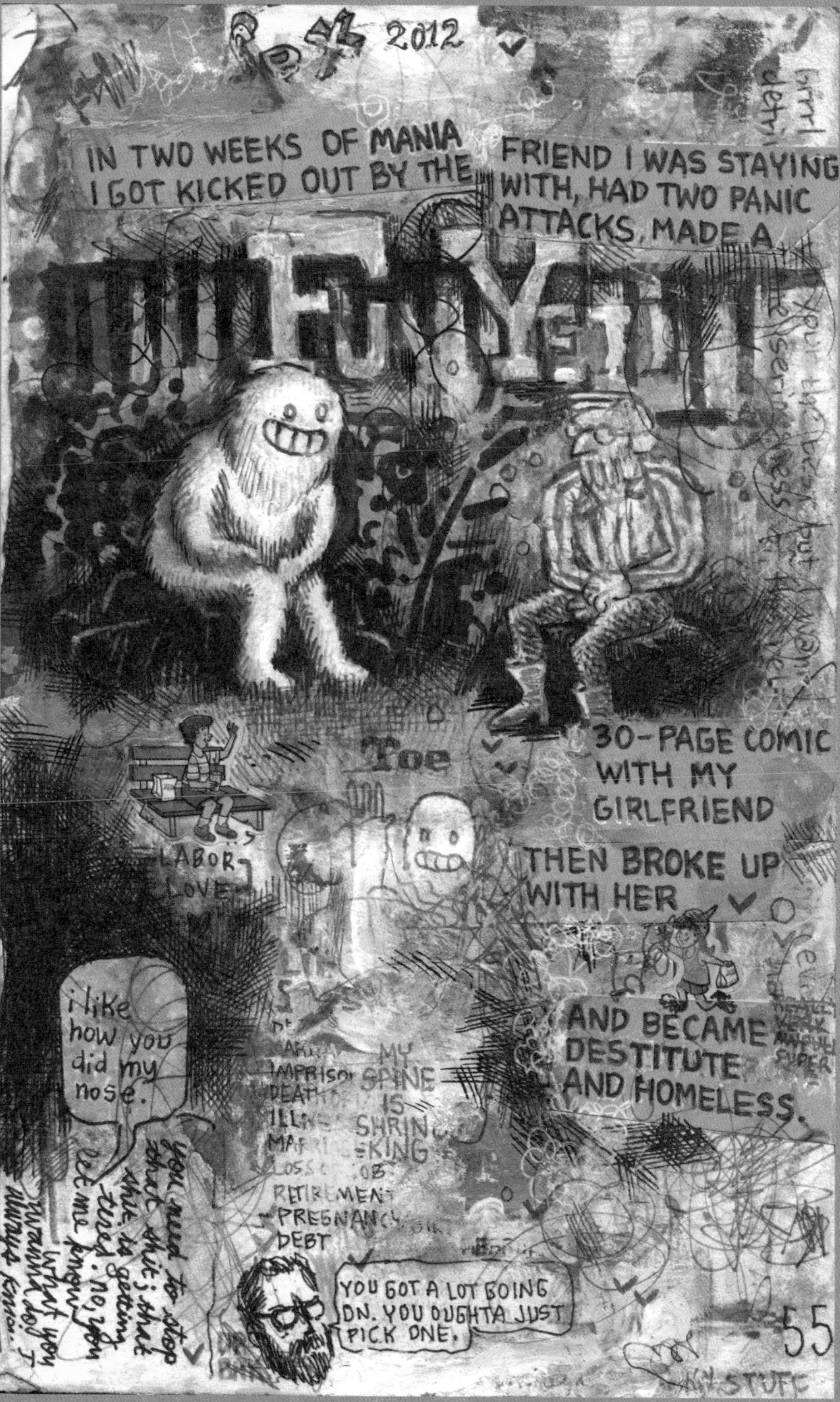
2012
IN TWO WEEKS OF MANIA I GOT KICKED OUT BY THE
FRIEND I WAS STAYING WITH, HAD TWO PANIC ATTACKS, MADE A
Toe
LABOR LOVE
30-PAGE COMIC WITH MY GIRLFRIEND
THEN BROKE UP WITH HER
AND BECAME DESTITUTE AND HOMELESS.
i like how you did my nose.
MY SPINE IS SHRINKING
RETIREMENT
PREGNANCY
DEBT
YOU GOT A LOT GOING ON. YOU OUGHTA JUST PICK ONE.

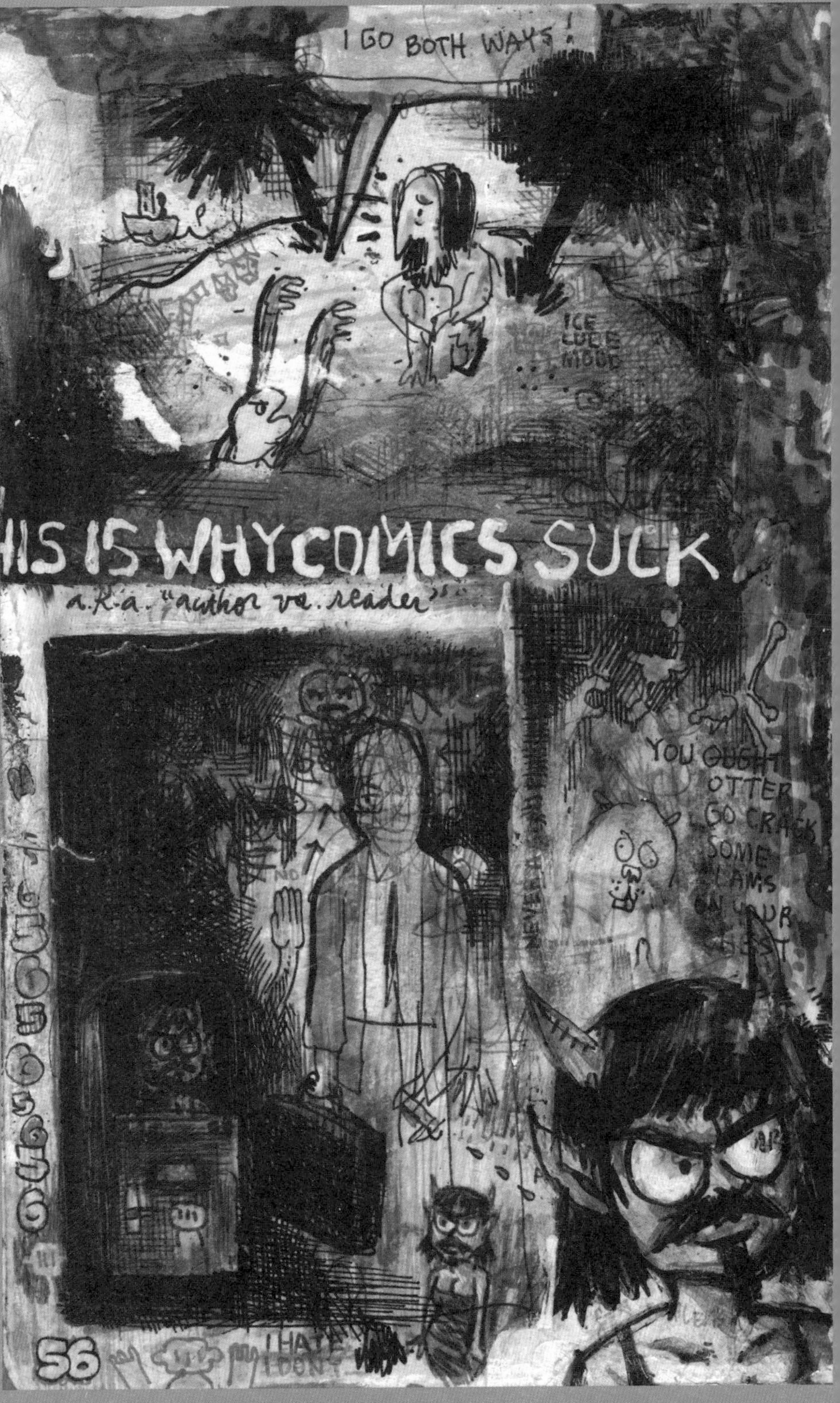

I GO BOTH WAYS!
HIS IS WHY COMICS SUCK
a.k.a. "author vs. reader"
YOU OUGHT OTTER GO CRACK SOME CLAMS

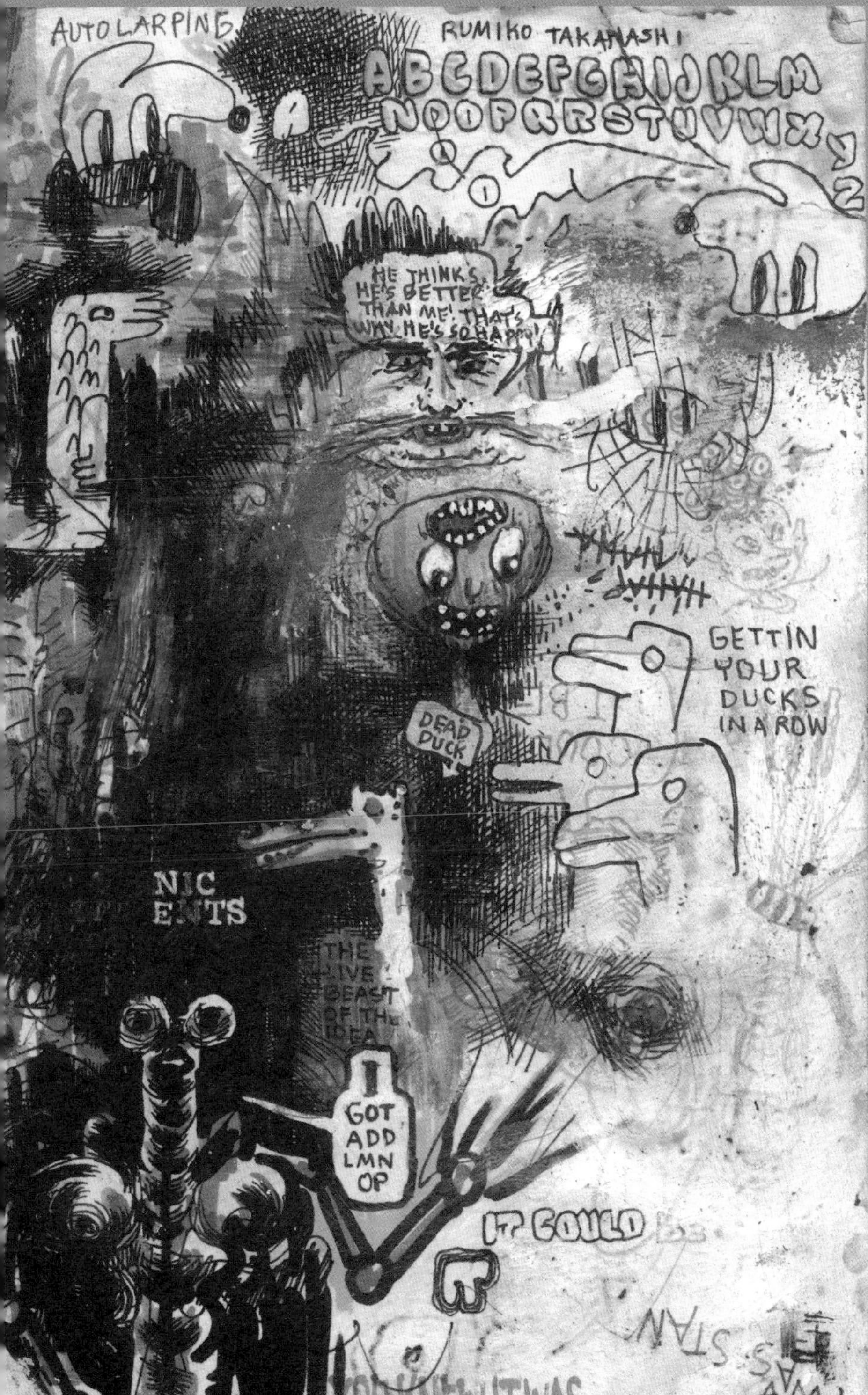
AUTOLARPING
RUMIKO TAKAHASHI
ABCDEFGHIJKLM
NOOPRRSTUVWXYZ
HE THINKS HE'S BETTER THAN ME! THAT'S WHY HE'S SO HAPPY!
GETTIN YOUR DUCKS IN A ROW
DEAD DUCK
NIC ENTS
THE LIVE BEAST OF THE IDEA
I GOT ADD LMN OP
IT COULD BE
YOU KNEW IT WAS

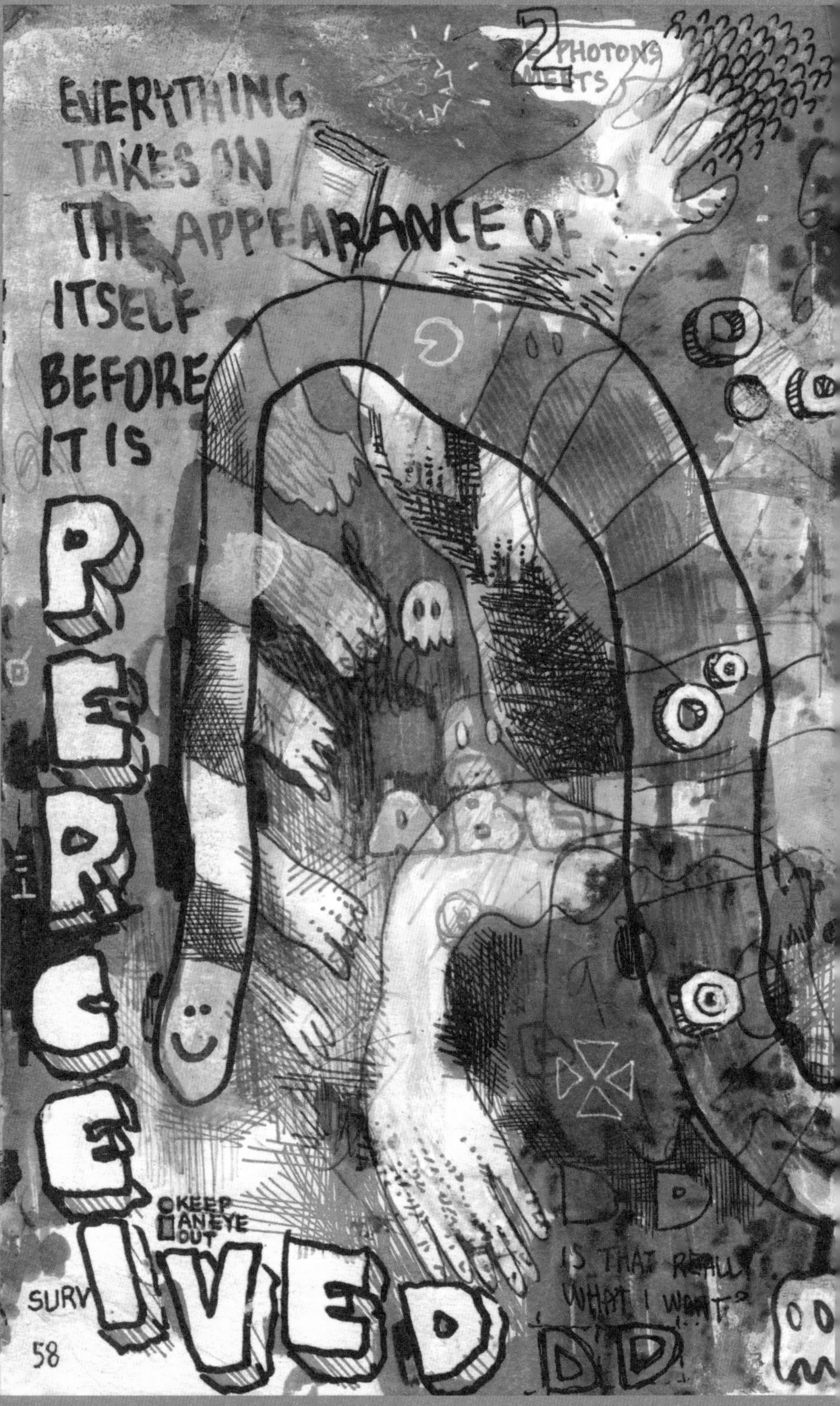

EVERYTHING TAKES ON THE APPEARANCE OF ITSELF BEFORE IT IS PERCEIVED
PHOTONS MEETS
KEEP AN EYE OUT
SURV
IS THAT REALLY WHAT I WANT?

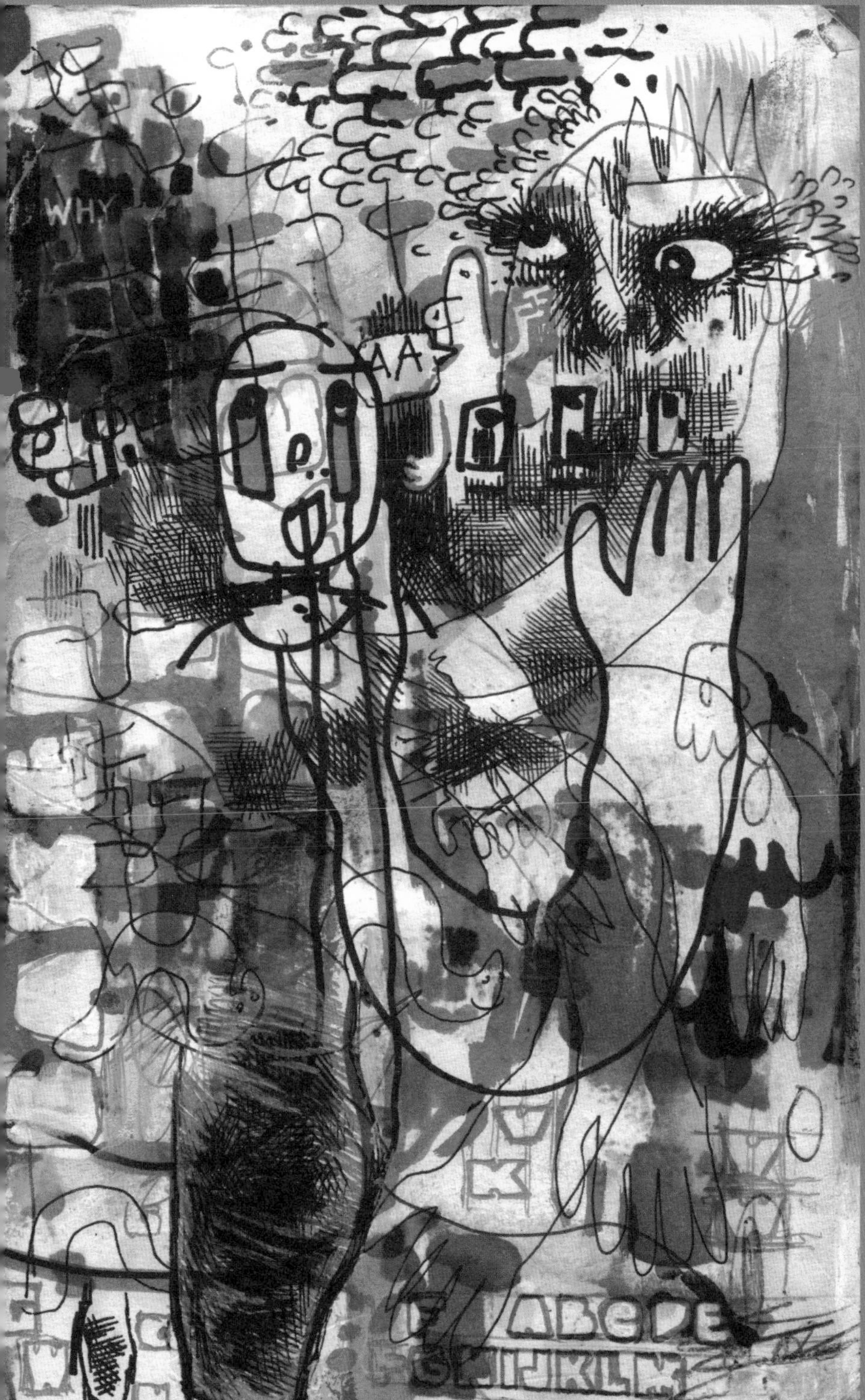
WHY
AA
ABCDE

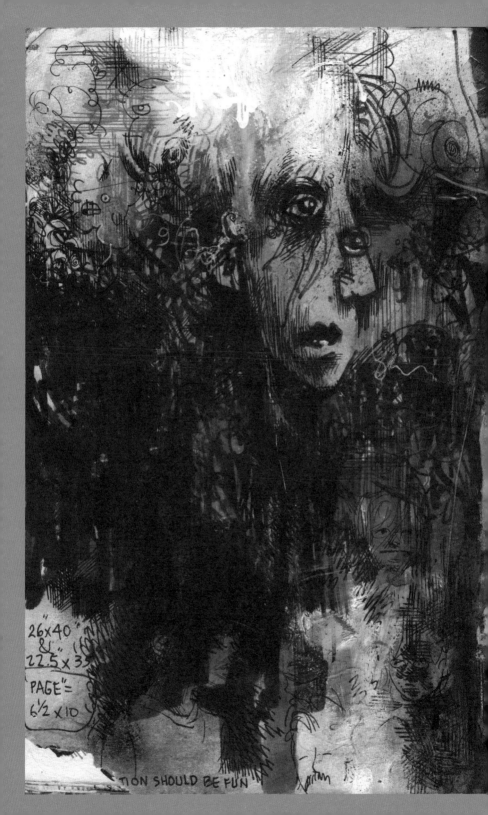

26"x40"
&′ "
22.5 x 3?

PAGE"=
6½ x 10

TION SHOULD BE FUN

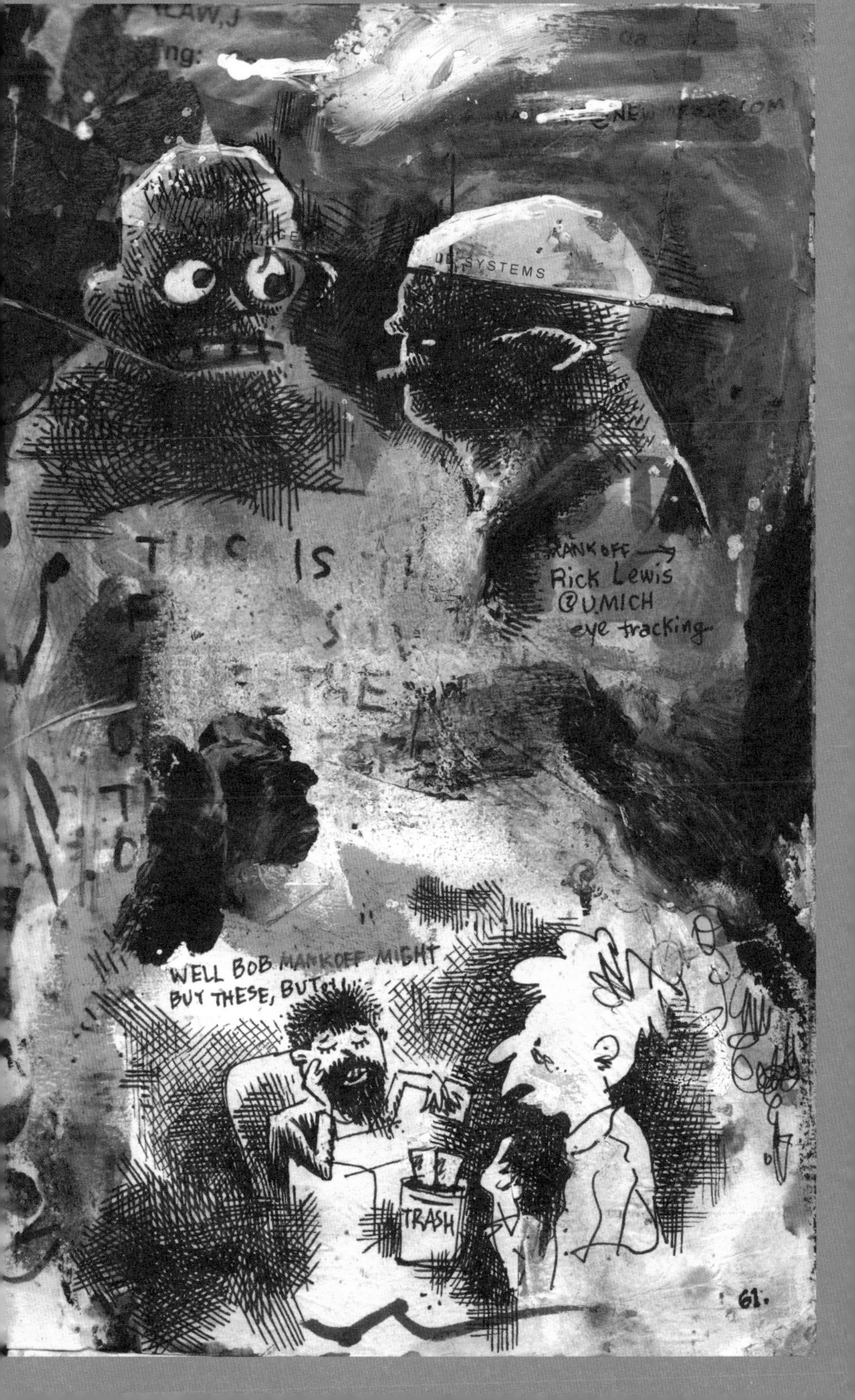
SYSTEMS
IS
RANKOFF →
Rick Lewis
@U.MICH
eye tracking
WELL BOB MANKOFF MIGHT
BUY THESE, BUT...
TRASH

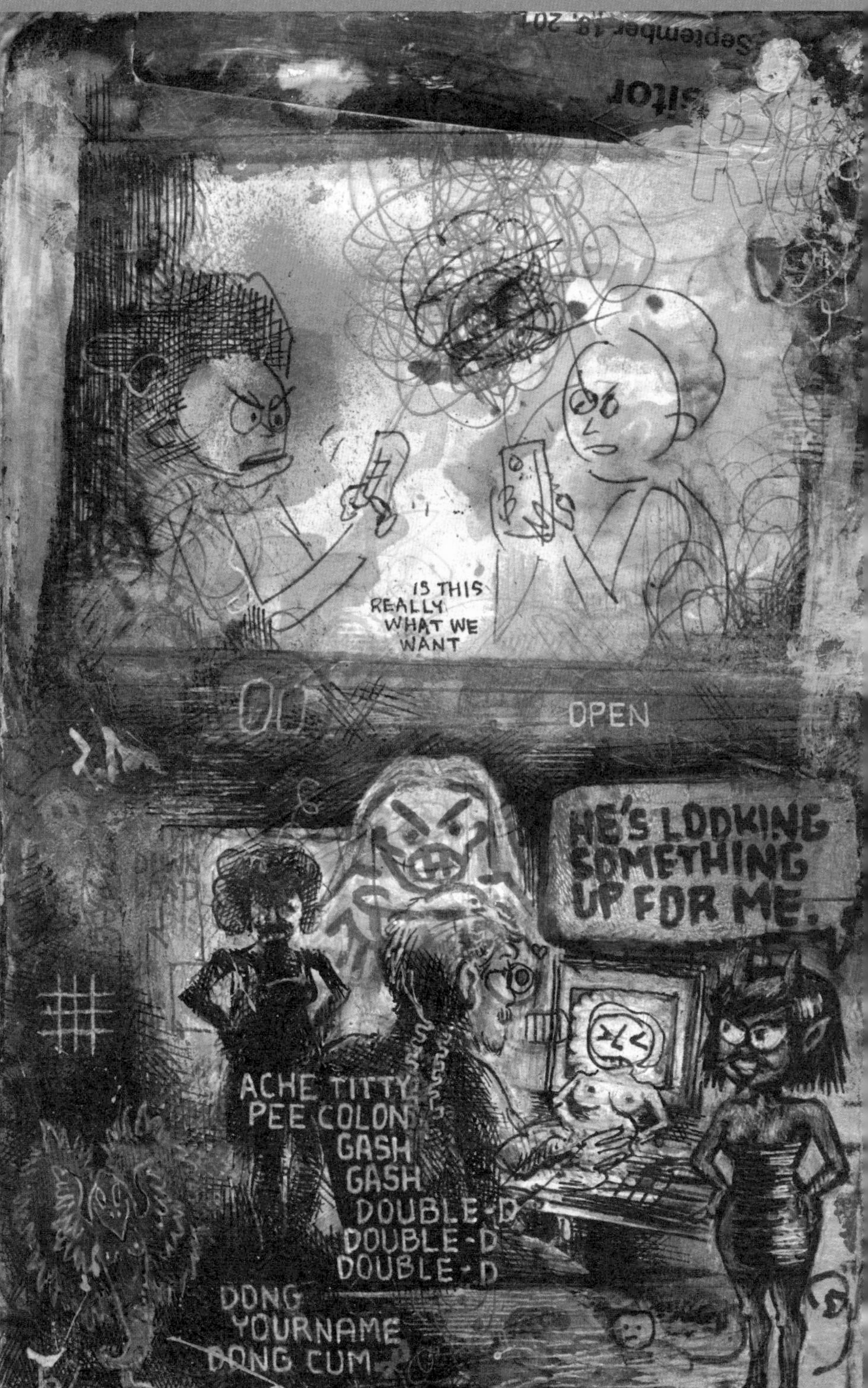
IS THIS REALLY WHAT WE WANT
OPEN
HE'S LOOKING SOMETHING UP FOR ME.
ACHE TITTY
PEE COLON
GASH
GASH
DOUBLE-D
DOUBLE-D
DOUBLE-D
DONG
YOURNAME
DONG CUM

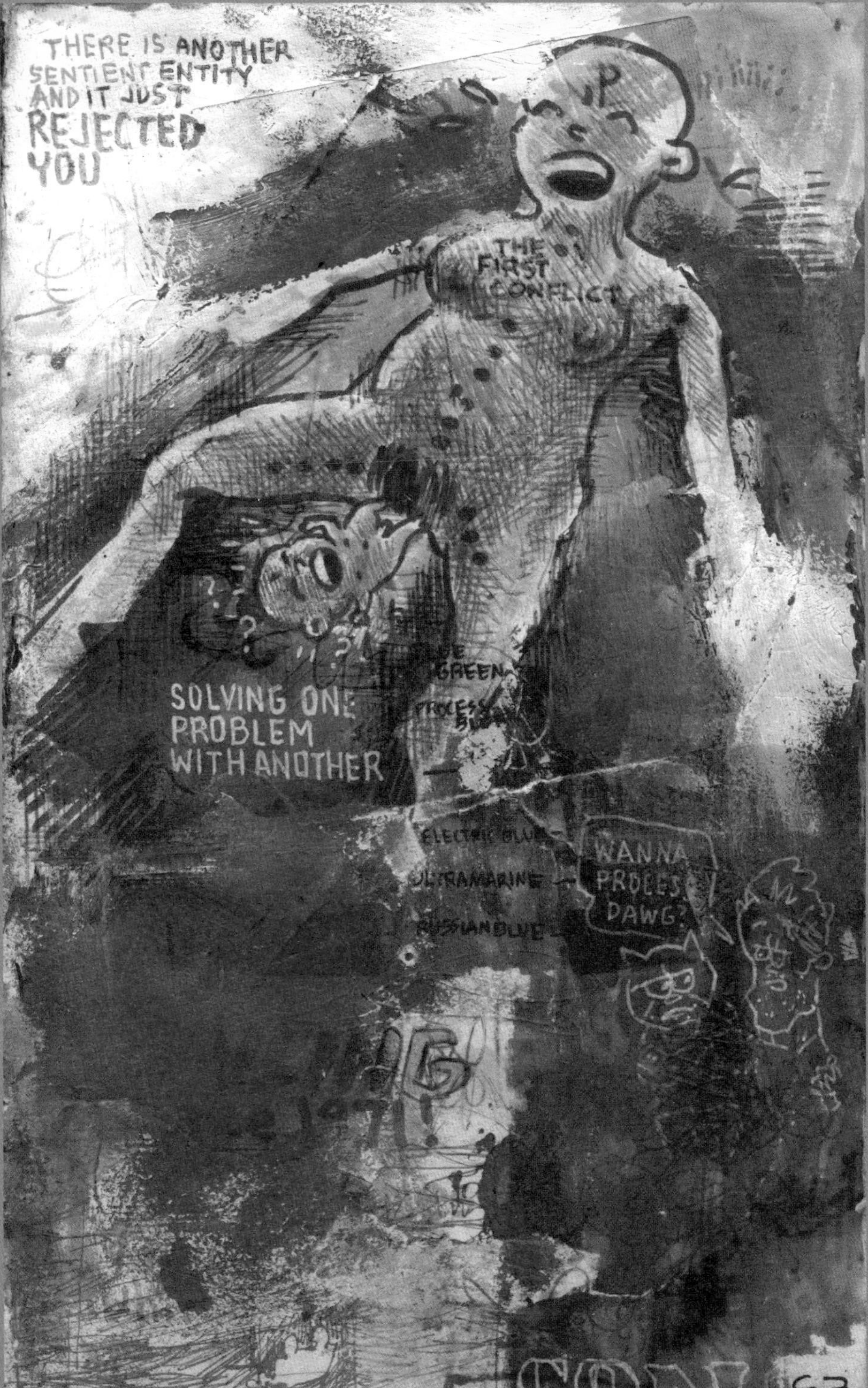
THERE IS ANOTHER SENTIENT ENTITY AND IT JUST REJECTED YOU
THE FIRST CONFLICT
SOLVING ONE PROBLEM WITH ANOTHER
GREEN
ELECTRIC BLUE
ULTRAMARINE
RUSSIAN BLUE
WANNA PROCESS DAWG?
KNOW THAT SONG MOM KNOW THAT
SON

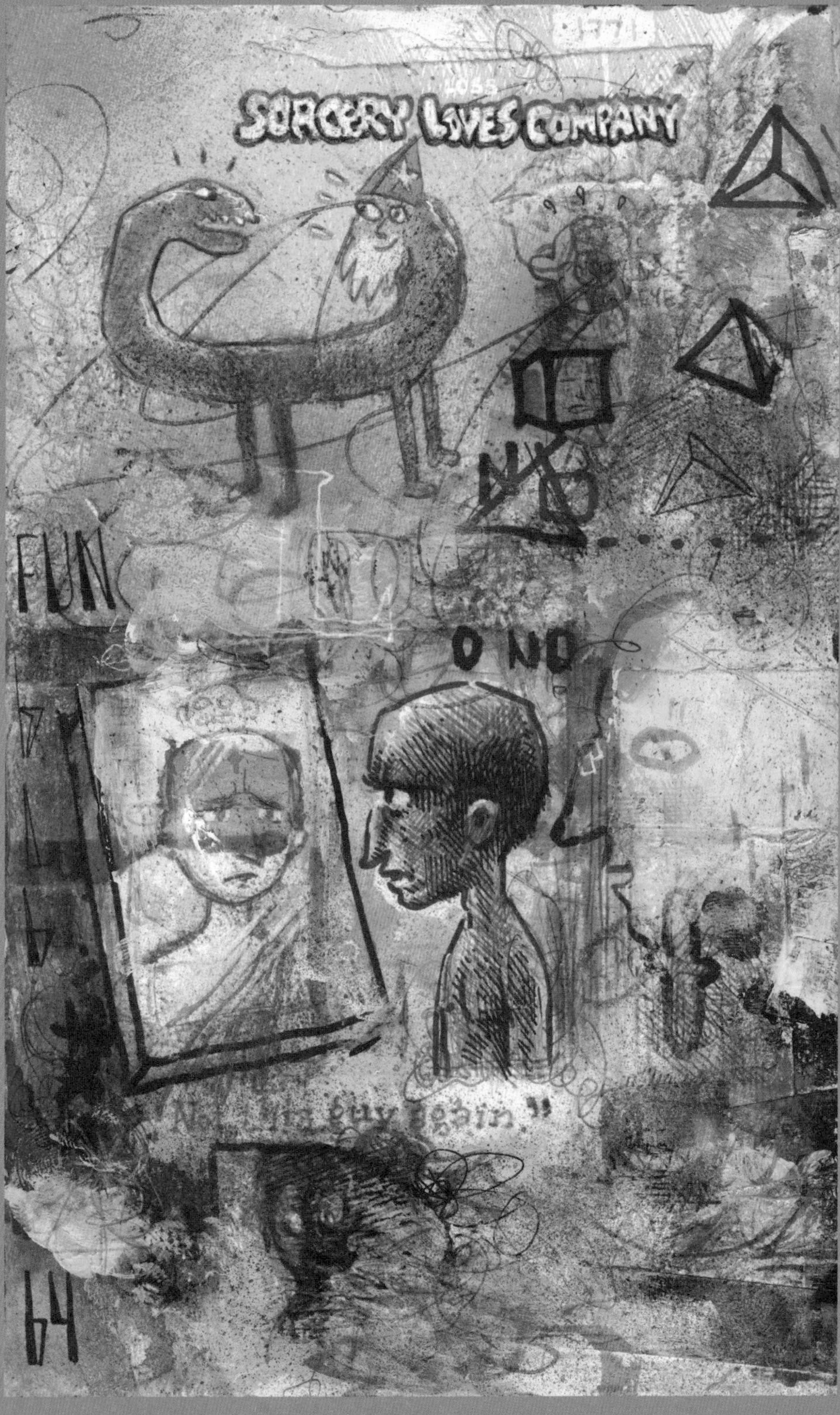
SORCERY LOVES COMPANY
FUN
O NO
guy again
64

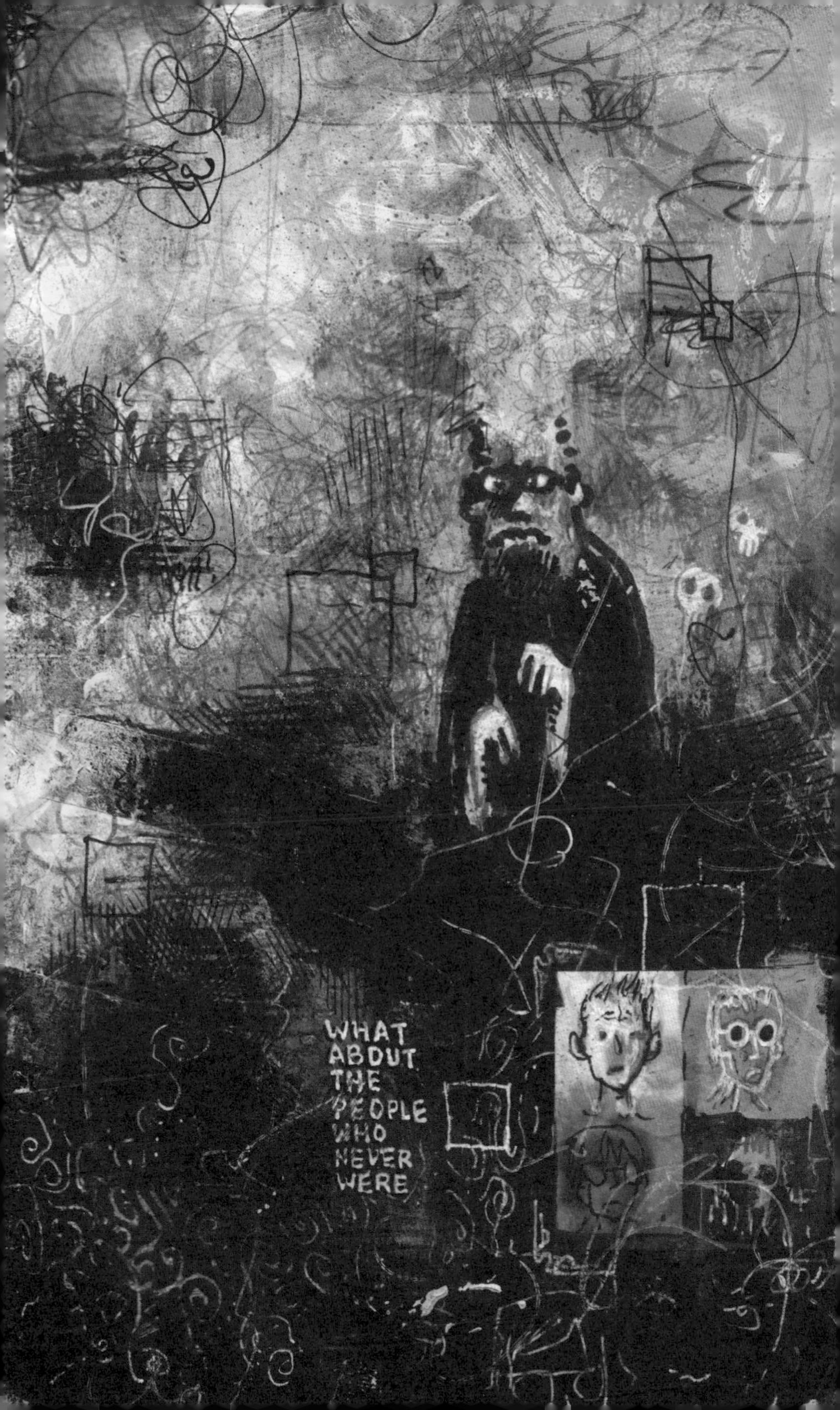
WHAT
ABOUT
THE
PEOPLE
WHO
NEVER
WERE

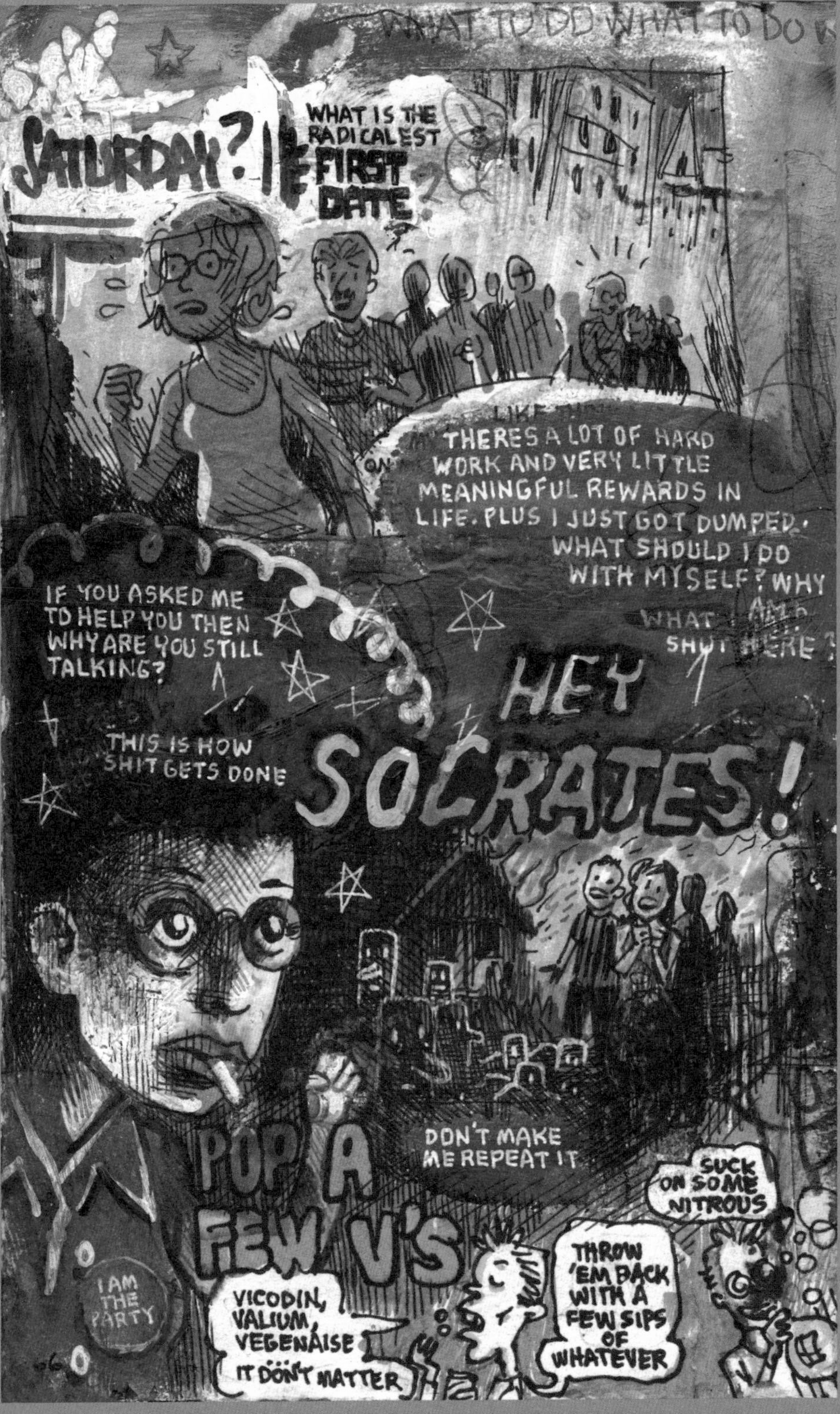
WHAT TO DO WHAT TO DO
SATURDAY?
WHAT IS THE RADICALEST FIRST DATE?
THERES A LOT OF HARD WORK AND VERY LITTLE MEANINGFUL REWARDS IN LIFE. PLUS I JUST GOT DUMPED. WHAT SHOULD I DO WITH MYSELF? WHY WHAT AM SHUT HERE?
IF YOU ASKED ME TO HELP YOU THEN WHY ARE YOU STILL TALKING?
THIS IS HOW SHIT GETS DONE
HEY SOCRATES!
DON'T MAKE ME REPEAT IT
POP A FEW V'S
SUCK ON SOME NITROUS
THROW 'EM BACK WITH A FEW SIPS OF WHATEVER
VICODIN, VALIUM, VEGENAISE IT DON'T MATTER
I AM THE PARTY

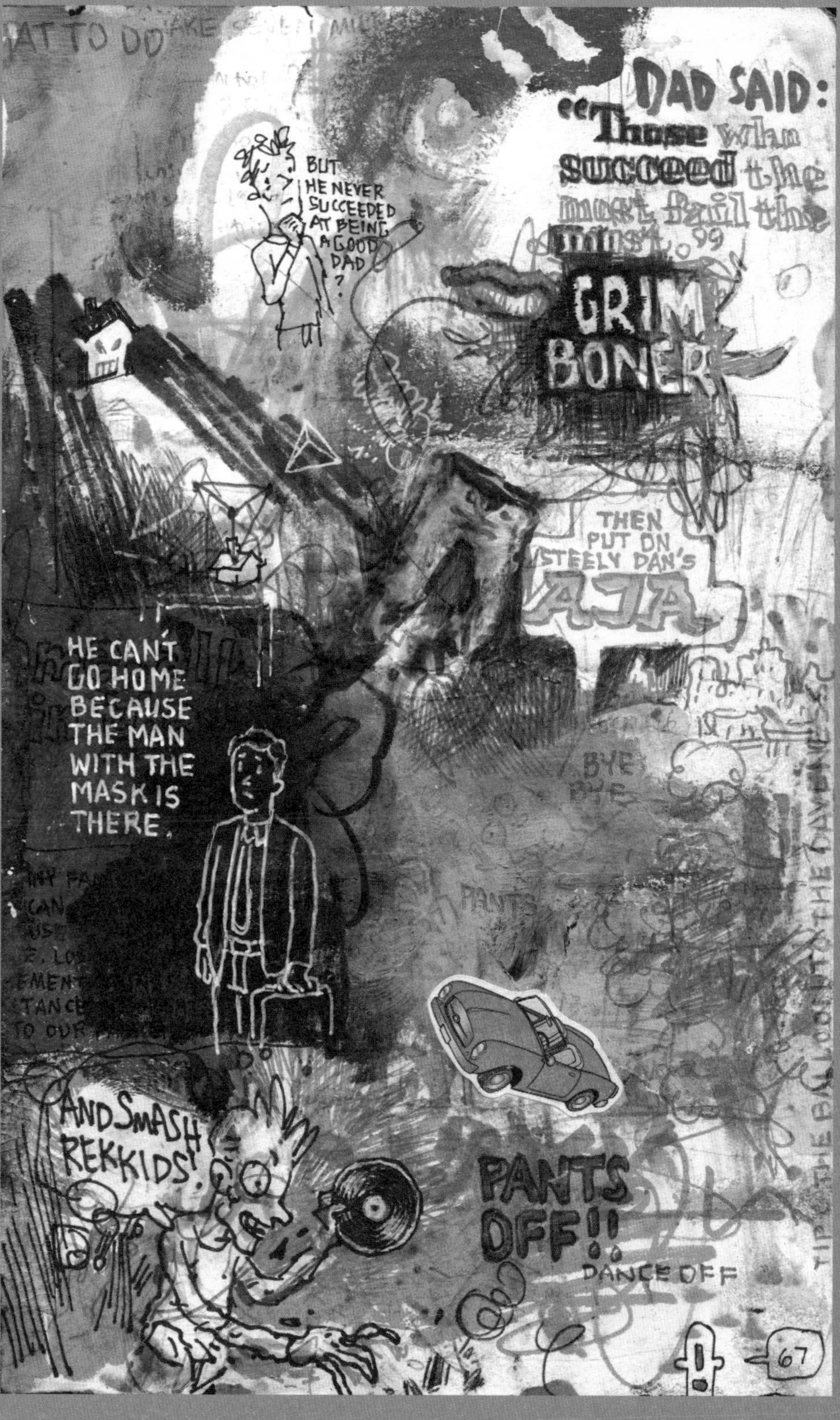

DAD SAID:
"Those who succeed the most fail the most."
BUT HE NEVER SUCCEEDED AT BEING A GOOD DAD?
GRIM BONER
THEN PUT ON STEELY DAN'S AJA
HE CAN'T GO HOME BECAUSE THE MAN WITH THE MASK IS THERE.
BYE BYE
AND SMASH REKKIDS!
PANTS OFF!!
DANCE OFF
TIP THE BALLOON TO THE DAVENCES

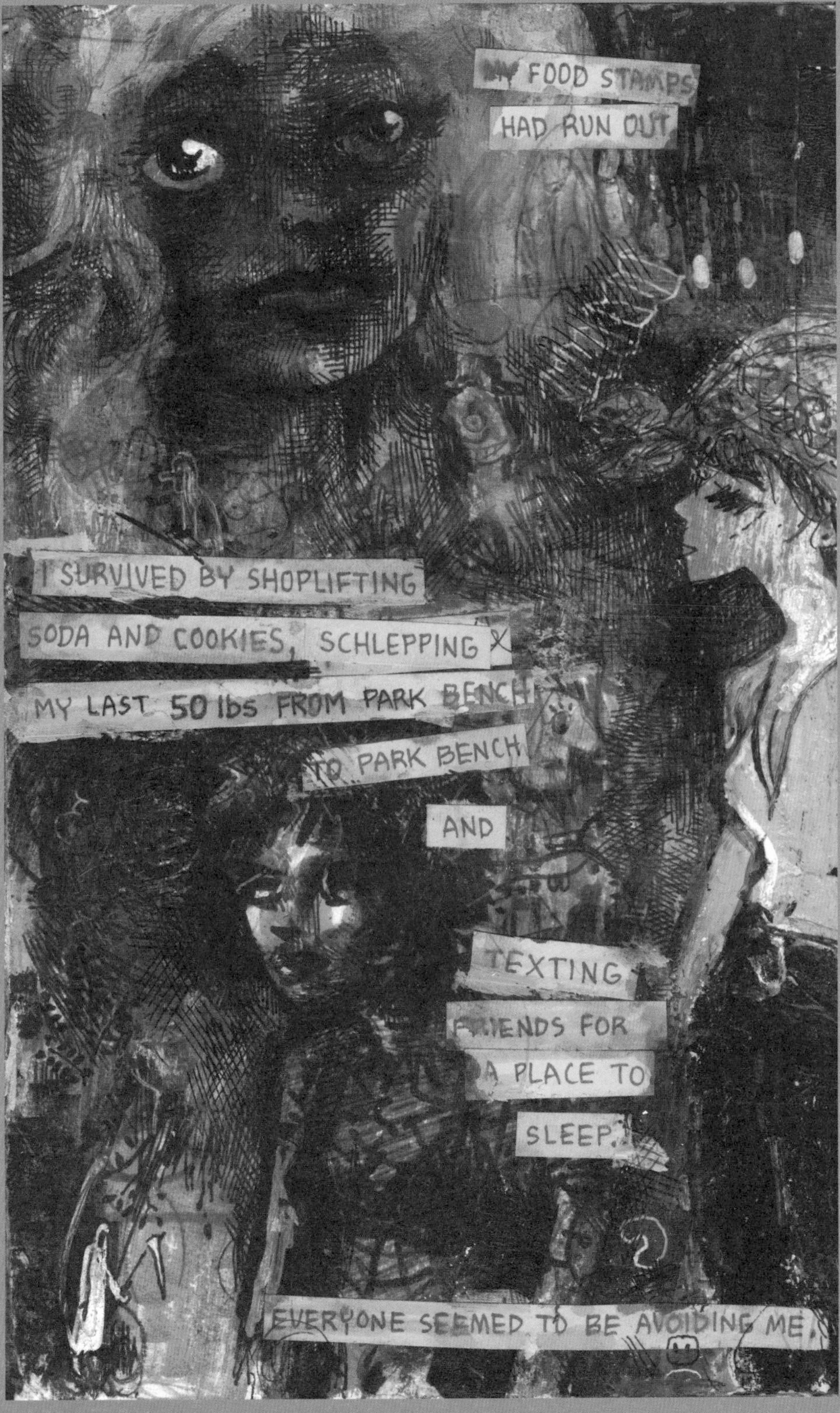
FOOD STAMPS
HAD RUN OUT
I SURVIVED BY SHOPLIFTING
SODA AND COOKIES, SCHLEPPING
MY LAST 50 lbs FROM PARK BENCH
TO PARK BENCH
AND
TEXTING
FRIENDS FOR
A PLACE TO
SLEEP.
EVERYONE SEEMED TO BE AVOIDING ME.

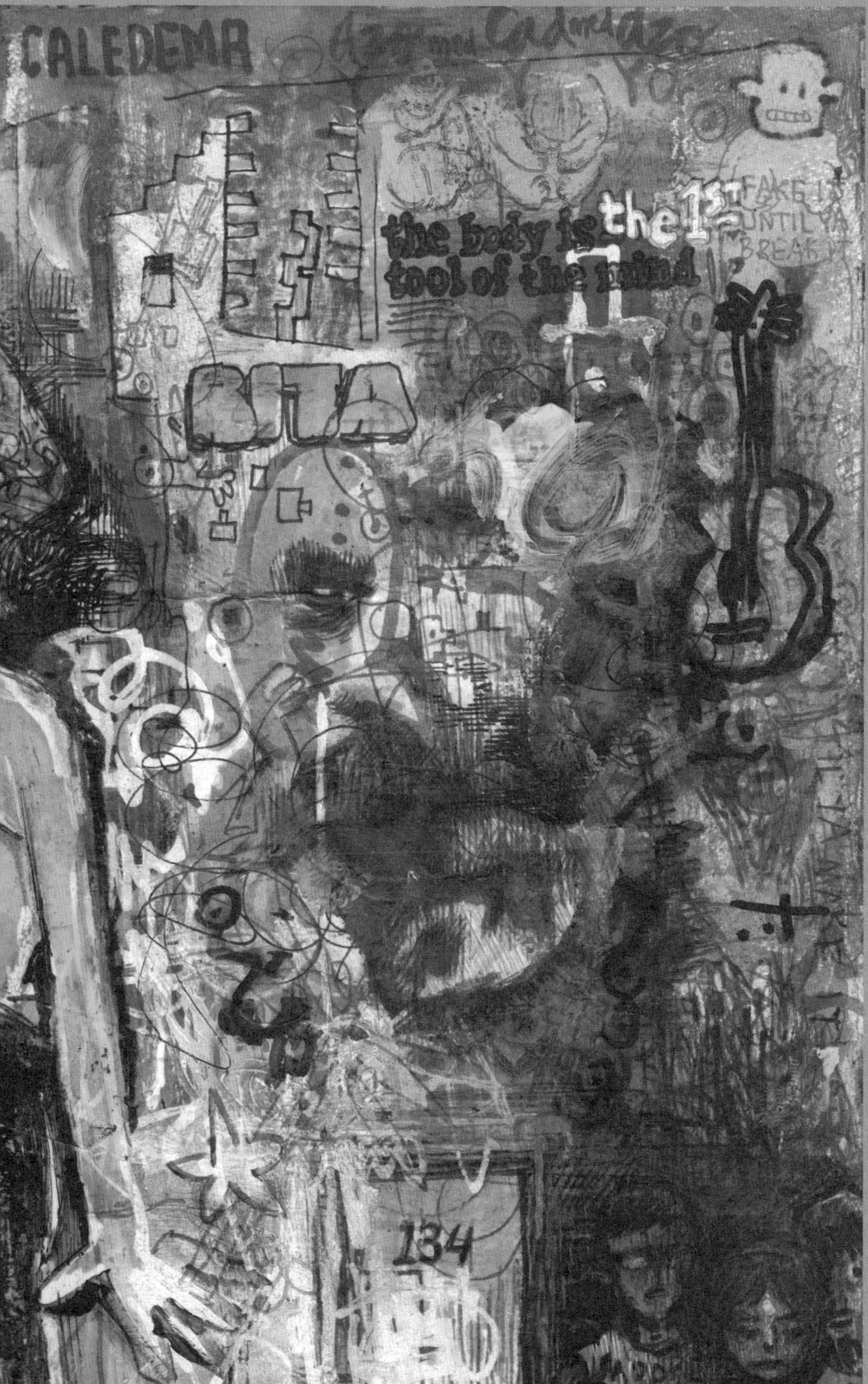
CALEDEMA
the body is the 1st
tool of the mind
134

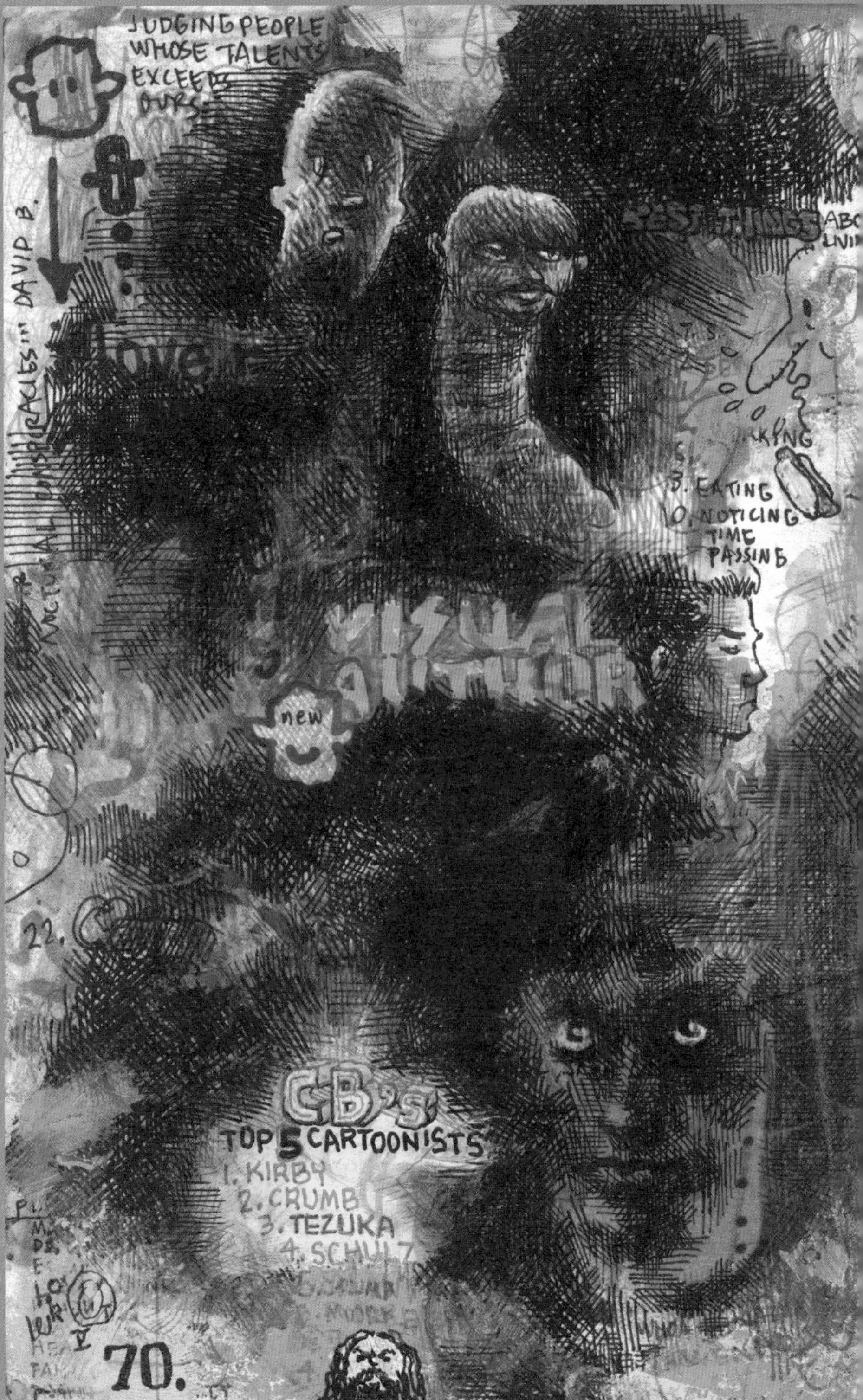
JUDGING PEOPLE WHOSE TALENTS EXCEEDS OURS.
DAVID B.
3. EATING
10. NOTICING TIME PASSING
new
22.
CB's
TOP 5 CARTOONISTS
1. KIRBY
2. CRUMB
3. TEZUKA
4. SCHULZ
70.

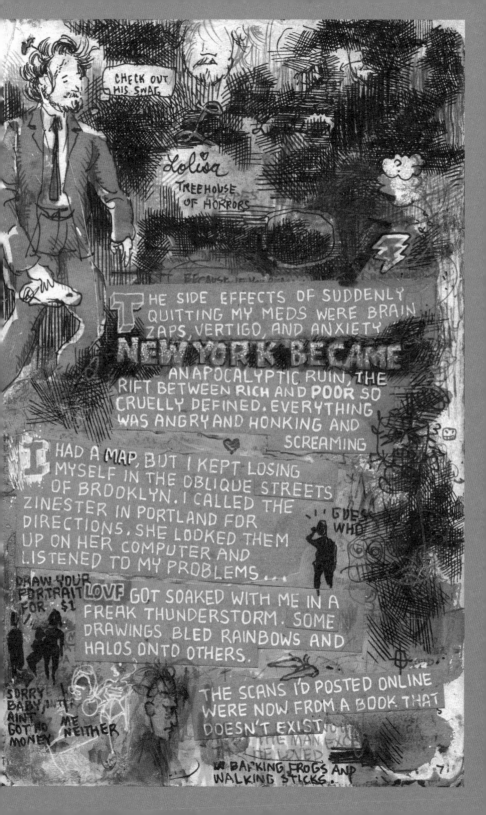

CHECK OUT HIS SWAG

Lolisa
TREEHOUSE OF HORRORS

THE SIDE EFFECTS OF SUDDENLY QUITTING MY MEDS WERE BRAIN ZAPS, VERTIGO, AND ANXIETY

NEW YORK BECAME AN APOCALYPTIC RUIN, THE RIFT BETWEEN RICH AND POOR SO CRUELLY DEFINED. EVERYTHING WAS ANGRY AND HONKING AND SCREAMING

I HAD A MAP, BUT I KEPT LOSING MYSELF IN THE OBLIQUE STREETS OF BROOKLYN. I CALLED THE ZINESTER IN PORTLAND FOR DIRECTIONS. SHE LOOKED THEM UP ON HER COMPUTER AND LISTENED TO MY PROBLEMS...

GUESS WHO

DRAW YOUR PORTRAIT FOR $1

LOVE GOT SOAKED WITH ME IN A FREAK THUNDERSTORM. SOME DRAWINGS BLED RAINBOWS AND HALOS ONTO OTHERS.

SORRY BABY AINT GOT NO MONEY

ME NEITHER

THE SCANS I'D POSTED ONLINE WERE NOW FROM A BOOK THAT DOESN'T EXIST

BARKING FROGS AND WALKING STICKS.

7

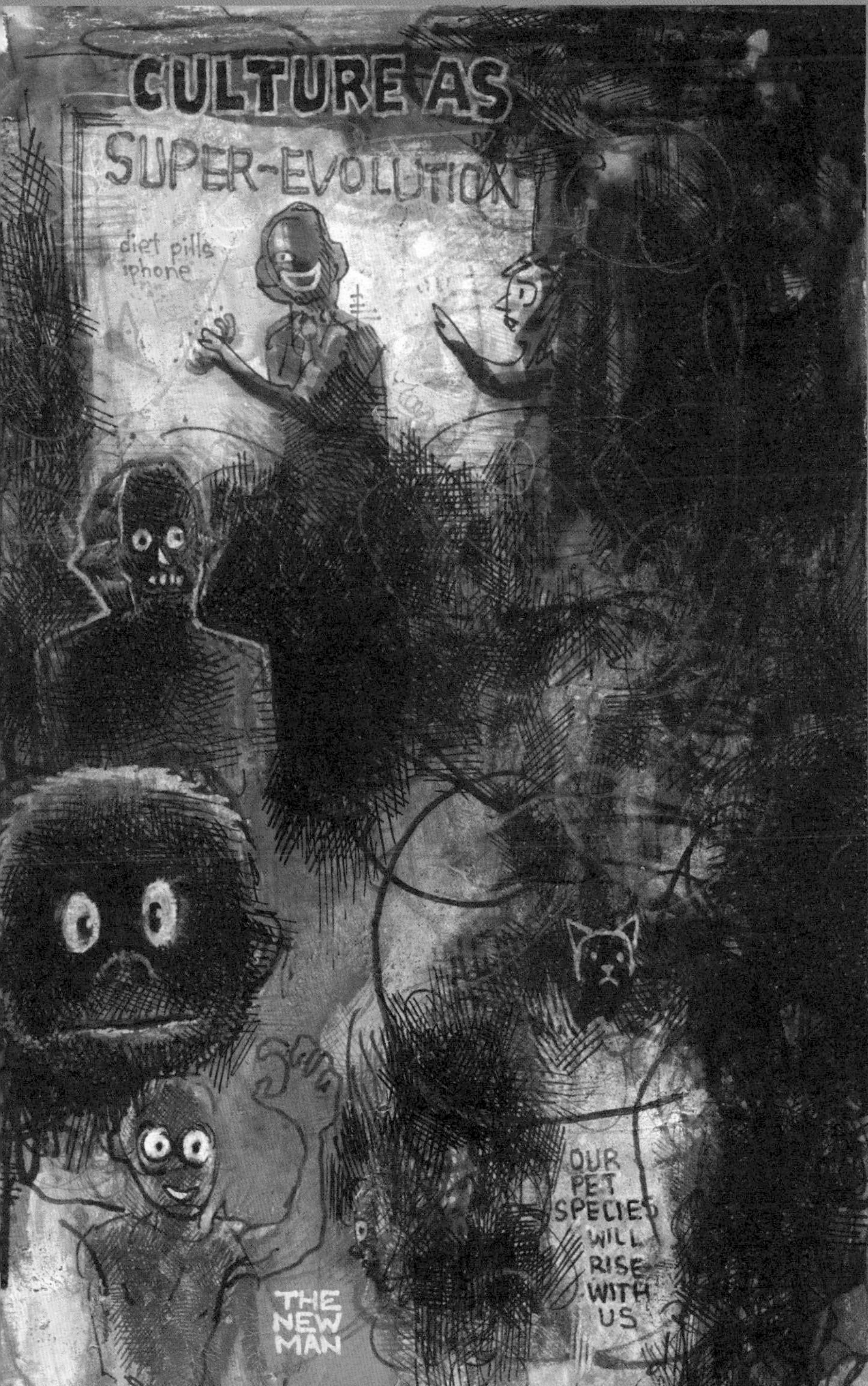
CULTURE AS
SUPER-EVOLUTION
diet pills
iphone
THE
NEW
MAN
OUR
PET
SPECIES
WILL
RISE
WITH
US

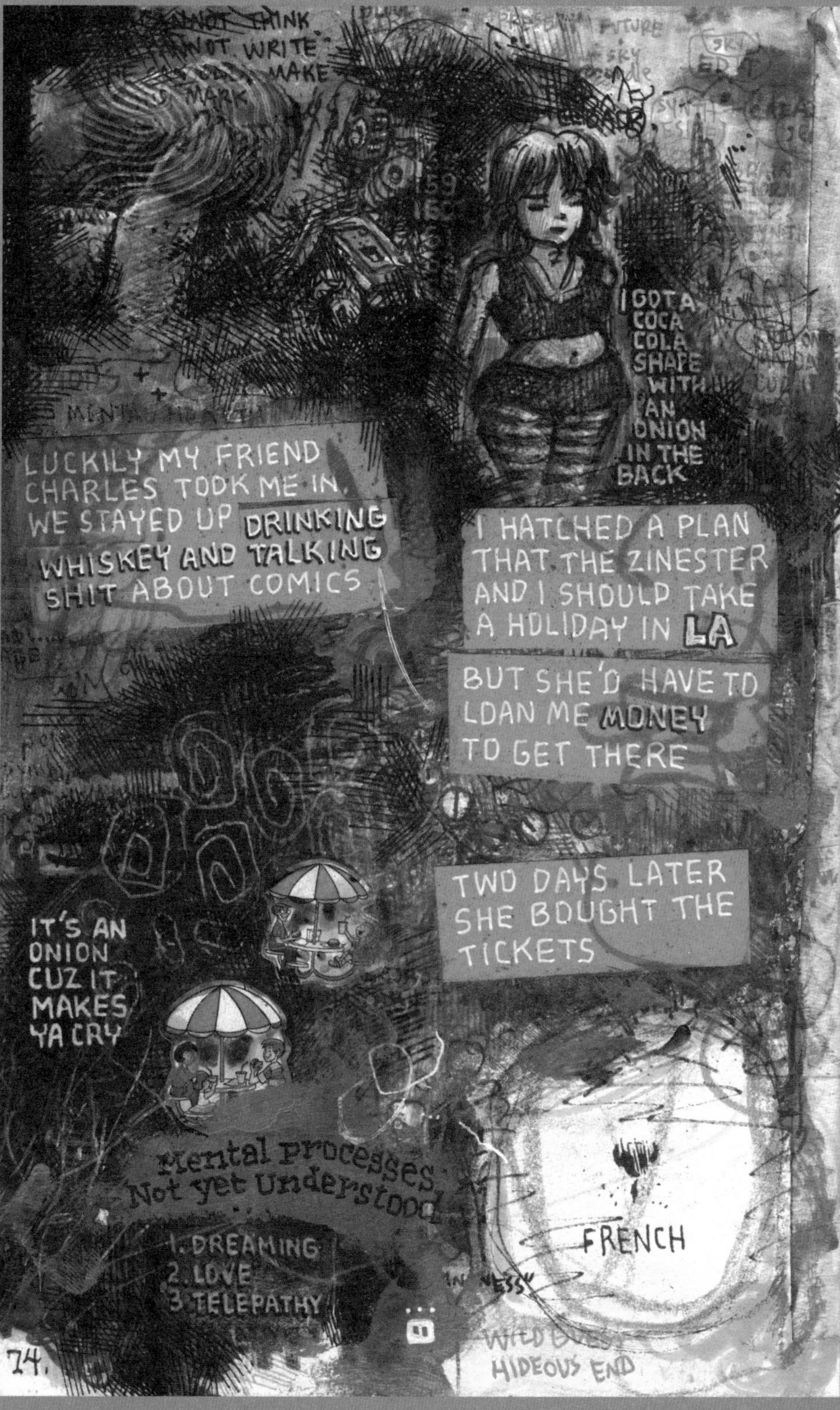

I GOT A COCA COLA SHAPE WITH AN ONION IN THE BACK
LUCKILY MY FRIEND CHARLES TOOK ME IN. WE STAYED UP DRINKING WHISKEY AND TALKING SHIT ABOUT COMICS
I HATCHED A PLAN THAT THE ZINESTER AND I SHOULD TAKE A HOLIDAY IN LA
BUT SHE'D HAVE TO LOAN ME MONEY TO GET THERE
TWO DAYS LATER SHE BOUGHT THE TICKETS
IT'S AN ONION CUZ IT MAKES YA CRY
Mental Processes Not yet Understood
1. DREAMING
2. LOVE
3. TELEPATHY
FRENCH
HIDEOUS END

Why is it so hard to trust me?

I don't see the point in arguing if you're just going to look it up on the Internet.

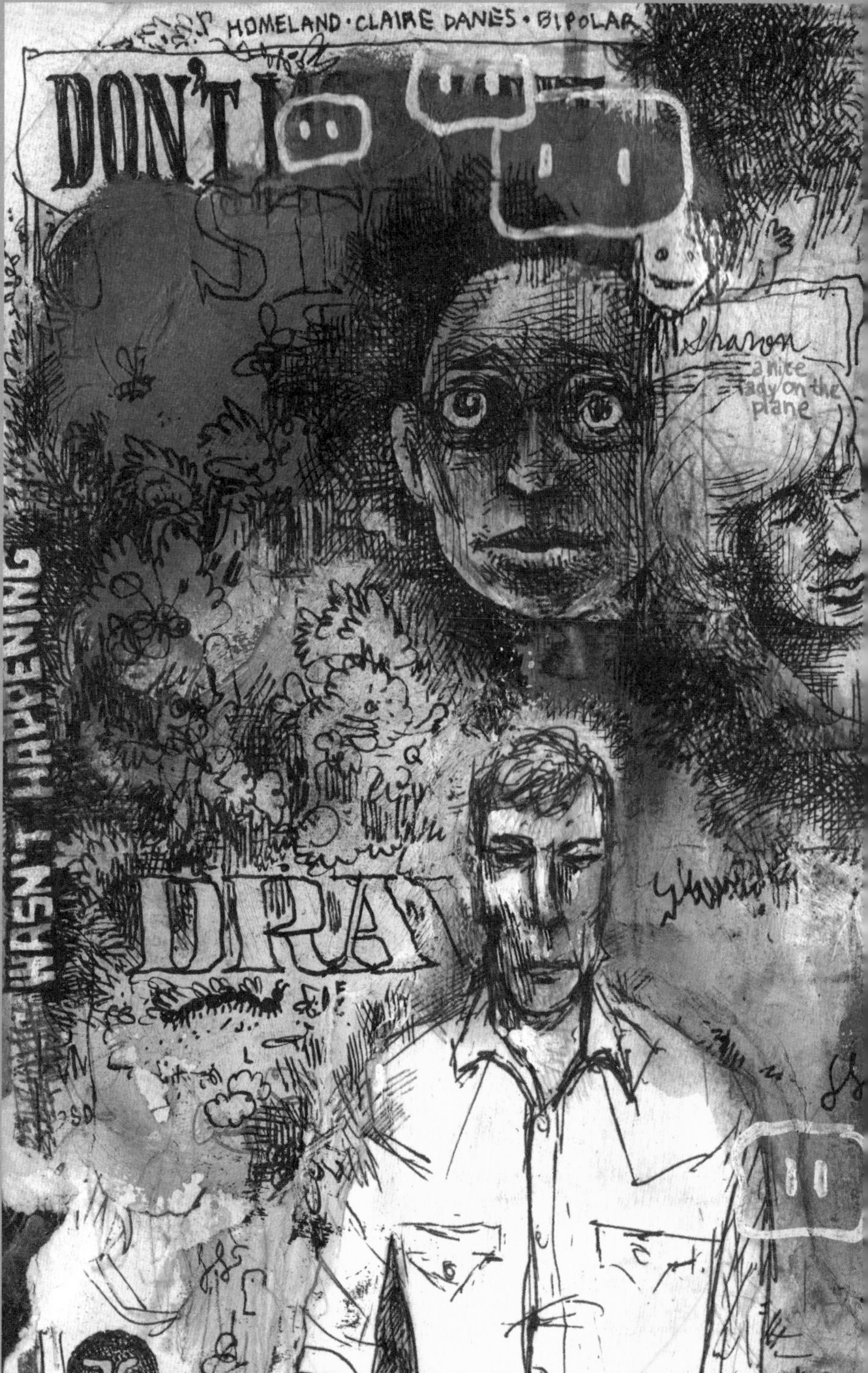
HOMELAND · CLAIRE DANES · BIPOLAR
DON'T
Sharon
a nice lady on the plane
WASN'T HAPPENING
76
WACO 2012

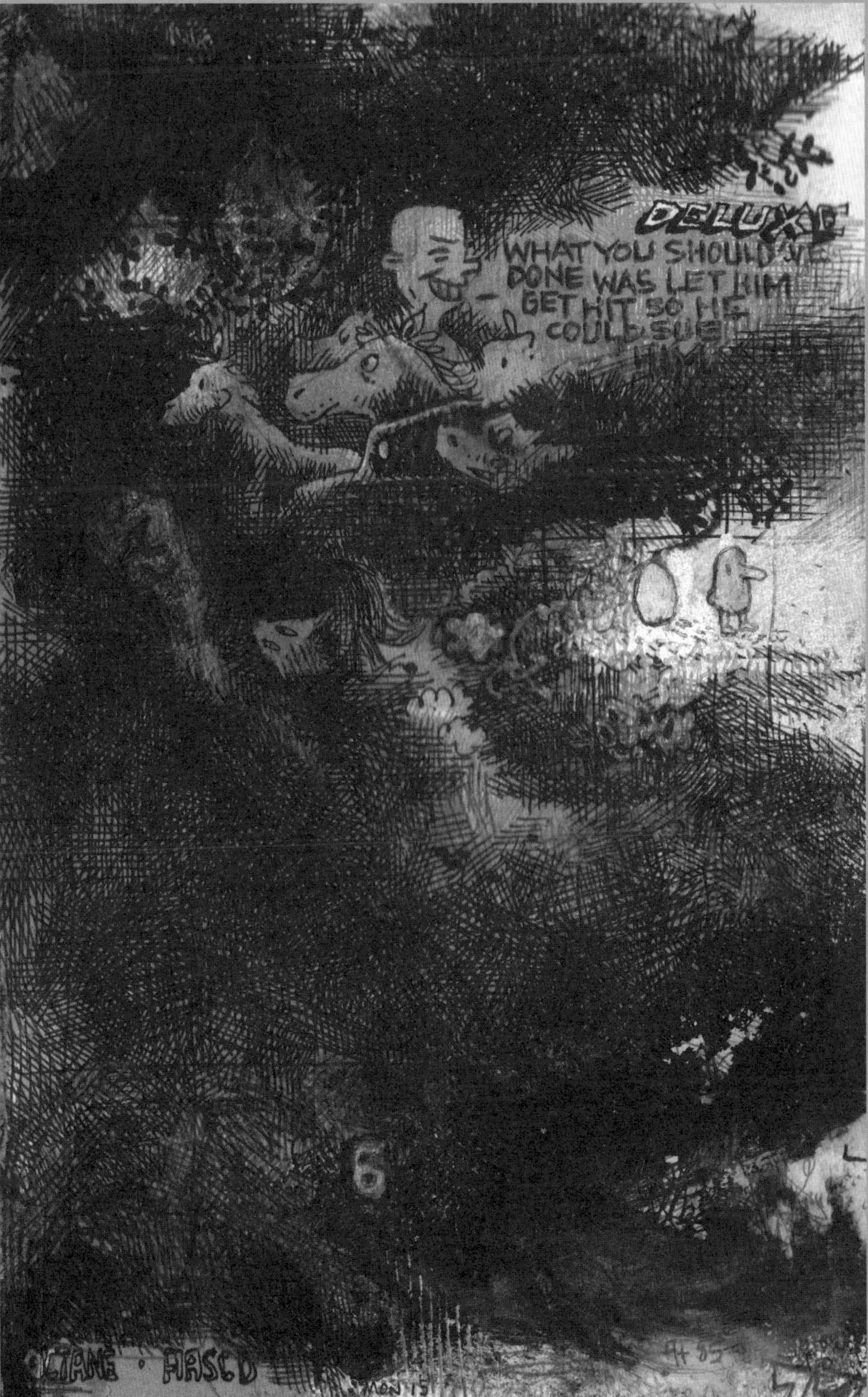
DELUXE
WHAT YOU SHOULD'VE DONE WAS LET HIM GET HIT SO HE COULD SUE HIM
6
FASCD
SPERMFIST
MON 15
5/9

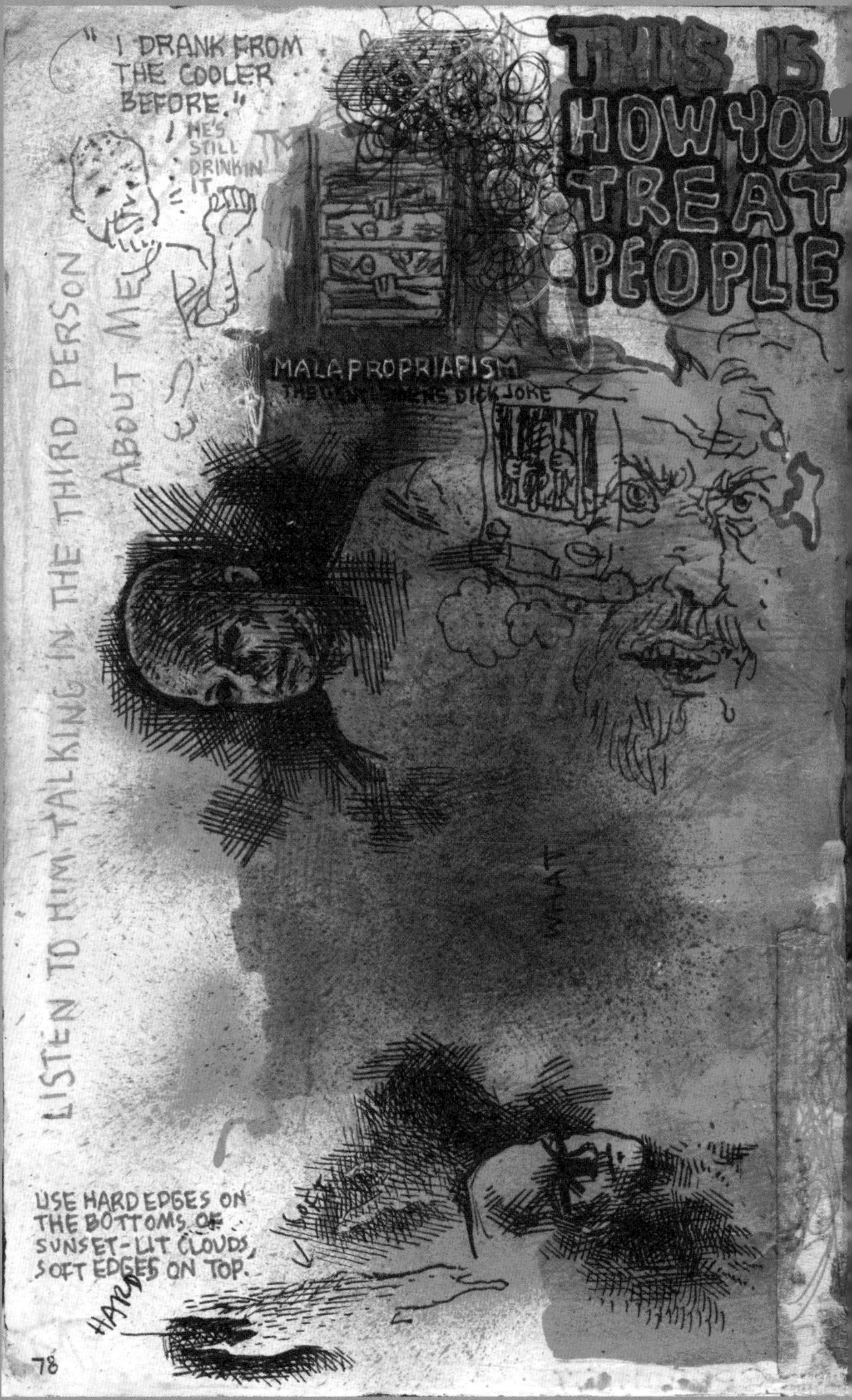
"I DRANK FROM THE COOLER BEFORE."
HE'S STILL DRINKIN' IT
THIS IS HOW YOU TREAT PEOPLE
MALAPROPRIAPISM
LISTEN TO HIM TALKING IN THE THIRD PERSON ABOUT ME
WHAT
USE HARD EDGES ON THE BOTTOMS OF SUNSET-LIT CLOUDS, SOFT EDGES ON TOP.
SOFT
HARD

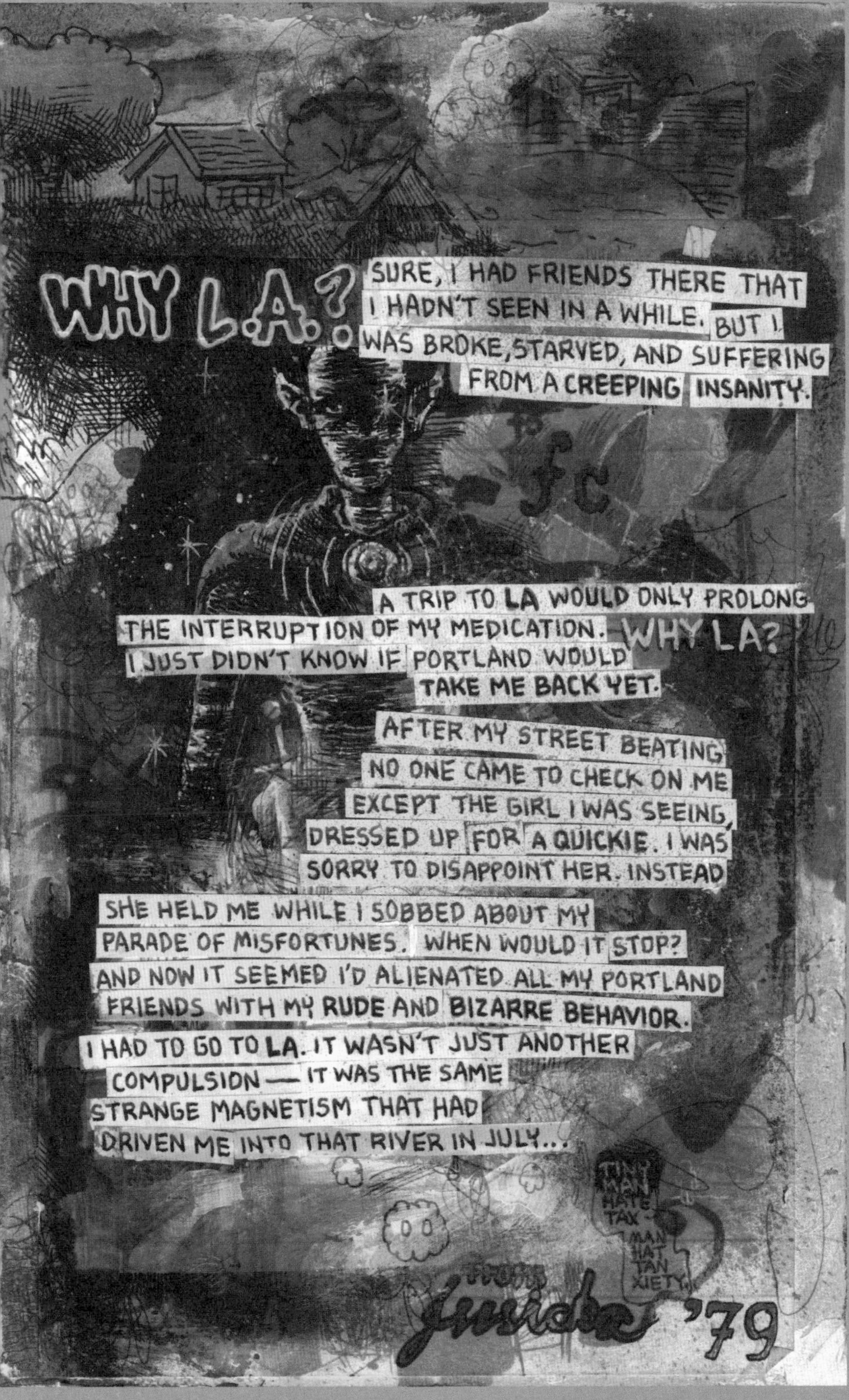
WHY L.A.?
SURE, I HAD FRIENDS THERE THAT I HADN'T SEEN IN A WHILE. BUT I WAS BROKE, STARVED, AND SUFFERING FROM A CREEPING INSANITY.
fc
A TRIP TO LA WOULD ONLY PROLONG THE INTERRUPTION OF MY MEDICATION. WHY LA? I JUST DIDN'T KNOW IF PORTLAND WOULD TAKE ME BACK YET.
AFTER MY STREET BEATING NO ONE CAME TO CHECK ON ME EXCEPT THE GIRL I WAS SEEING, DRESSED UP FOR A QUICKIE. I WAS SORRY TO DISAPPOINT HER. INSTEAD SHE HELD ME WHILE I SOBBED ABOUT MY PARADE OF MISFORTUNES. WHEN WOULD IT STOP? AND NOW IT SEEMED I'D ALIENATED ALL MY PORTLAND FRIENDS WITH MY RUDE AND BIZARRE BEHAVIOR. I HAD TO GO TO LA. IT WASN'T JUST ANOTHER COMPULSION — IT WAS THE SAME STRANGE MAGNETISM THAT HAD DRIVEN ME INTO THAT RIVER IN JULY...
TINY MAN HATE TAX - MAN HAT TAN XIETY
'79

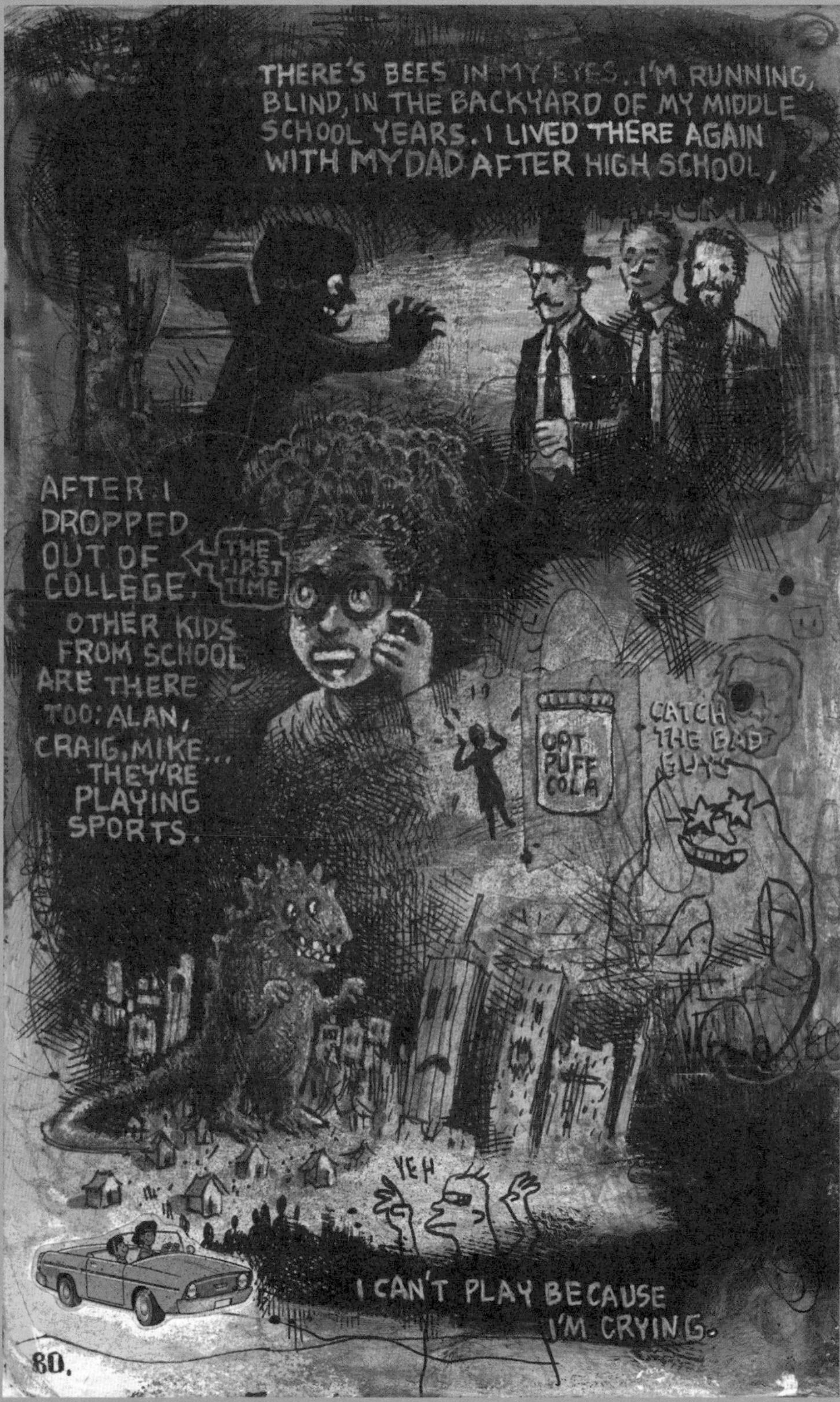
THERE'S BEES IN MY EYES. I'M RUNNING, BLIND, IN THE BACKYARD OF MY MIDDLE SCHOOL YEARS. I LIVED THERE AGAIN WITH MY DAD AFTER HIGH SCHOOL,
AFTER I DROPPED OUT OF COLLEGE.
THE FIRST TIME
OTHER KIDS FROM SCHOOL ARE THERE TOO: ALAN, CRAIG, MIKE... THEY'RE PLAYING SPORTS.
OAT PUFF COLA
CATCH THE BAD GUYS
YEH
I CAN'T PLAY BECAUSE I'M CRYING.

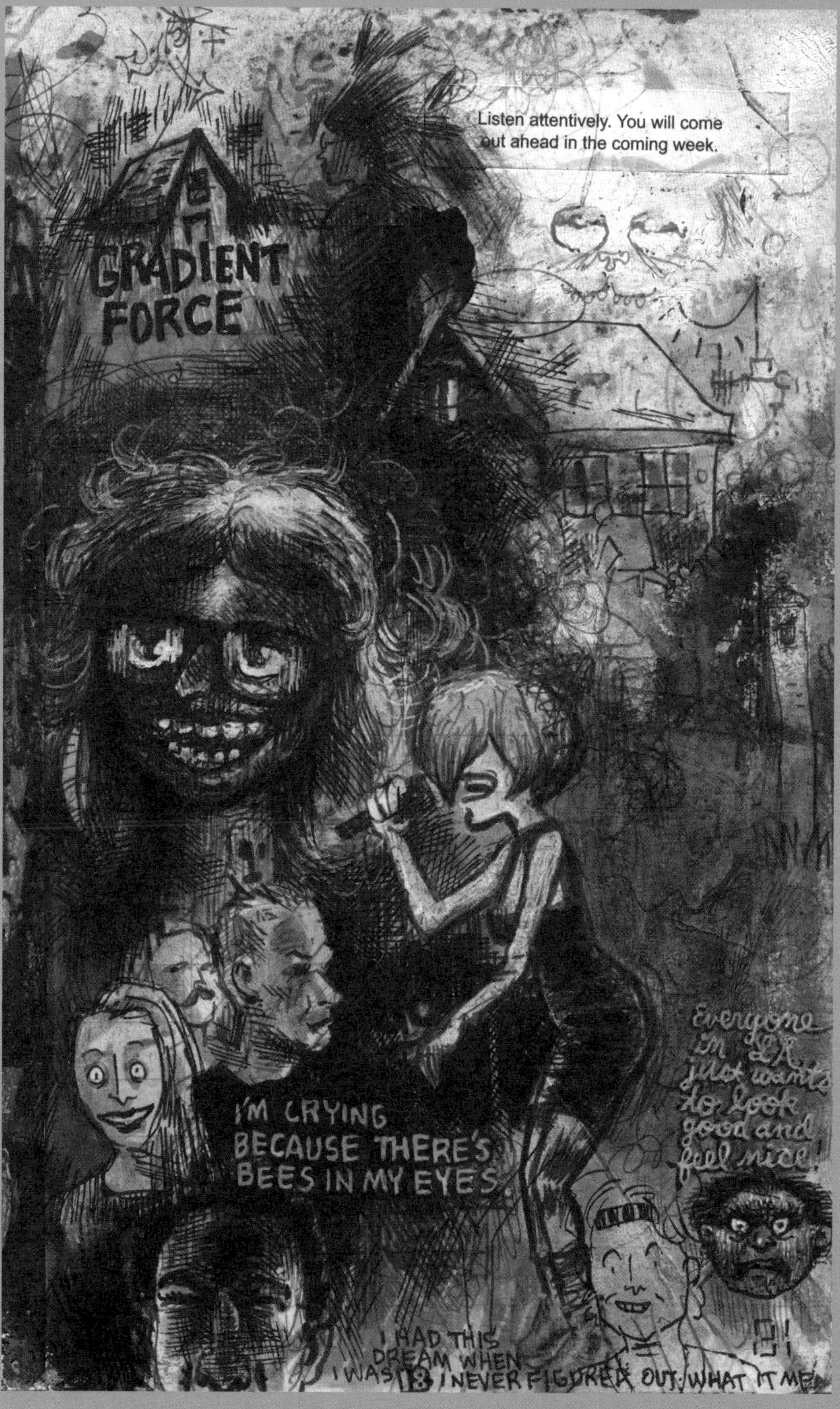

GRADIENT FORCE
Listen attentively. You will come out ahead in the coming week.
Everyone in L.A. just wants to look good and feel nice!
I'M CRYING BECAUSE THERE'S BEES IN MY EYES.
I HAD THIS DREAM WHEN I WAS 13 I NEVER FIGURED OUT WHAT IT ME

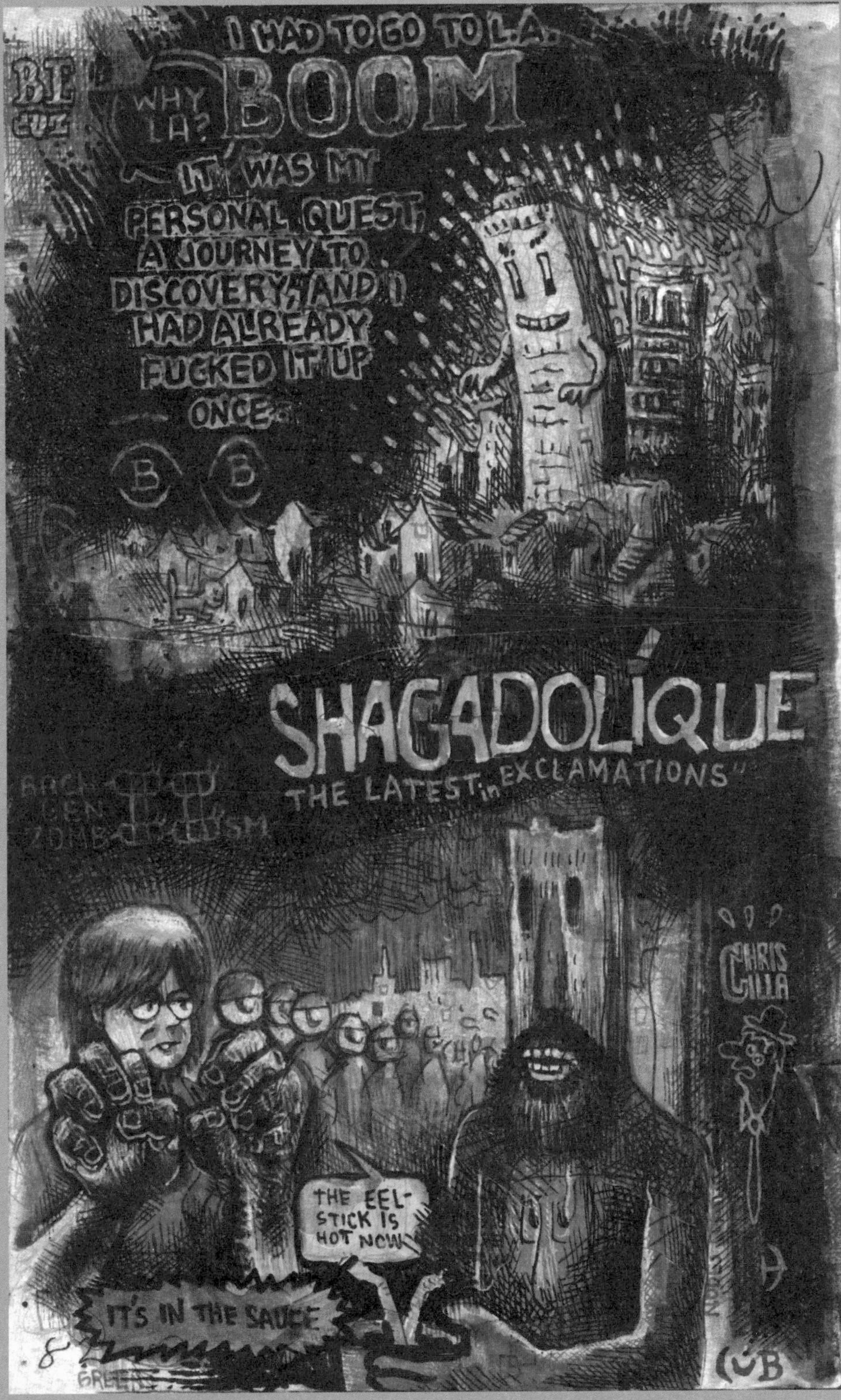
I HAD TO GO TO L.A.
WHY LA?
BOOM
IT WAS MY PERSONAL QUEST, A JOURNEY TO DISCOVERY, AND I HAD ALREADY FUCKED IT UP ONCE.
SHAGADOLÍQUE
"THE LATEST in EXCLAMATIONS"
CHRIS CILLA
THE EEL-STICK IS HOT NOW
IT'S IN THE SAUCE

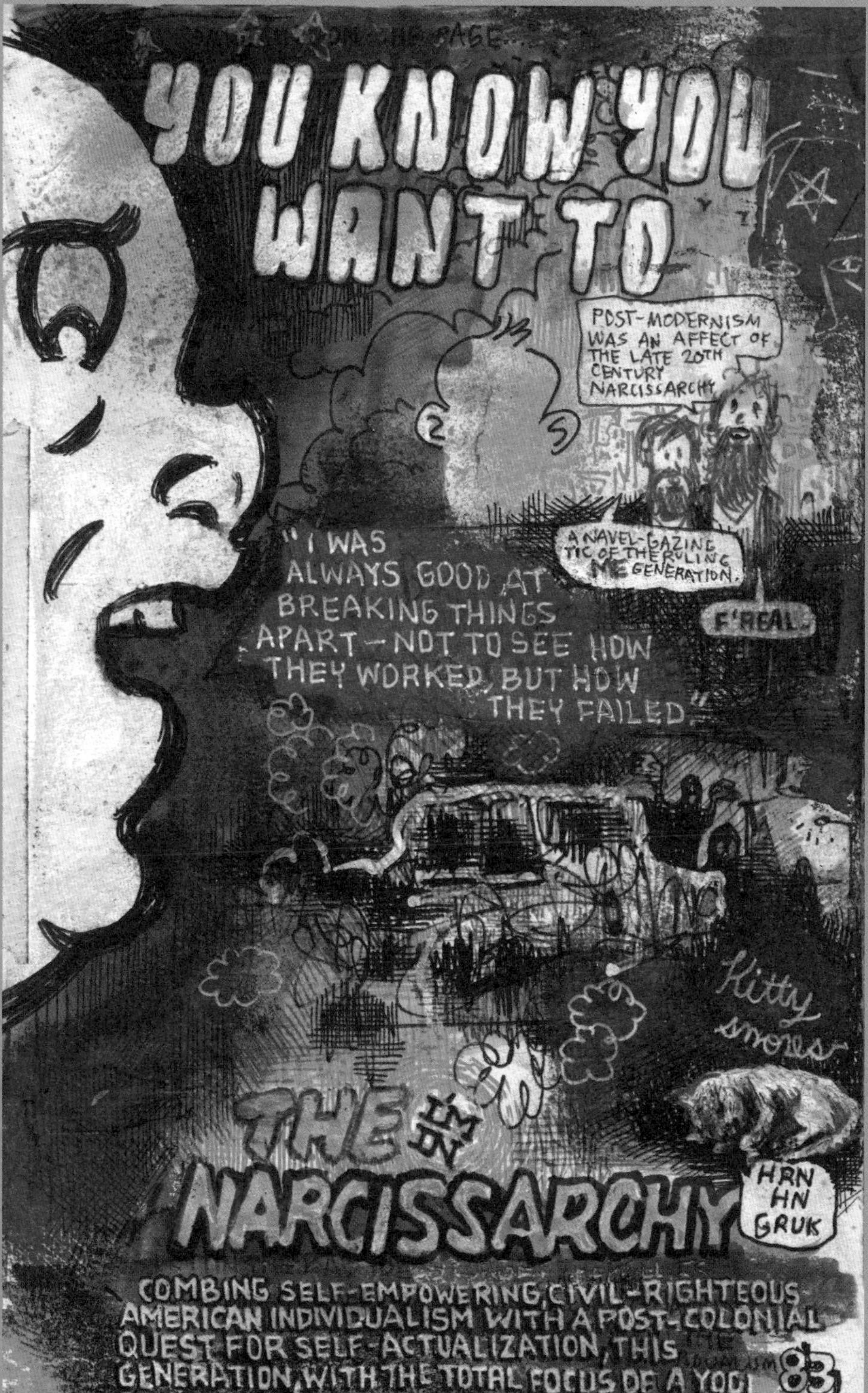

YOU KNOW YOU WANT TO
POST-MODERNISM WAS AN AFFECT OF THE LATE 20TH CENTURY NARCISSARCHY
A NAVEL-GAZING TIC OF THE RULING ME GENERATION.
F'REAL.
"I WAS ALWAYS GOOD AT BREAKING THINGS APART — NOT TO SEE HOW THEY WORKED, BUT HOW THEY FAILED."
Kitty snores
THE I'M IN NARCISSARCHY
HRN HN GRUK
COMBING SELF-EMPOWERING, CIVIL-RIGHTEOUS AMERICAN INDIVIDUALISM WITH A POST-COLONIAL QUEST FOR SELF-ACTUALIZATION, THIS GENERATION, WITH THE TOTAL FOCUS OF A YODI ARMY, BLAZED A TRAIL INWARDS!!!
83

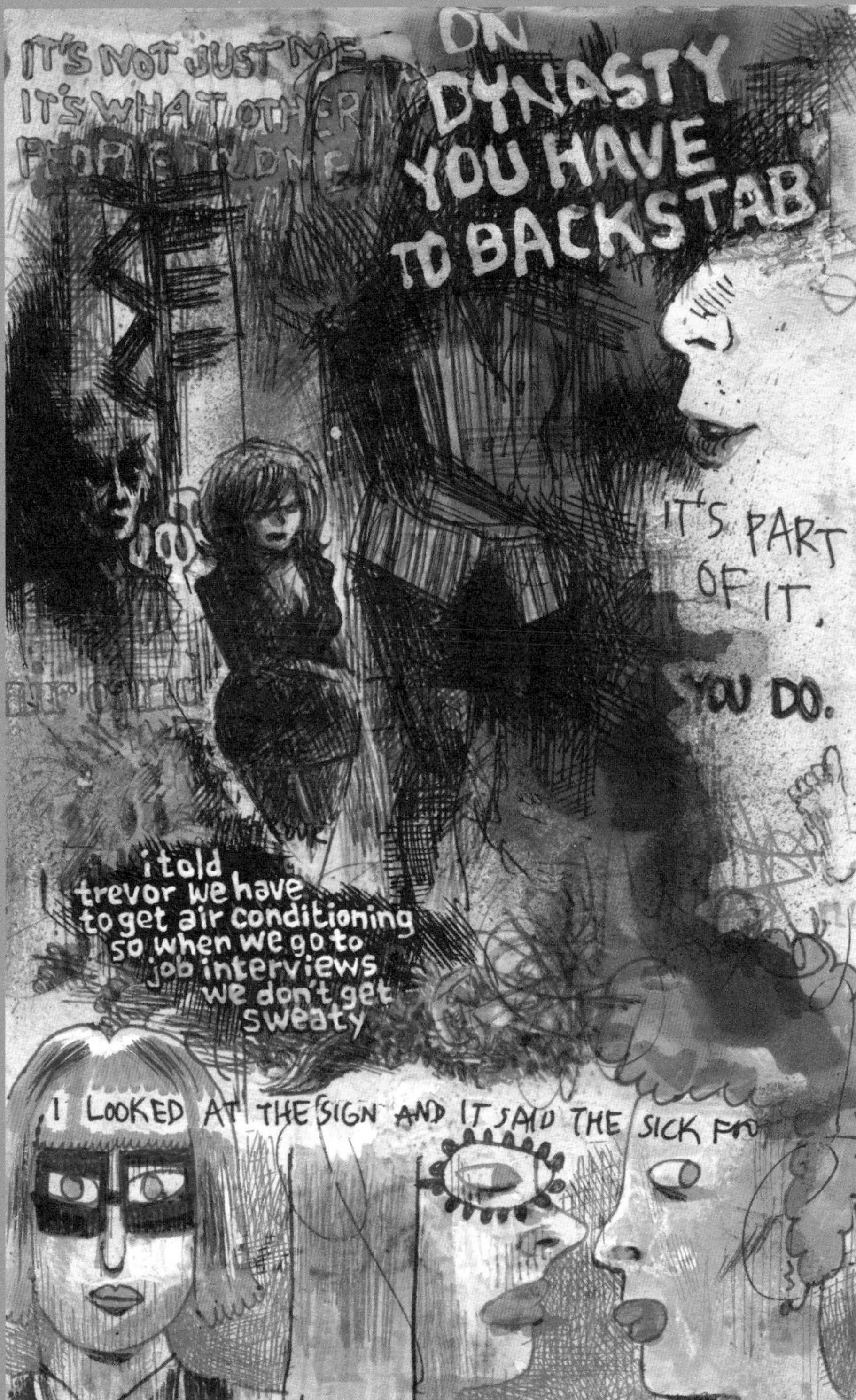
IT'S NOT JUST ME
IT'S WHAT OTHER PEOPLE TOLD ME
ON DYNASTY YOU HAVE TO BACKSTAB
IT'S PART OF IT.
YOU DO.
i told trevor we have to get air conditioning so when we go to job interviews we don't get sweaty
I LOOKED AT THE SIGN AND IT SAID THE SICK

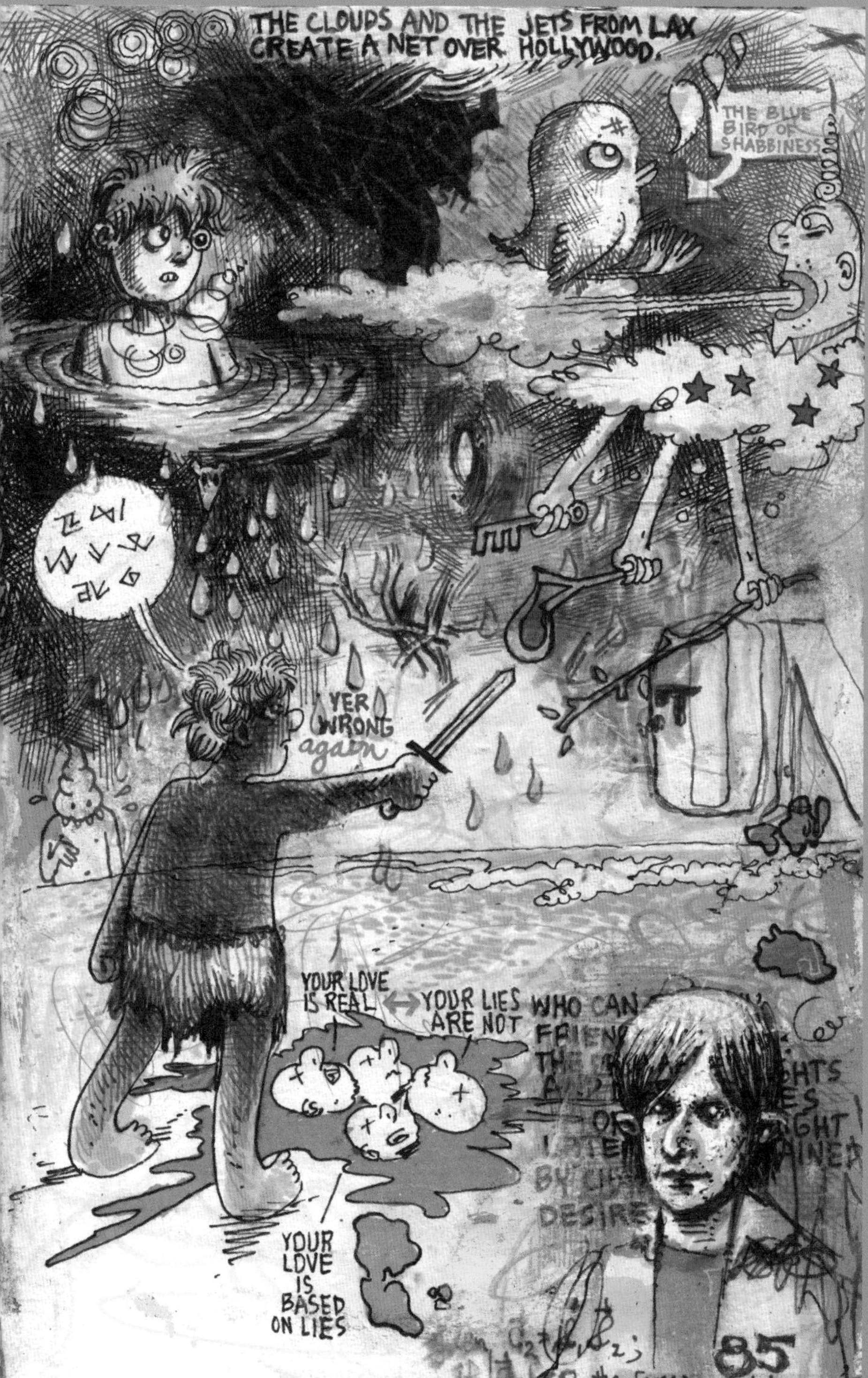
THE CLOUDS AND THE JETS FROM LAX CREATE A NET OVER HOLLYWOOD.
THE BLUE BIRD OF SHABBINESS
YER WRONG again
YOUR LOVE IS REAL
YOUR LIES ARE NOT
WHO CAN
DESIRE
YOUR LOVE IS BASED ON LIES
85
, the force is repulsive
"THAT EXPRESSION JAIME DREW INFLUENCED MY TWEETING STYLE"

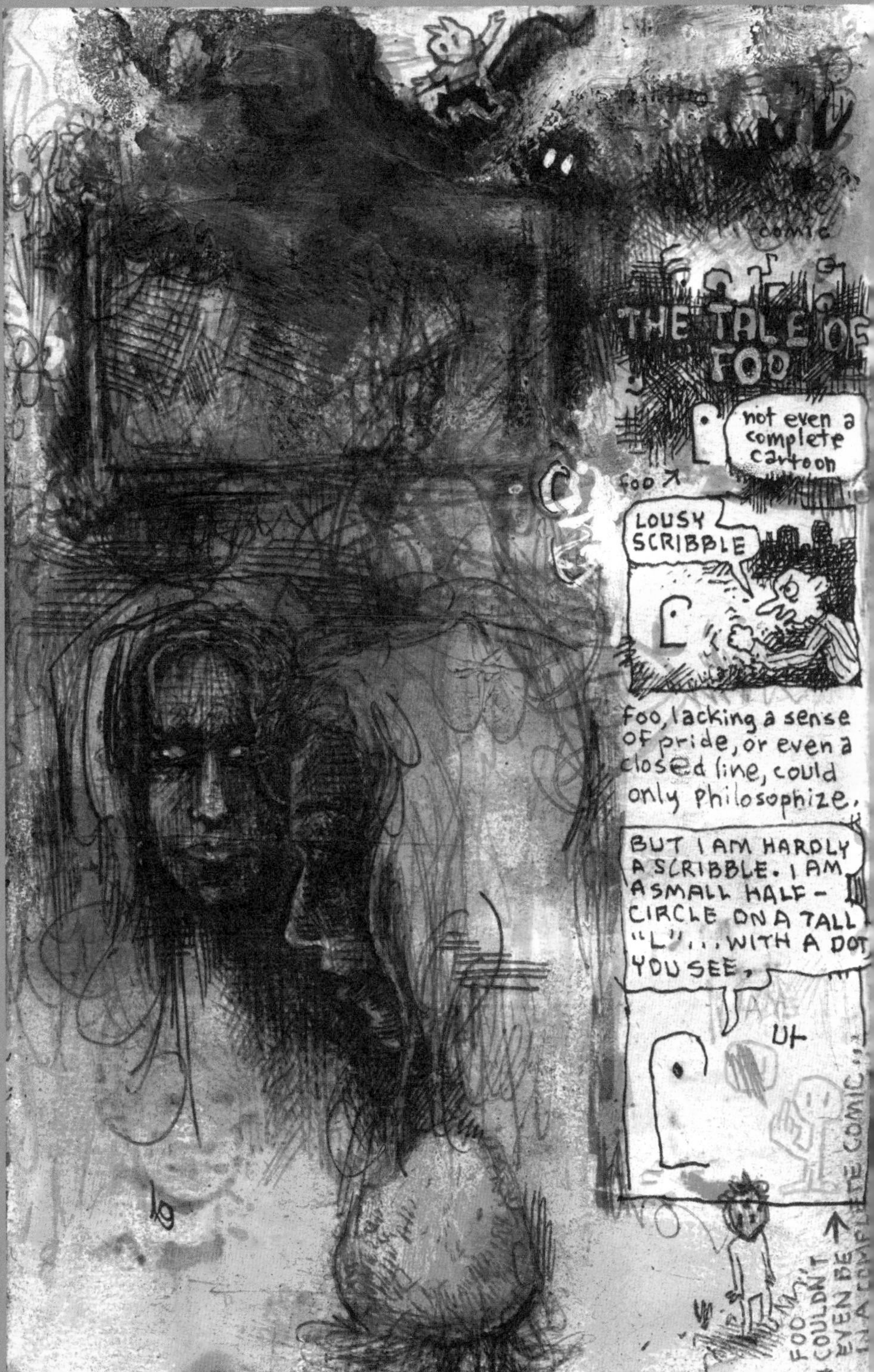

COMIC
THE TALE OF FOO
not even a complete cartoon
foo
LOUSY SCRIBBLE
foo, lacking a sense of pride, or even a closed line, could only philosophize.
BUT I AM HARDLY A SCRIBBLE. I AM A SMALL HALF-CIRCLE ON A TALL "L"... WITH A DOT YOU SEE.
FOO COULDN'T EVEN BE IN A COMPLETE COMIC

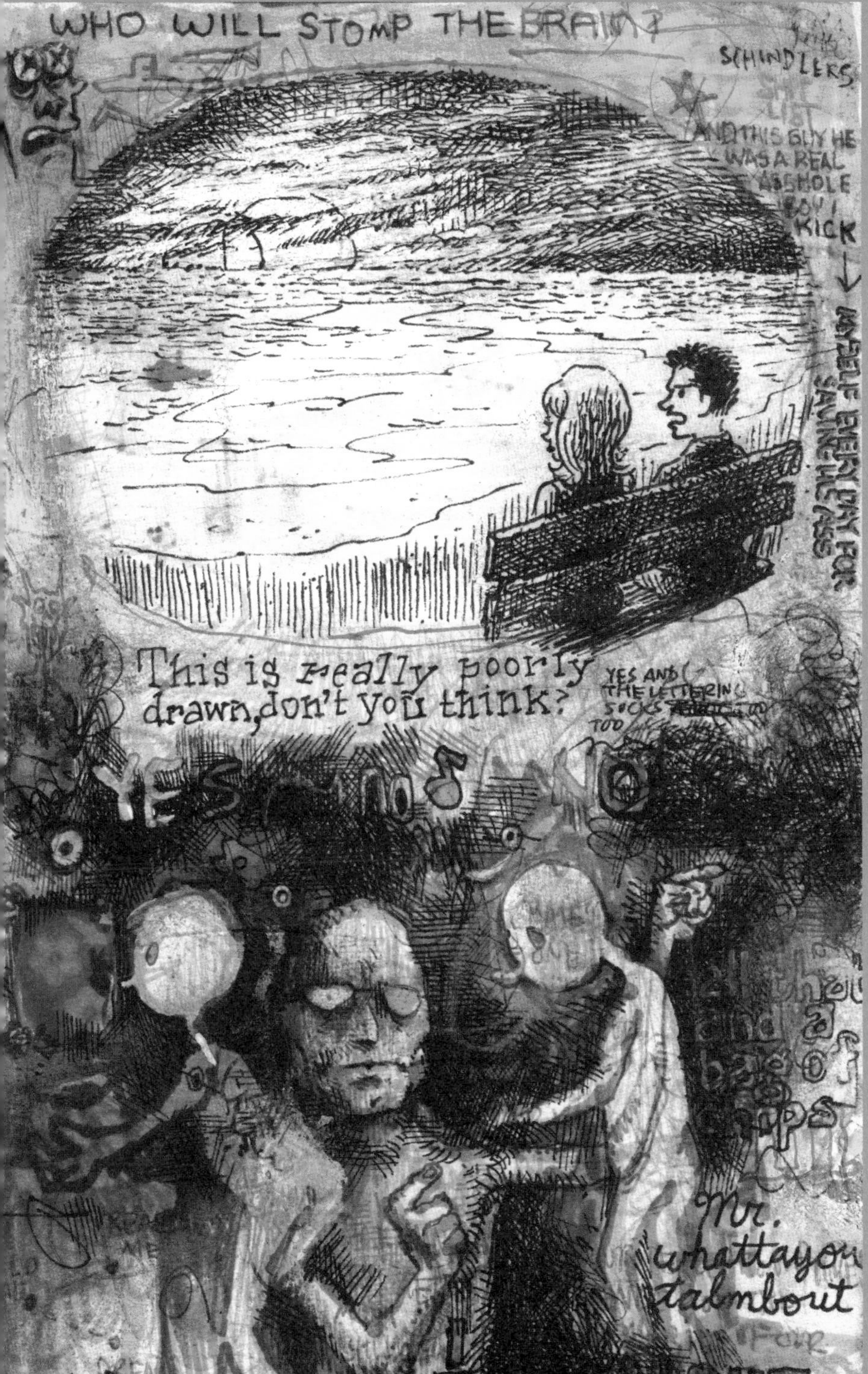
WHO WILL STOMP THE BRAIN?
SCHINDLERS
AND THIS GUY HE WAS A REAL ASSHOLE BOY I KICK
MYSELF EVERY DAY FOR SAVING HIS ASS
This is really poorly drawn, don't you think?
YES AND THE LETTERING SUCKS TOO
Mr. whattayou talmbout
OUT

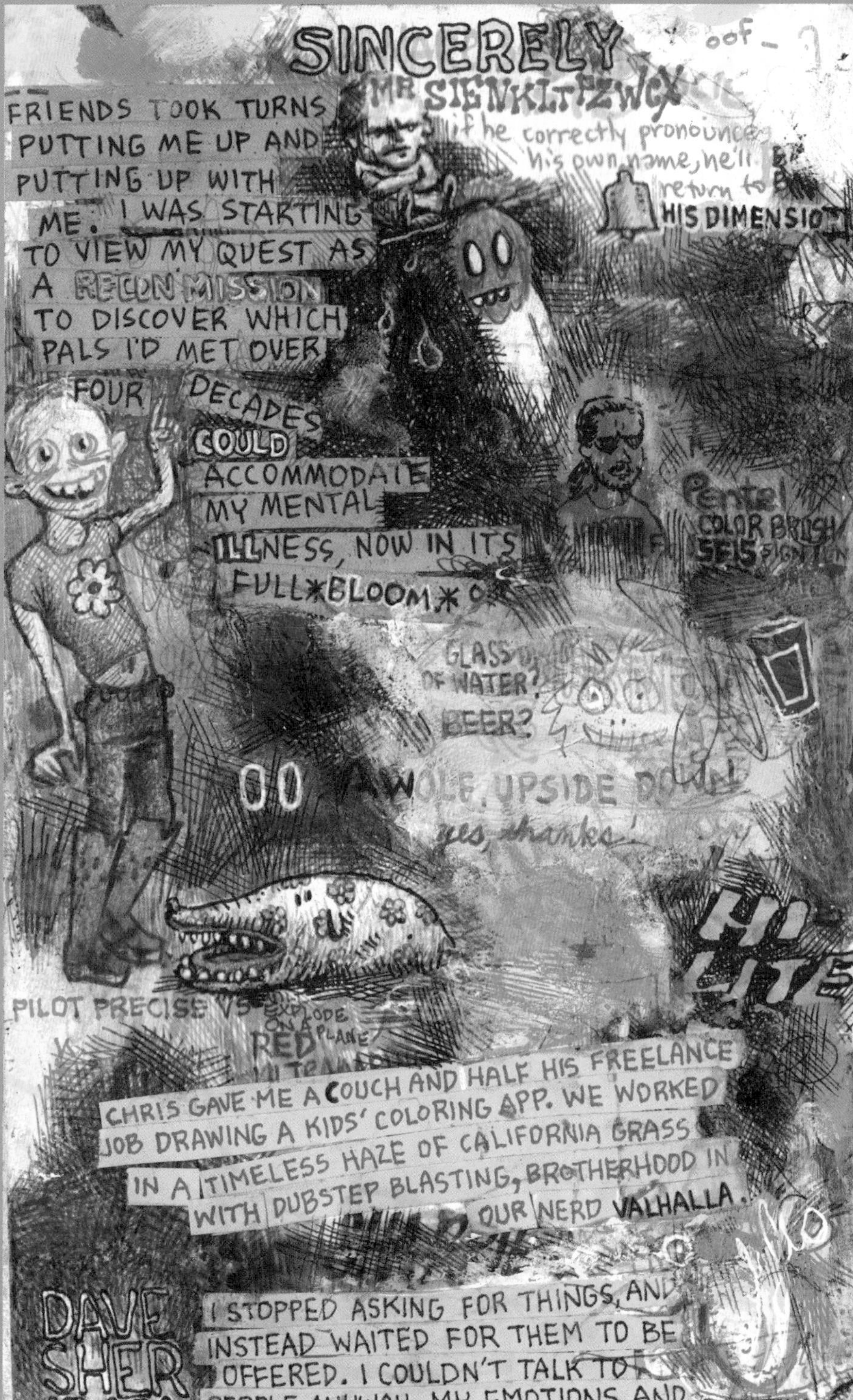
SINCERELY
MR SIENKLTIZWCX
if he correctly pronounces his own name, he'll return to HIS DIMENSIO
FRIENDS TOOK TURNS PUTTING ME UP AND PUTTING UP WITH ME. I WAS STARTING TO VIEW MY QUEST AS A RECON MISSION TO DISCOVER WHICH PALS I'D MET OVER FOUR DECADES COULD ACCOMMODATE MY MENTAL ILLNESS, NOW IN ITS FULL*BLOOM*
Pentel COLOR BRUSH
GLASS OF WATER?
BEER?
A WOLF UPSIDE DOWN
yes, thanks
HI LITE
PILOT PRECISE VS
EXPLODE ON A PLANE
RED
CHRIS GAVE ME A COUCH AND HALF HIS FREELANCE JOB DRAWING A KIDS' COLORING APP. WE WORKED IN A TIMELESS HAZE OF CALIFORNIA GRASS WITH DUBSTEP BLASTING, BROTHERHOOD IN OUR NERD VALHALLA.
DAVE SHERIDAN
I STOPPED ASKING FOR THINGS, AND INSTEAD WAITED FOR THEM TO BE OFFERED. I COULDN'T TALK TO PEOPLE ANYWAY. MY EMOTIONS AND MY THOUGHTS WERE ALL SCRAMBLED.

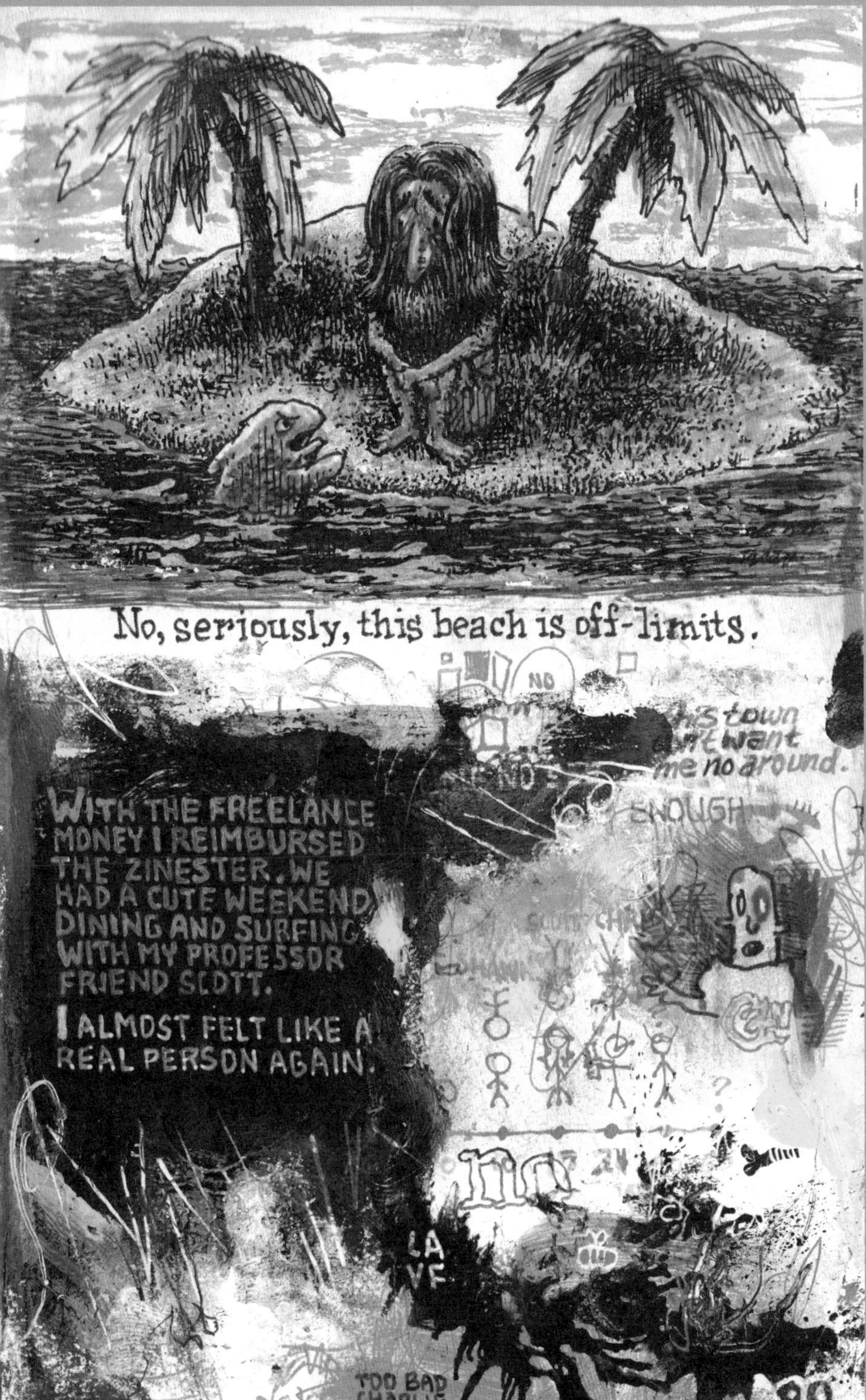
No, seriously, this beach is off-limits.
NO
ENOUGH
WITH THE FREELANCE MONEY I REIMBURSED THE ZINESTER. WE HAD A CUTE WEEKEND DINING AND SURFING WITH MY PROFESSOR FRIEND SCOTT.
I ALMOST FELT LIKE A REAL PERSON AGAIN.
no
LA VF
TOO BAD CHARLIE YOU WOULDA HAD 3 8'S.

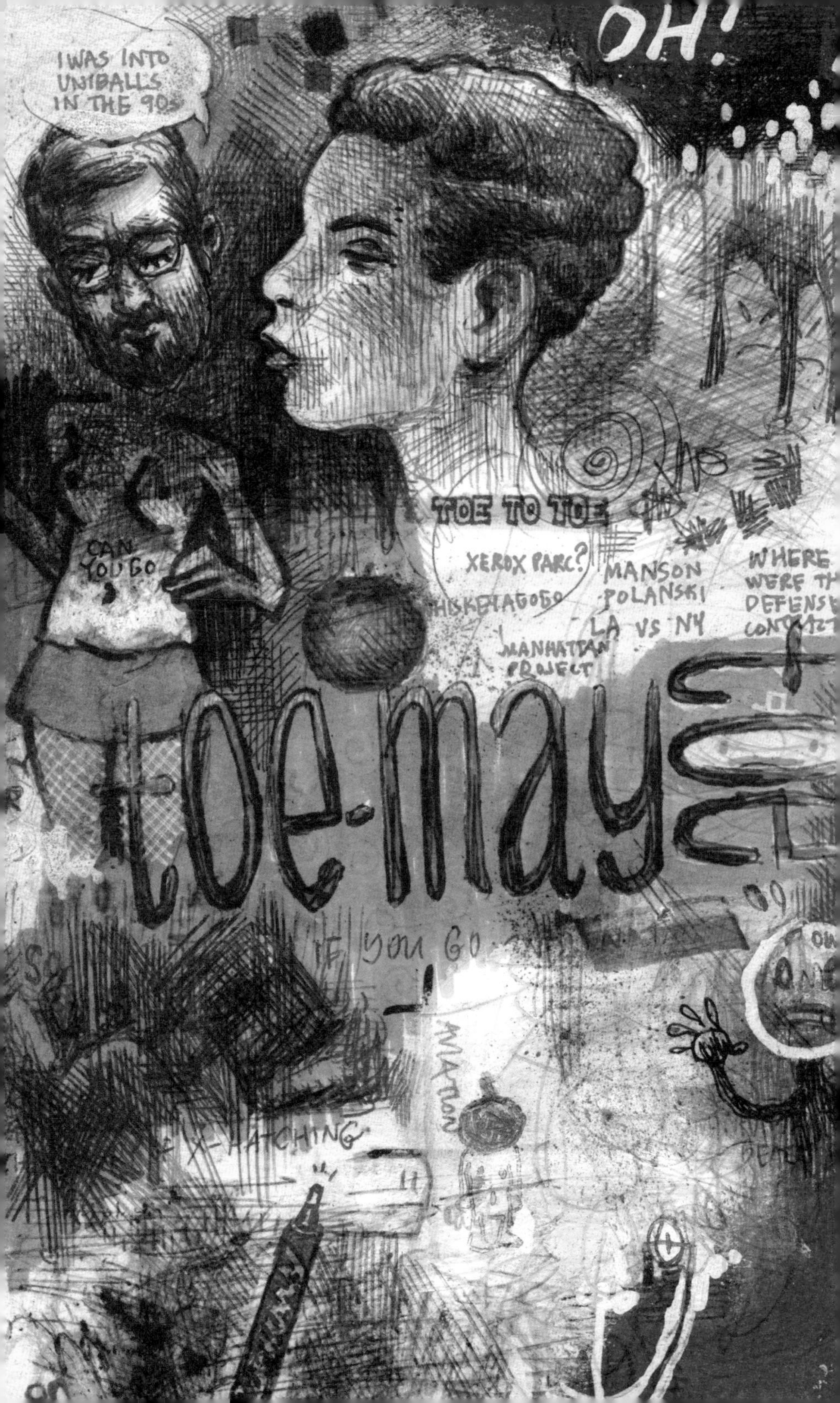
I WAS INTO UNIBALLS IN THE 90s
OH!
TOE TO TOE
CAN YOU GO
XEROX PARC?
MANSON POLANSKI
LA VS NY
MANHATTAN PROJECT
toe-may
IF you GO
X-HATCHING
AMATION

THE ARTIST AS MISANTHROPE,

HERMENEUTICALLY SEALED IN A SHACK,
FORTRESS, OR SHADOWY TRAILER
ISSUING SATIRIC SCREEDS 'N THE SERVICE
OF SOCIETAL CONDEMNATION; THE
ARTIST AS A KEEPER OF THE SACRED
TRUTH; A BEACON ISSUING THE ONE
CLARION MANTRA THAT DISCOURAGES

HUMANITY IS A FAILURE

NAW

MAN

SIT AND PONDER
AT YOUR

THIS IS THE KINDA BRAIN
SPEED ONLY GOOD FOR
MAKING UP ANAGRAMS &
CROSSHATCHIN

IDEAS? GIVE ME
ONE WORD AND
I'LL FILL
A BIBLE!

BOO!   WEIRDO

GET
REAL

$\sqrt{5}$

NOT ME I'M A COURTESAN

91

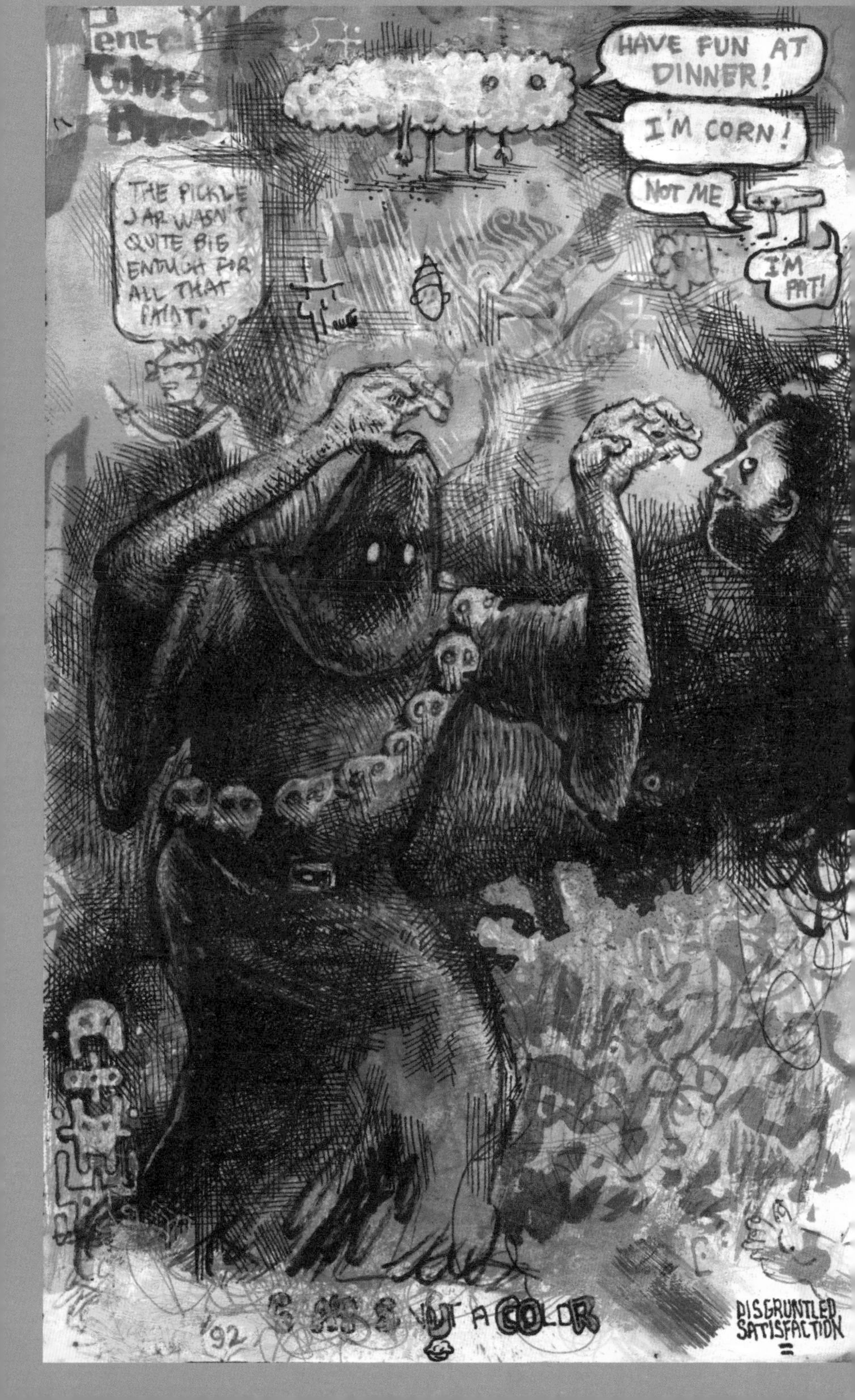
Pentel
HAVE FUN AT DINNER!
I'M CORN!
NOT ME
I'M PAT!
THE PICKLE JAR WASN'T QUITE BIG ENOUGH FOR ALL THAT PAINT!
'92
NOT A COLOR
DISGRUNTLED SATISFACTION =

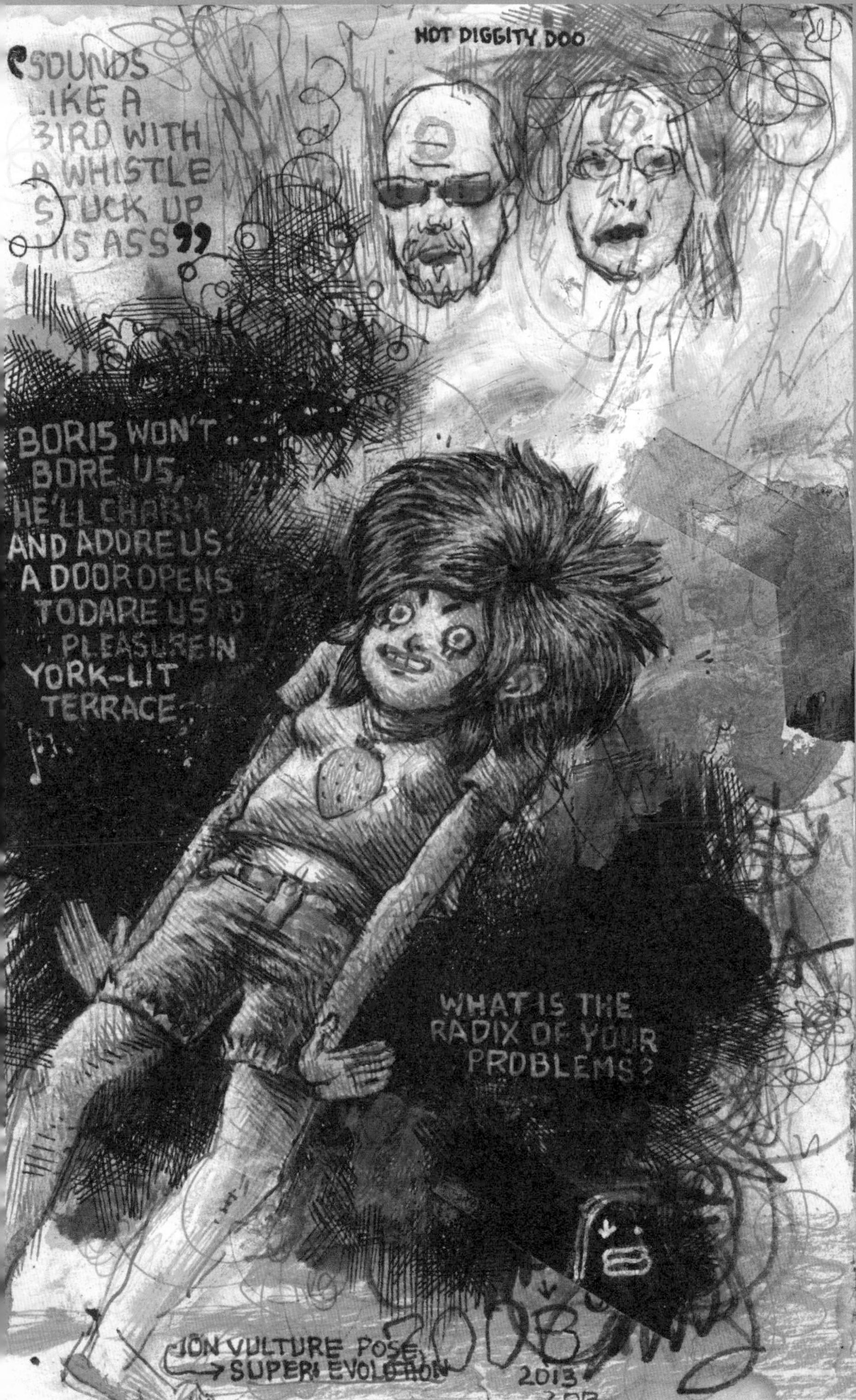

NOT DIGGITY DOO
"SOUNDS LIKE A BIRD WITH A WHISTLE STUCK UP HIS ASS"
BORIS WON'T BORE US, HE'LL CHARM AND ADORE US: A DOOR OPENS TO DARE US TO PLEASURE IN YORK-LIT TERRACE
WHAT IS THE RADIX OF YOUR PROBLEMS?
JON VULTURE POSE → SUPER EVOLUTION
2013 ZDB

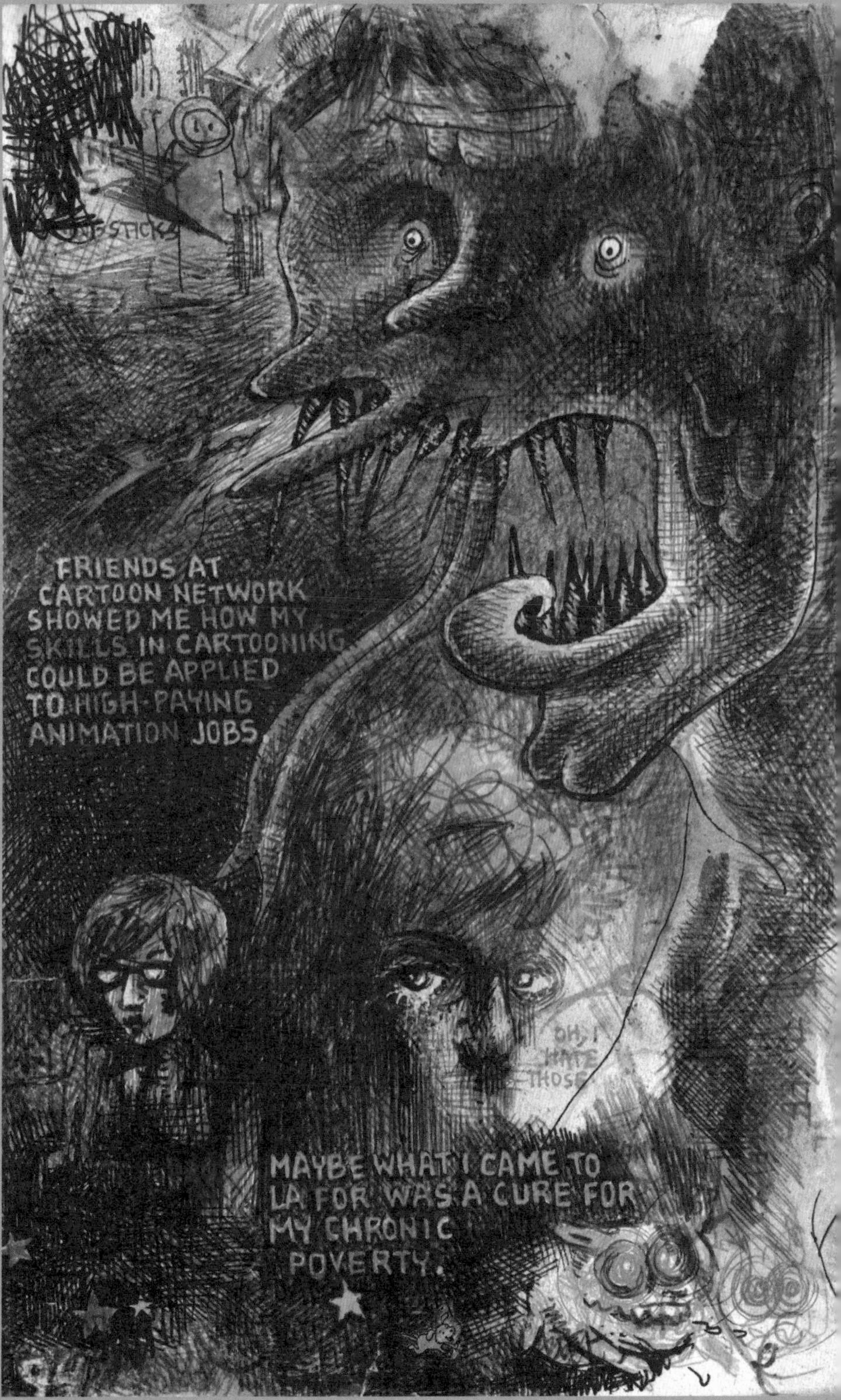
FRIENDS AT CARTOON NETWORK SHOWED ME HOW MY SKILLS IN CARTOONING COULD BE APPLIED TO HIGH-PAYING ANIMATION JOBS.
OH, I HATE THOSE
MAYBE WHAT I CAME TO LA FOR WAS A CURE FOR MY CHRONIC POVERTY.

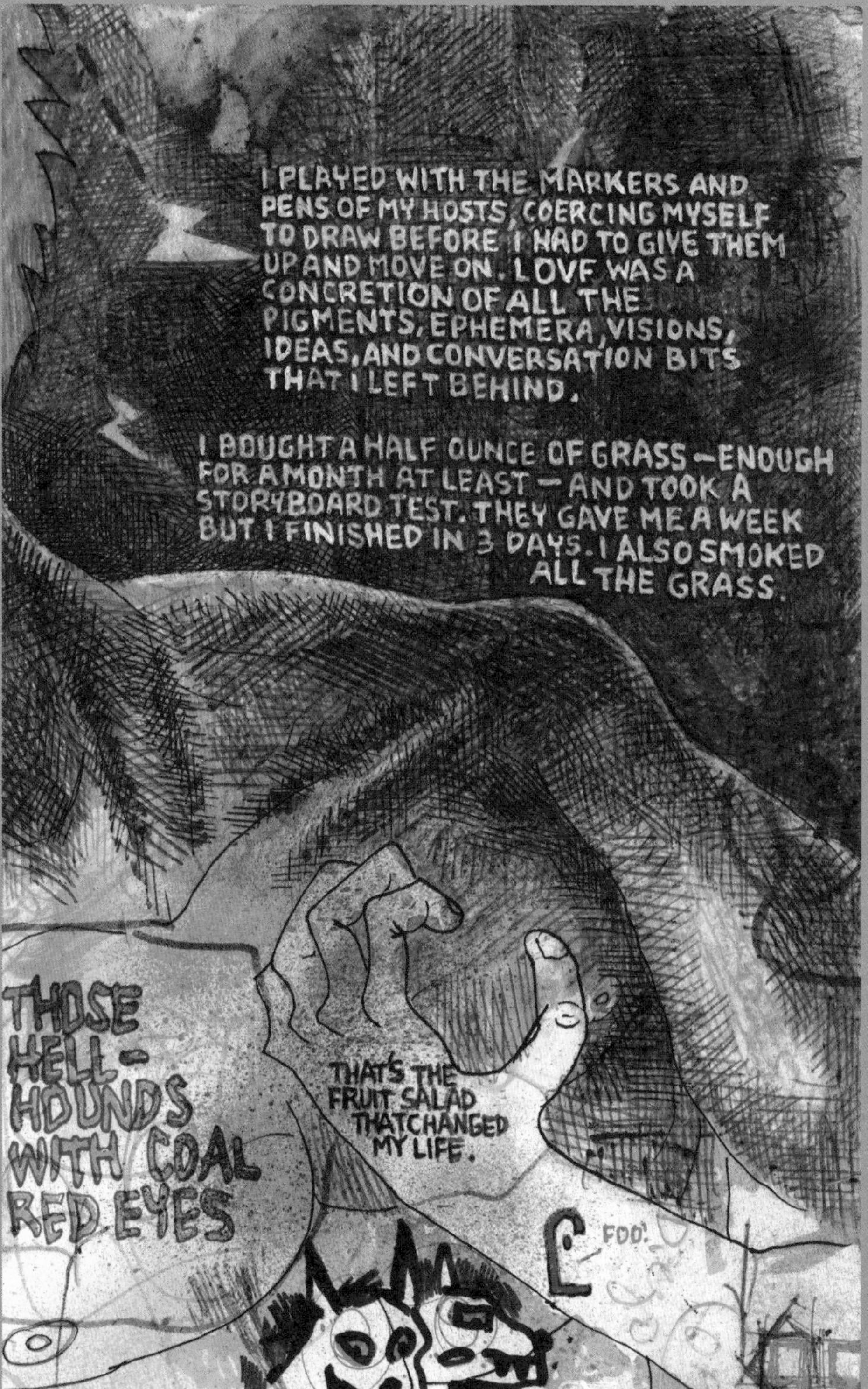
I PLAYED WITH THE MARKERS AND PENS OF MY HOSTS, COERCING MYSELF TO DRAW BEFORE I HAD TO GIVE THEM UP AND MOVE ON. LOVE WAS A CONCRETION OF ALL THE PIGMENTS, EPHEMERA, VISIONS, IDEAS, AND CONVERSATION BITS THAT I LEFT BEHIND.
I BOUGHT A HALF OUNCE OF GRASS — ENOUGH FOR A MONTH AT LEAST — AND TOOK A STORYBOARD TEST. THEY GAVE ME A WEEK BUT I FINISHED IN 3 DAYS. I ALSO SMOKED ALL THE GRASS.
THOSE HELL-HOUNDS WITH COAL RED EYES
THAT'S THE FRUIT SALAD THAT CHANGED MY LIFE.
FOO.
ARE YOU GONNA SMASH MY RECORD TOO?

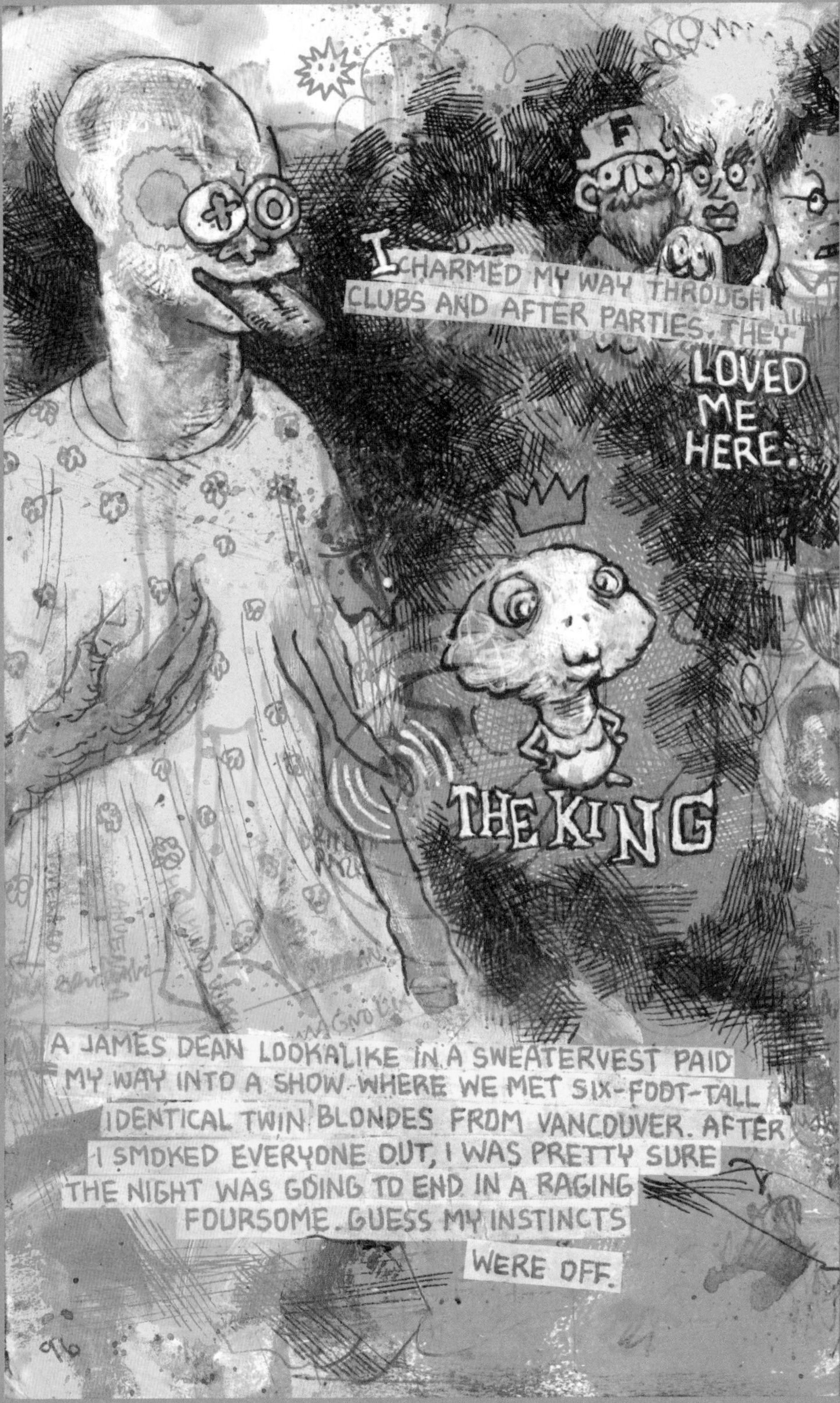
I CHARMED MY WAY THROUGH CLUBS AND AFTER PARTIES. THEY LOVED ME HERE.
THE KING
A JAMES DEAN LOOKALIKE IN A SWEATERVEST PAID MY WAY INTO A SHOW WHERE WE MET SIX-FOOT-TALL IDENTICAL TWIN BLONDES FROM VANCOUVER. AFTER I SMOKED EVERYONE OUT, I WAS PRETTY SURE THE NIGHT WAS GOING TO END IN A RAGING FOURSOME. GUESS MY INSTINCTS WERE OFF.

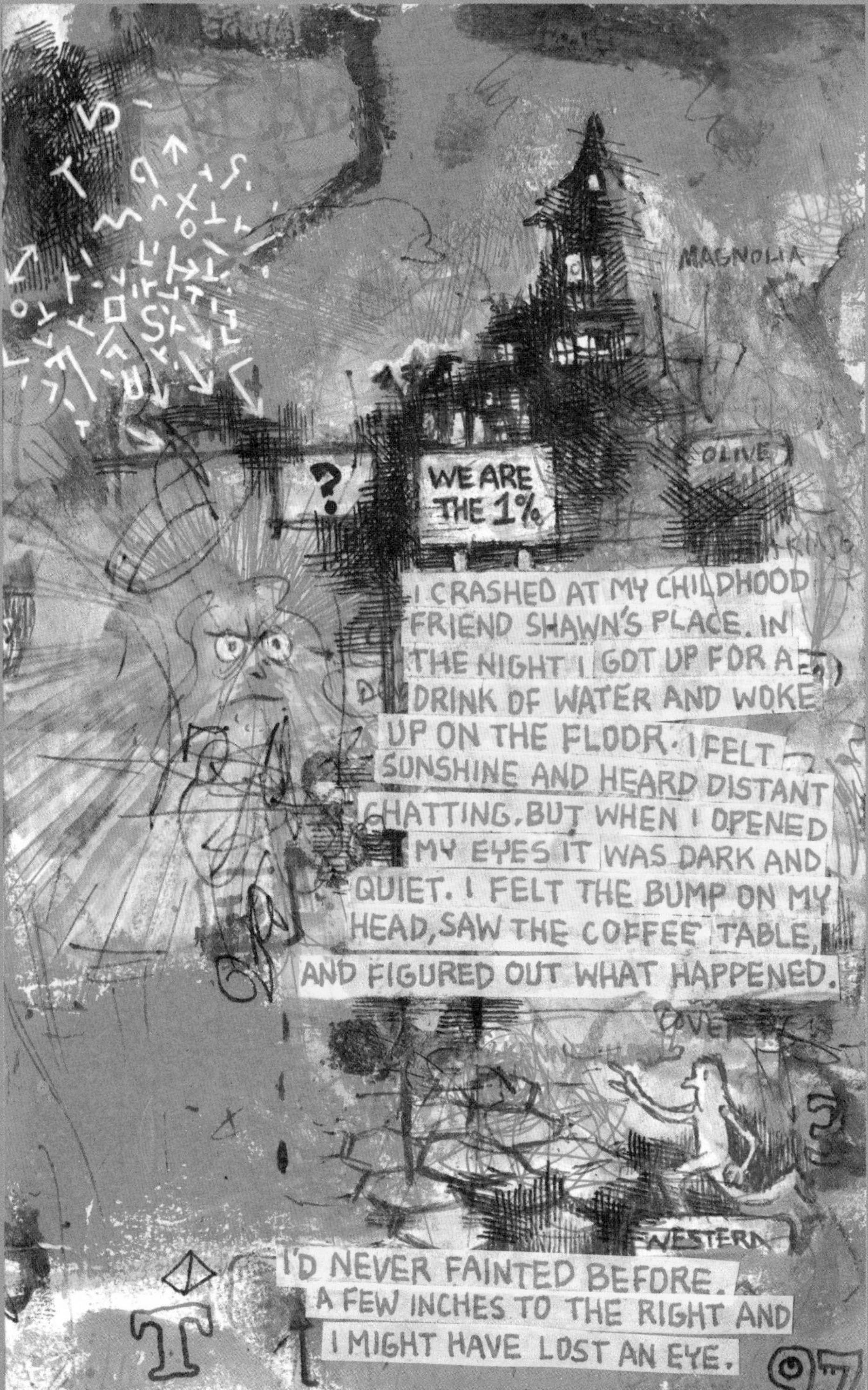
MAGNOLIA
OLIVE
?
WE ARE THE 1%
I CRASHED AT MY CHILDHOOD FRIEND SHAWN'S PLACE. IN THE NIGHT I GOT UP FOR A DRINK OF WATER AND WOKE UP ON THE FLOOR. I FELT SUNSHINE AND HEARD DISTANT CHATTING, BUT WHEN I OPENED MY EYES IT WAS DARK AND QUIET. I FELT THE BUMP ON MY HEAD, SAW THE COFFEE TABLE, AND FIGURED OUT WHAT HAPPENED.
WESTERN
I'D NEVER FAINTED BEFORE. A FEW INCHES TO THE RIGHT AND I MIGHT HAVE LOST AN EYE.
T
GLENOAKS

AN HOMAGE TO BAD DESIGN

NO

MIXTAPE of databases

.index

encyc

RARY

ASE

98

GRAD- DBA OF INFOR
SYSTE

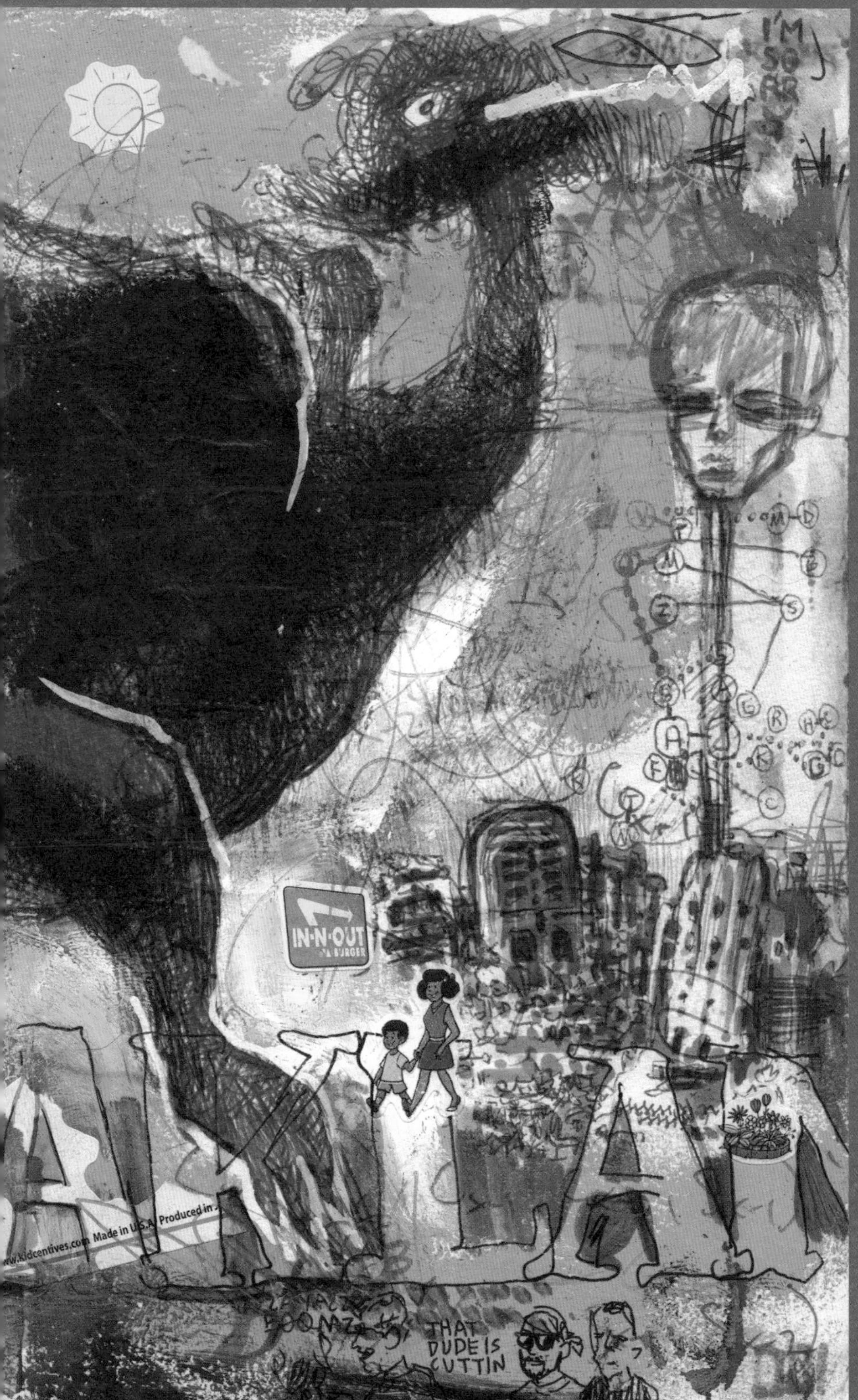

I'M SO
IN-N-OUT BURGER
www.kidcentives.com Made in U.S.A. Produced in
THAT DUDE IS CUTTIN

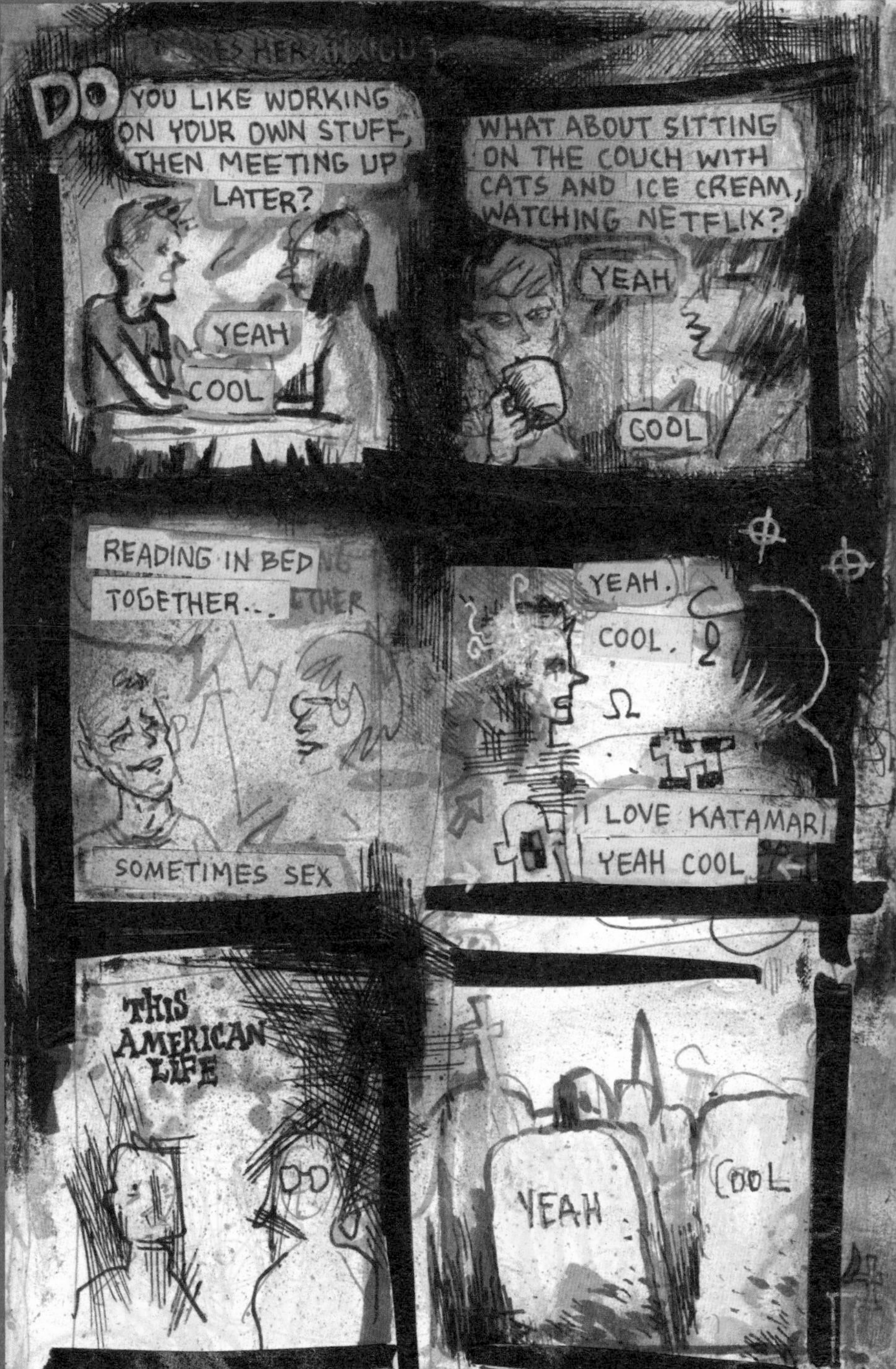
DO YOU LIKE WORKING ON YOUR OWN STUFF, THEN MEETING UP LATER?
YEAH
COOL
WHAT ABOUT SITTING ON THE COUCH WITH CATS AND ICE CREAM, WATCHING NETFLIX?
YEAH
COOL
READING IN BED TOGETHER...
SOMETIMES SEX
YEAH.
COOL.
I LOVE KATAMARI
YEAH COOL
THIS AMERICAN LIFE
YEAH
COOL

THIS ISN'T A COMIC ABOUT A RELATIONSHIP...

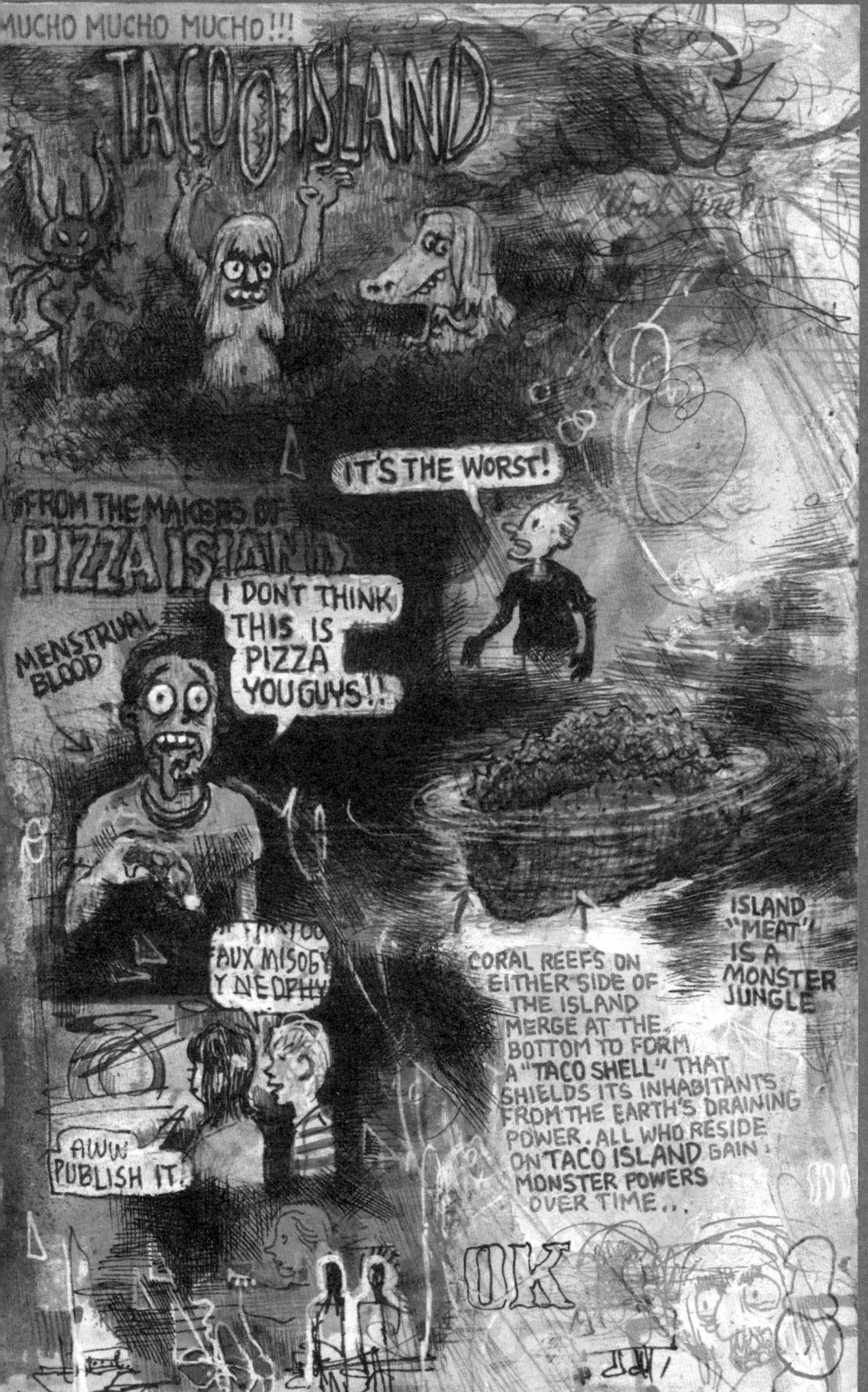

MUCHO MUCHO MUCHO!!!
TACO ISLAND
IT'S THE WORST!
FROM THE MAKERS OF
PIZZA ISLAND
I DON'T THINK THIS IS PIZZA YOU GUYS!!
MENSTRUAL BLOOD
ISLAND "MEAT" IS A MONSTER JUNGLE
CORAL REEFS ON EITHER SIDE OF THE ISLAND MERGE AT THE BOTTOM TO FORM A "TACO SHELL" THAT SHIELDS ITS INHABITANTS FROM THE EARTH'S DRAINING POWER. ALL WHO RESIDE ON TACO ISLAND GAIN MONSTER POWERS OVER TIME...
AUX MISOGY
AWW PUBLISH IT.
OK

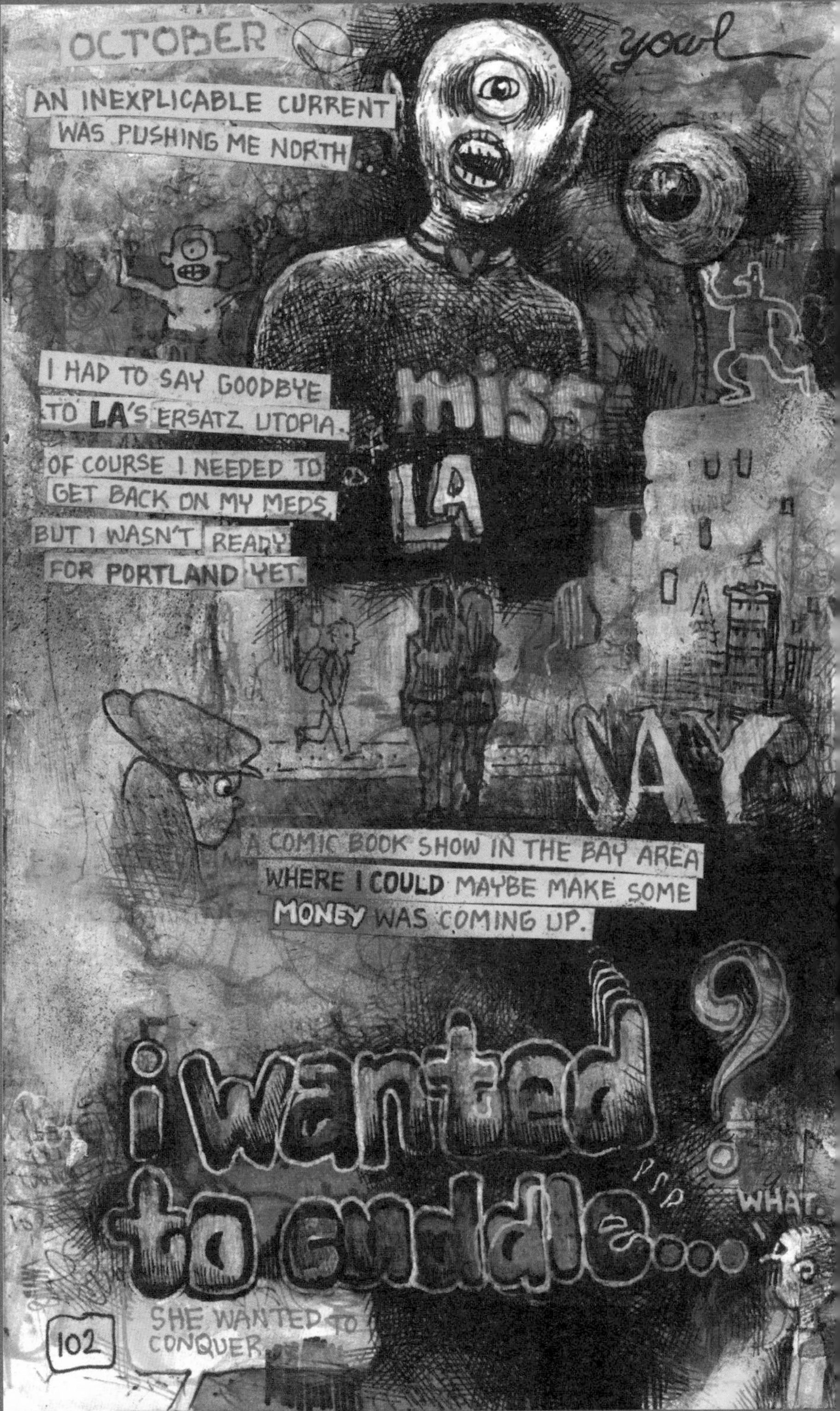
OCTOBER
yowl
AN INEXPLICABLE CURRENT WAS PUSHING ME NORTH
I HAD TO SAY GOODBYE TO LA'S ERSATZ UTOPIA.
miss LA
OF COURSE I NEEDED TO GET BACK ON MY MEDS,
BUT I WASN'T READY FOR PORTLAND YET.
AY
A COMIC BOOK SHOW IN THE BAY AREA WHERE I COULD MAYBE MAKE SOME MONEY WAS COMING UP.
i wanted to cuddle...
?
WHAT
SHE WANTED TO CONQUER
102

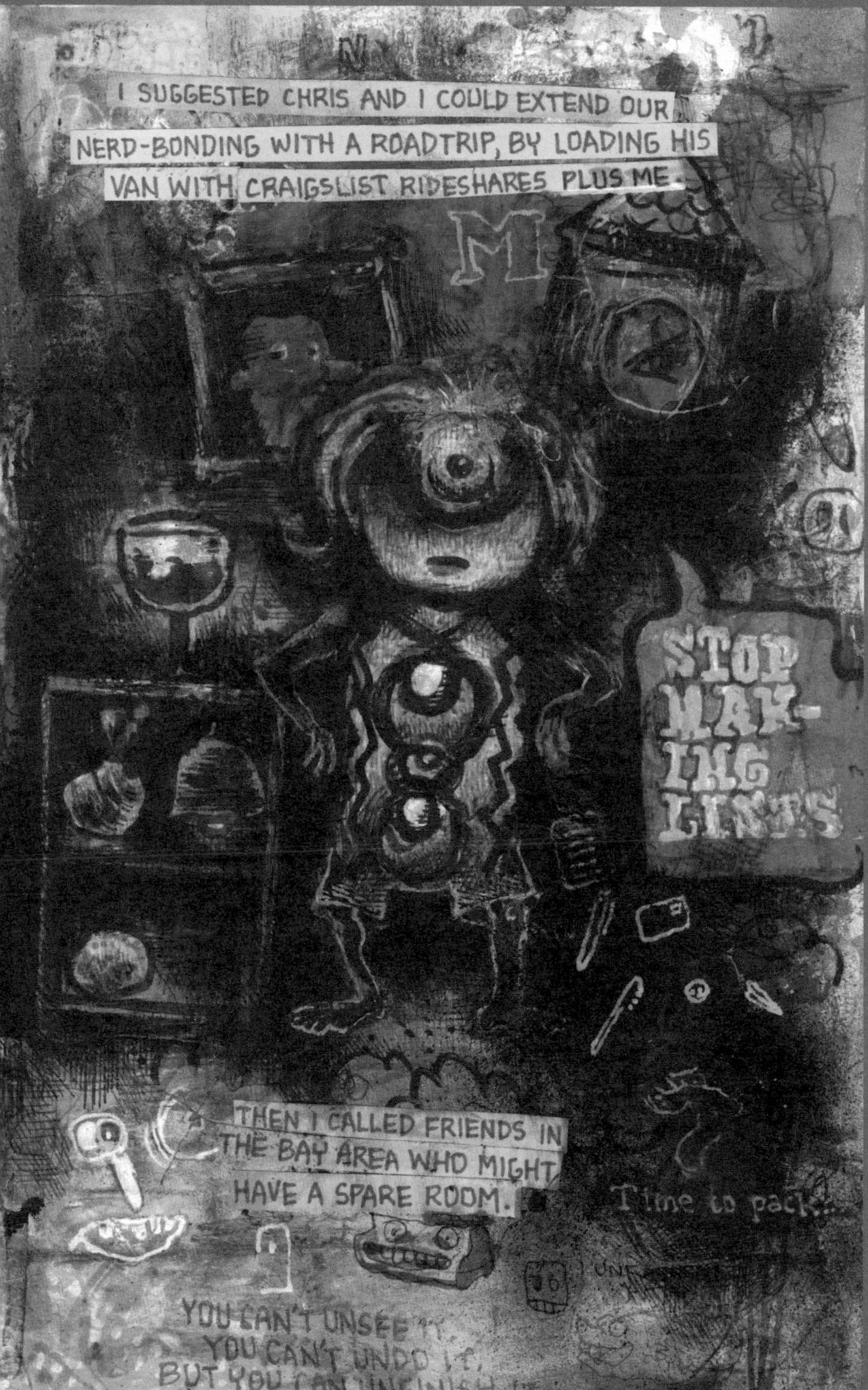
I SUGGESTED CHRIS AND I COULD EXTEND OUR NERD-BONDING WITH A ROADTRIP, BY LOADING HIS VAN WITH CRAIGSLIST RIDESHARES PLUS ME.
STOP MAKING LISTS
THEN I CALLED FRIENDS IN THE BAY AREA WHO MIGHT HAVE A SPARE ROOM.
Time to pack...
YOU CAN'T UNSEE IT. YOU CAN'T UNDO IT. BUT YOU CAN UNFINISH IT...

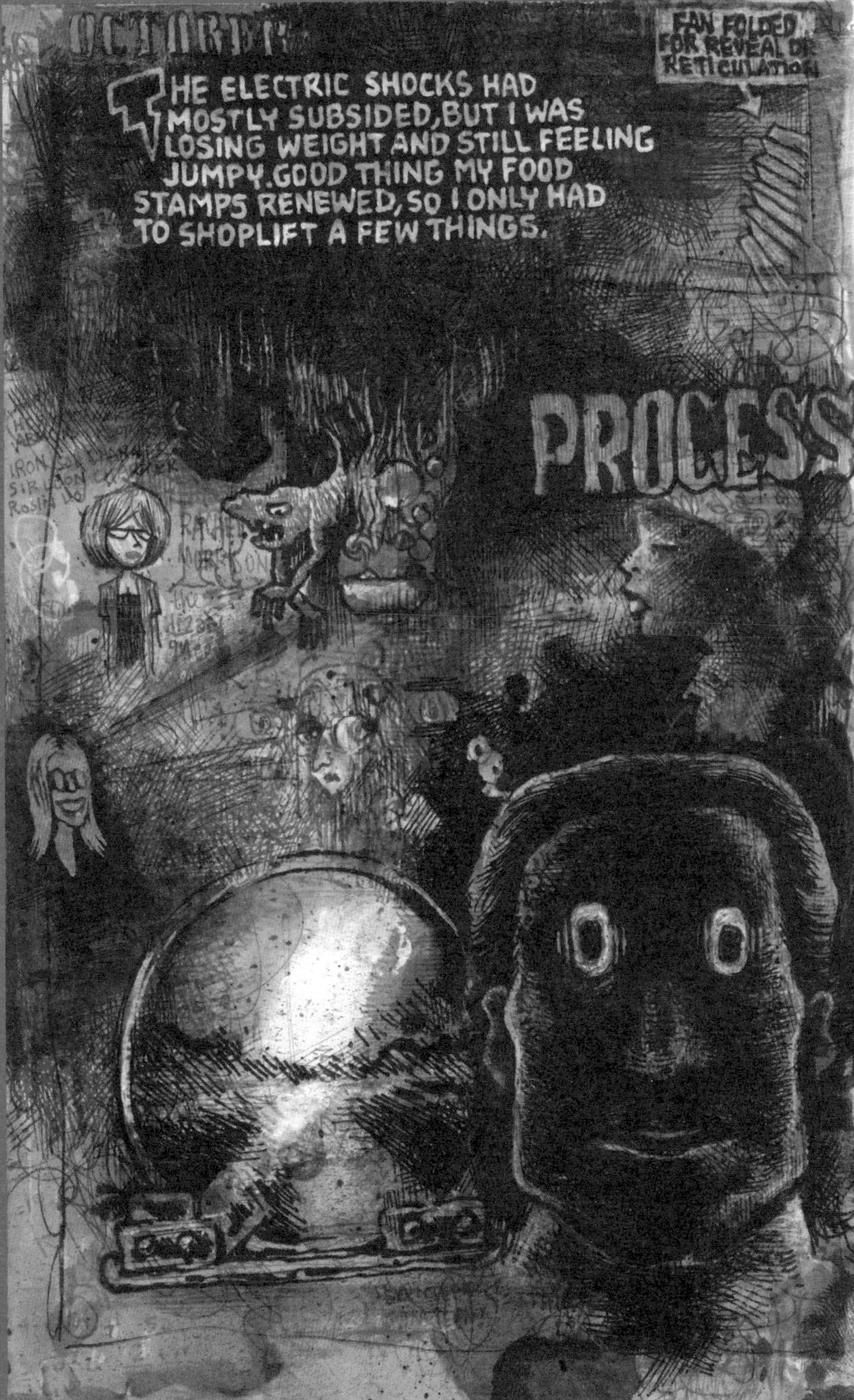

FAN FOLDED FOR REVEAL OF RETICULATION
THE ELECTRIC SHOCKS HAD MOSTLY SUBSIDED, BUT I WAS LOSING WEIGHT AND STILL FEELING JUMPY. GOOD THING MY FOOD STAMPS RENEWED, SO I ONLY HAD TO SHOPLIFT A FEW THINGS.
PROCESS

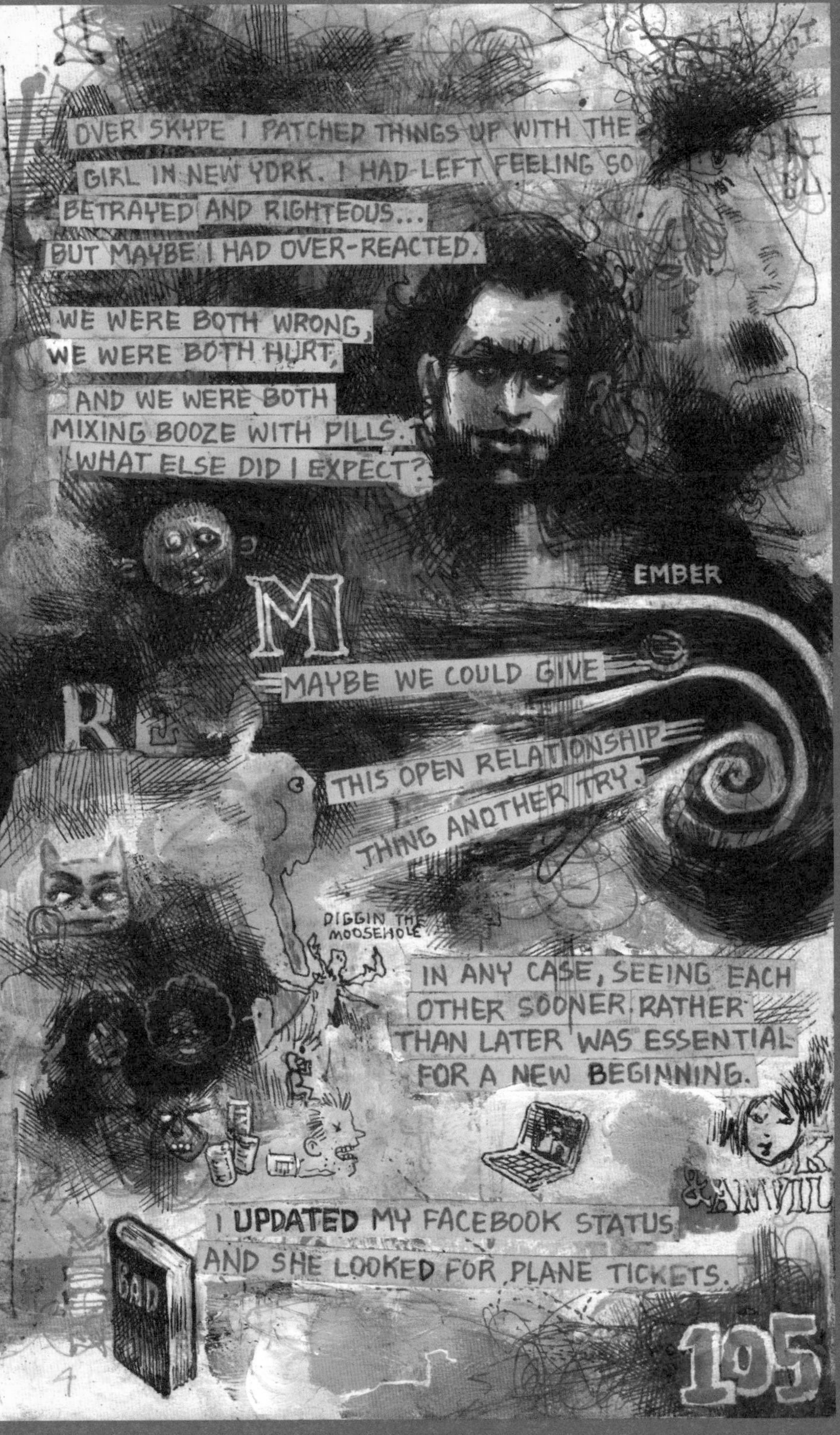
OVER SKYPE I PATCHED THINGS UP WITH THE
GIRL IN NEW YORK. I HAD LEFT FEELING SO
BETRAYED AND RIGHTEOUS...
BUT MAYBE I HAD OVER-REACTED.
WE WERE BOTH WRONG,
WE WERE BOTH HURT,
AND WE WERE BOTH
MIXING BOOZE WITH PILLS.
WHAT ELSE DID I EXPECT?
EMBER
M
MAYBE WE COULD GIVE
R
THIS OPEN RELATIONSHIP
THING ANOTHER TRY.
DIGGIN THE MOOSEHOLE
IN ANY CASE, SEEING EACH
OTHER SOONER RATHER
THAN LATER WAS ESSENTIAL
FOR A NEW BEGINNING.
I UPDATED MY FACEBOOK STATUS
AND SHE LOOKED FOR PLANE TICKETS.
BAD
105

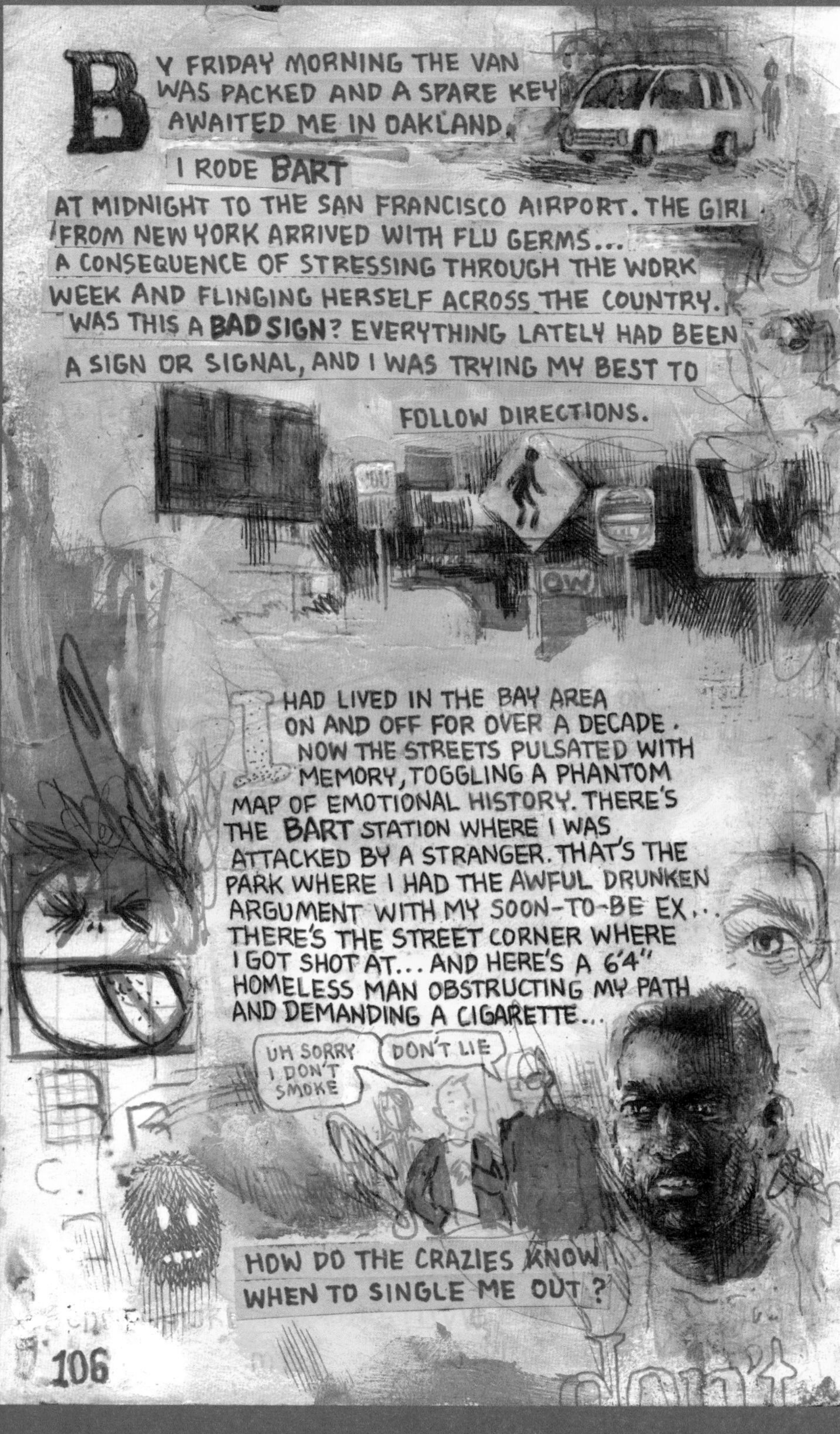
BY FRIDAY MORNING THE VAN WAS PACKED AND A SPARE KEY AWAITED ME IN OAKLAND.
I RODE BART
AT MIDNIGHT TO THE SAN FRANCISCO AIRPORT. THE GIRL FROM NEW YORK ARRIVED WITH FLU GERMS... A CONSEQUENCE OF STRESSING THROUGH THE WORK WEEK AND FLINGING HERSELF ACROSS THE COUNTRY.
WAS THIS A BAD SIGN? EVERYTHING LATELY HAD BEEN A SIGN OR SIGNAL, AND I WAS TRYING MY BEST TO
FOLLOW DIRECTIONS.
I HAD LIVED IN THE BAY AREA ON AND OFF FOR OVER A DECADE. NOW THE STREETS PULSATED WITH MEMORY, TOGGLING A PHANTOM MAP OF EMOTIONAL HISTORY. THERE'S THE BART STATION WHERE I WAS ATTACKED BY A STRANGER. THAT'S THE PARK WHERE I HAD THE AWFUL DRUNKEN ARGUMENT WITH MY SOON-TO-BE EX... THERE'S THE STREET CORNER WHERE I GOT SHOT AT... AND HERE'S A 6'4" HOMELESS MAN OBSTRUCTING MY PATH AND DEMANDING A CIGARETTE...
UH SORRY I DON'T SMOKE
DON'T LIE
HOW DO THE CRAZIES KNOW WHEN TO SINGLE ME OUT?

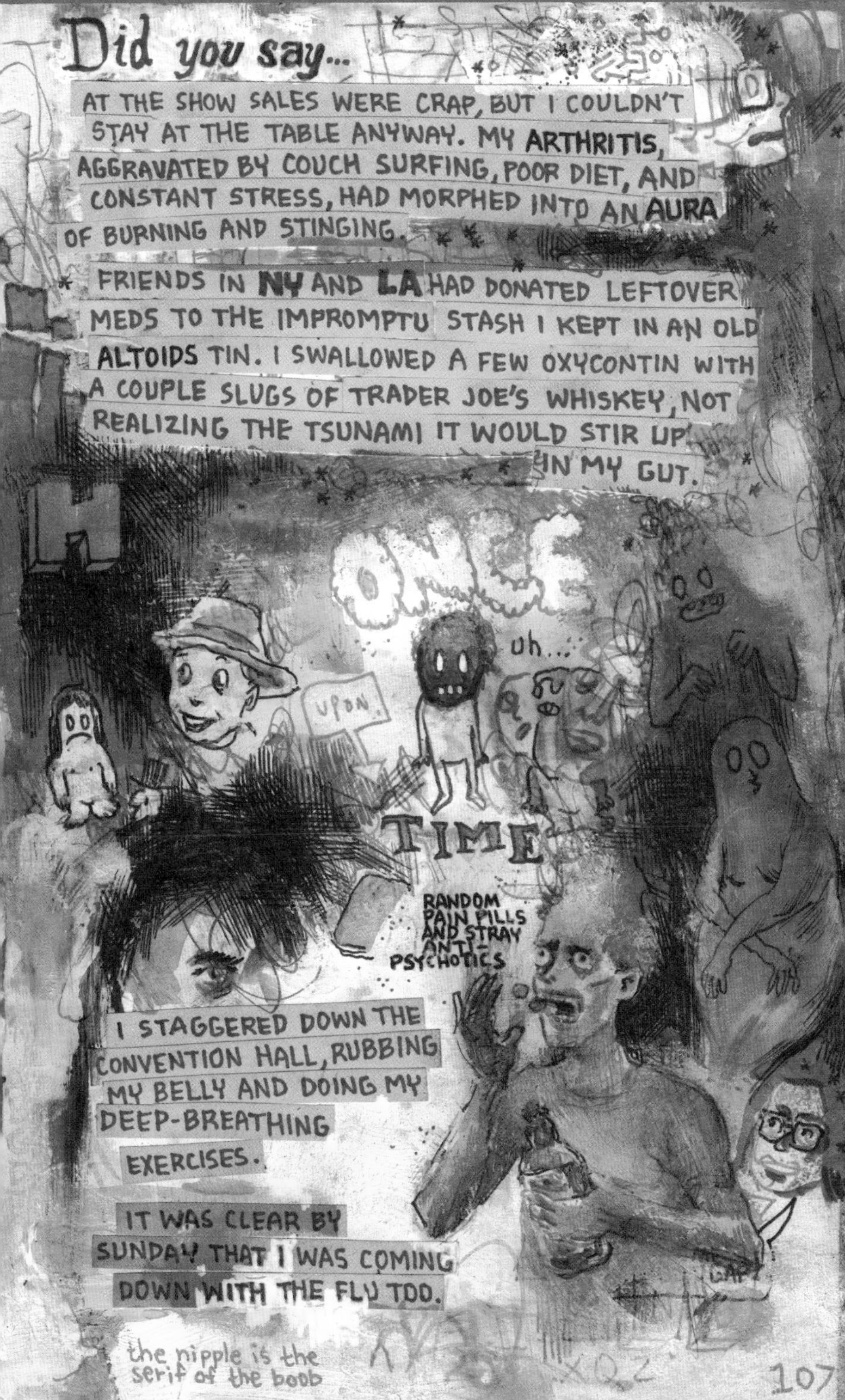
Did you say...
AT THE SHOW SALES WERE CRAP, BUT I COULDN'T STAY AT THE TABLE ANYWAY. MY ARTHRITIS, AGGRAVATED BY COUCH SURFING, POOR DIET, AND CONSTANT STRESS, HAD MORPHED INTO AN AURA OF BURNING AND STINGING.
FRIENDS IN NY AND LA HAD DONATED LEFTOVER MEDS TO THE IMPROMPTU STASH I KEPT IN AN OLD ALTOIDS TIN. I SWALLOWED A FEW OXYCONTIN WITH A COUPLE SLUGS OF TRADER JOE'S WHISKEY, NOT REALIZING THE TSUNAMI IT WOULD STIR UP IN MY GUT.
ONCE
UPON
uh...
TIME
RANDOM PAIN PILLS AND STRAY ANTI-PSYCHOTICS
I STAGGERED DOWN THE CONVENTION HALL, RUBBING MY BELLY AND DOING MY DEEP-BREATHING EXERCISES.
IT WAS CLEAR BY SUNDAY THAT I WAS COMING DOWN WITH THE FLU TOO.
the nipple is the serif of the boob

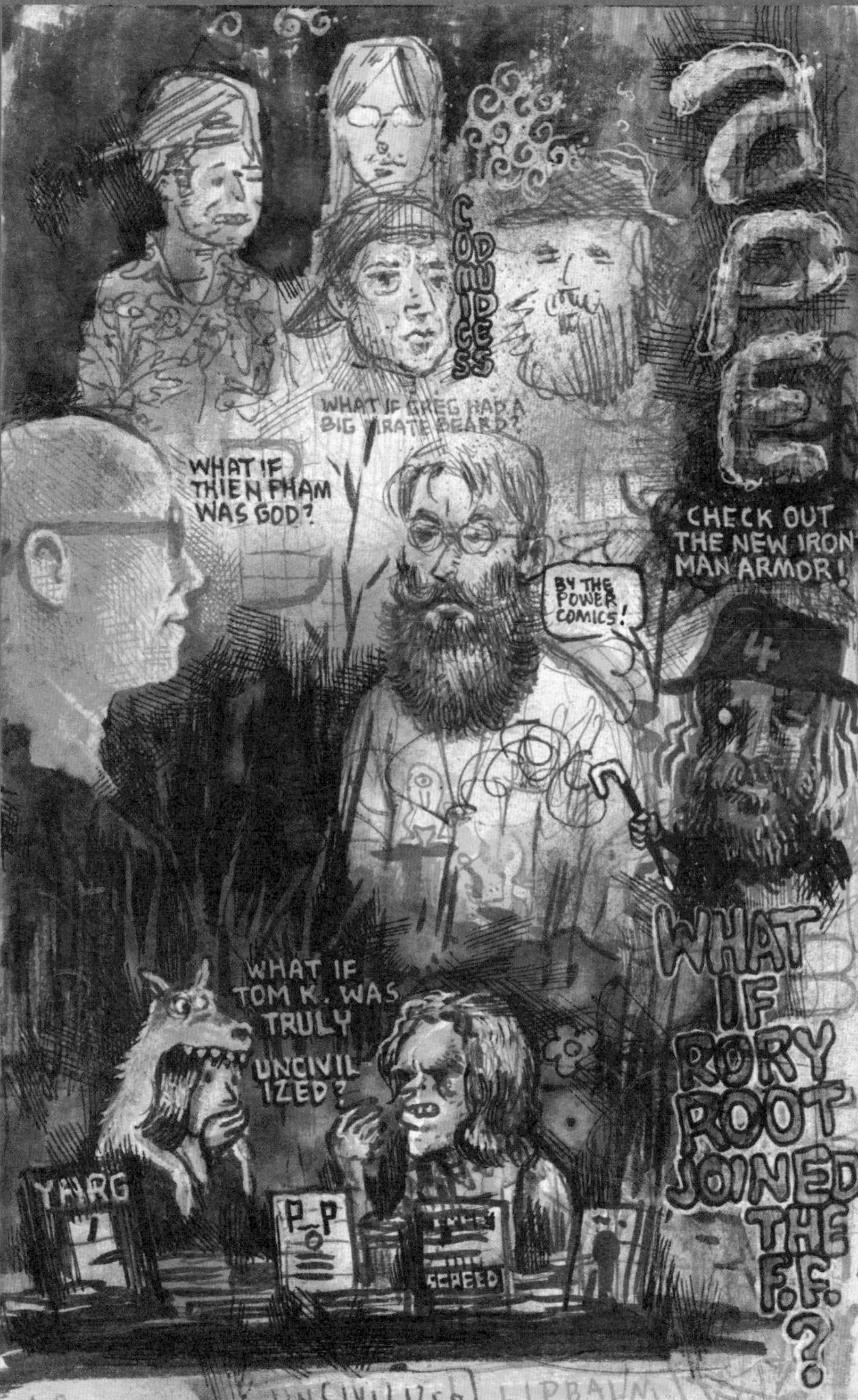
COMICS DUDES
WHAT IF GREG HAD A BIG PIRATE BEARD?
WHAT IF THIEN PHAM WAS GOD?
CHECK OUT THE NEW IRON MAN ARMOR!
BY THE POWER COMICS!
WHAT IF TOM K. WAS TRULY UNCIVILIZED?
WHAT IF RORY ROOT JOINED THE F.F.?
YHRG
SCREED
UNCIVILIZED BOOKS
LIPBALM SMILELIFE

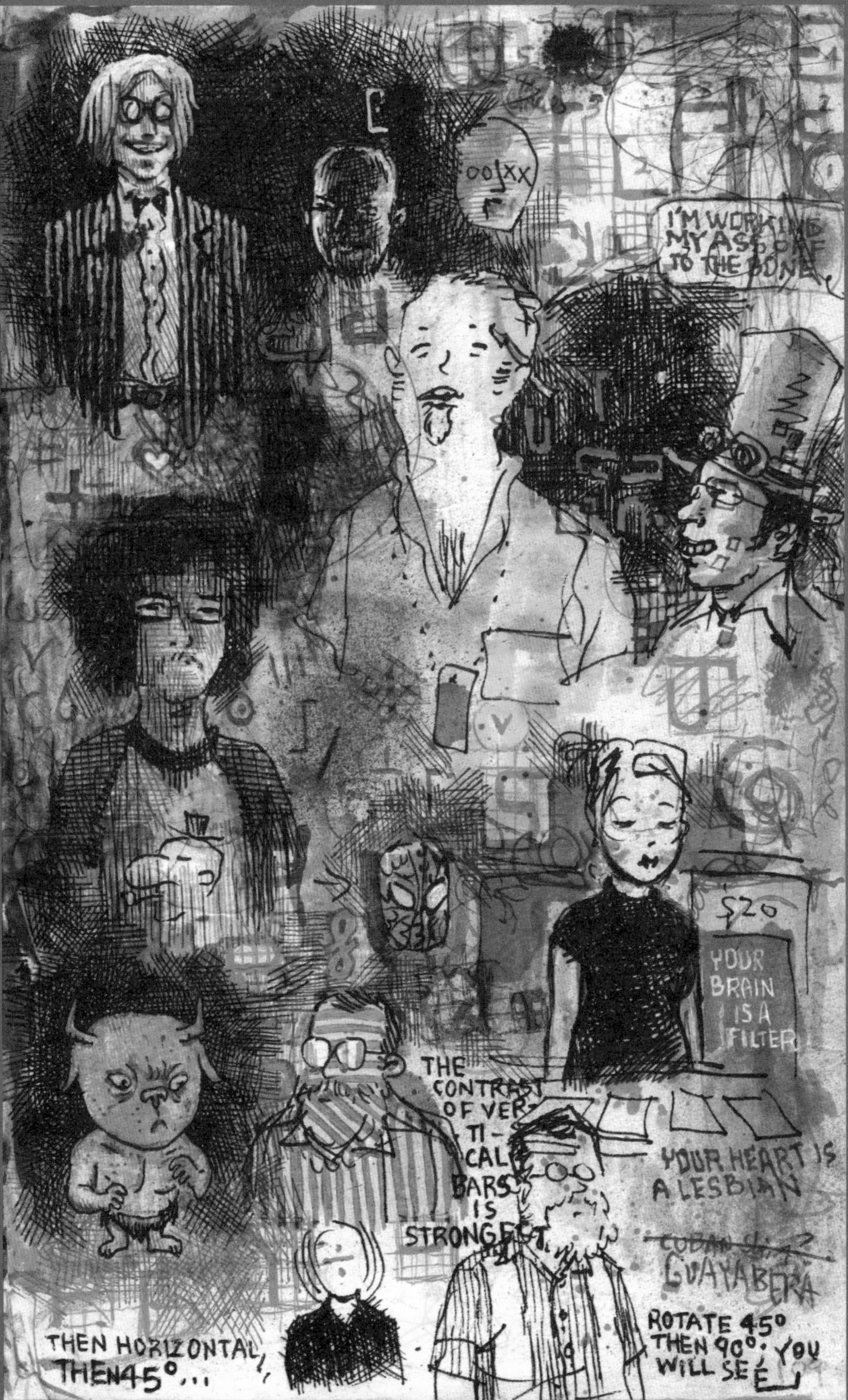

OO/XX
I'M WORKING MY ASS OFF TO THE BONE
$20
YOUR BRAIN IS A FILTER
THE CONTRAST OF VERTICAL BARS IS STRONGEST
YOUR HEART IS A LESBIAN
GUAYABERA
THEN HORIZONTAL, THEN 45°...
ROTATE 45° THEN 90°, YOU WILL SEE

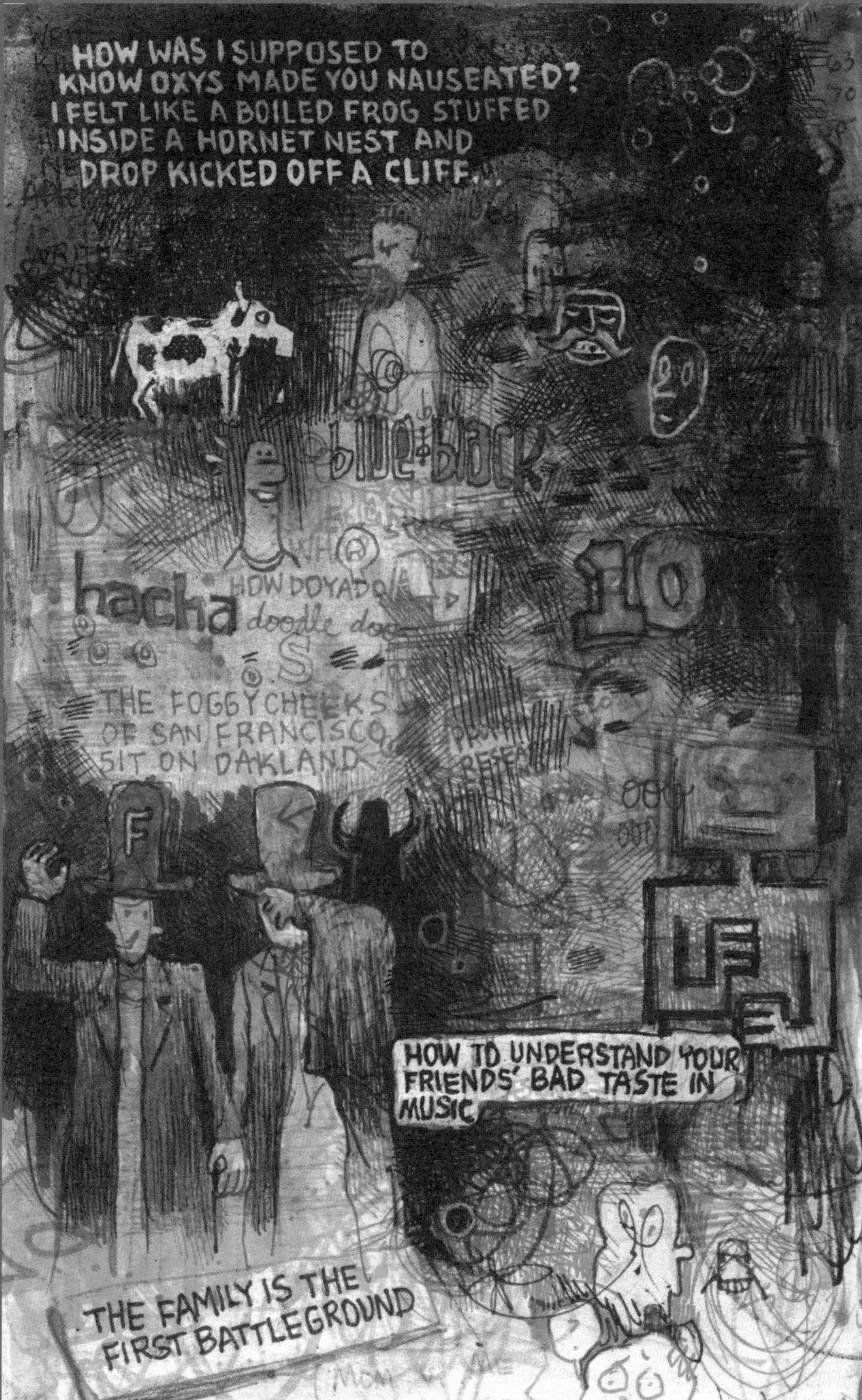

HOW WAS I SUPPOSED TO KNOW OXYS MADE YOU NAUSEATED? I FELT LIKE A BOILED FROG STUFFED INSIDE A HORNET NEST AND DROP KICKED OFF A CLIFF...
hacha
THE FOGGY CHEEKS OF SAN FRANCISCO SIT ON OAKLAND
10
HOW TO UNDERSTAND YOUR FRIENDS' BAD TASTE IN MUSIC
THE FAMILY IS THE FIRST BATTLEGROUND

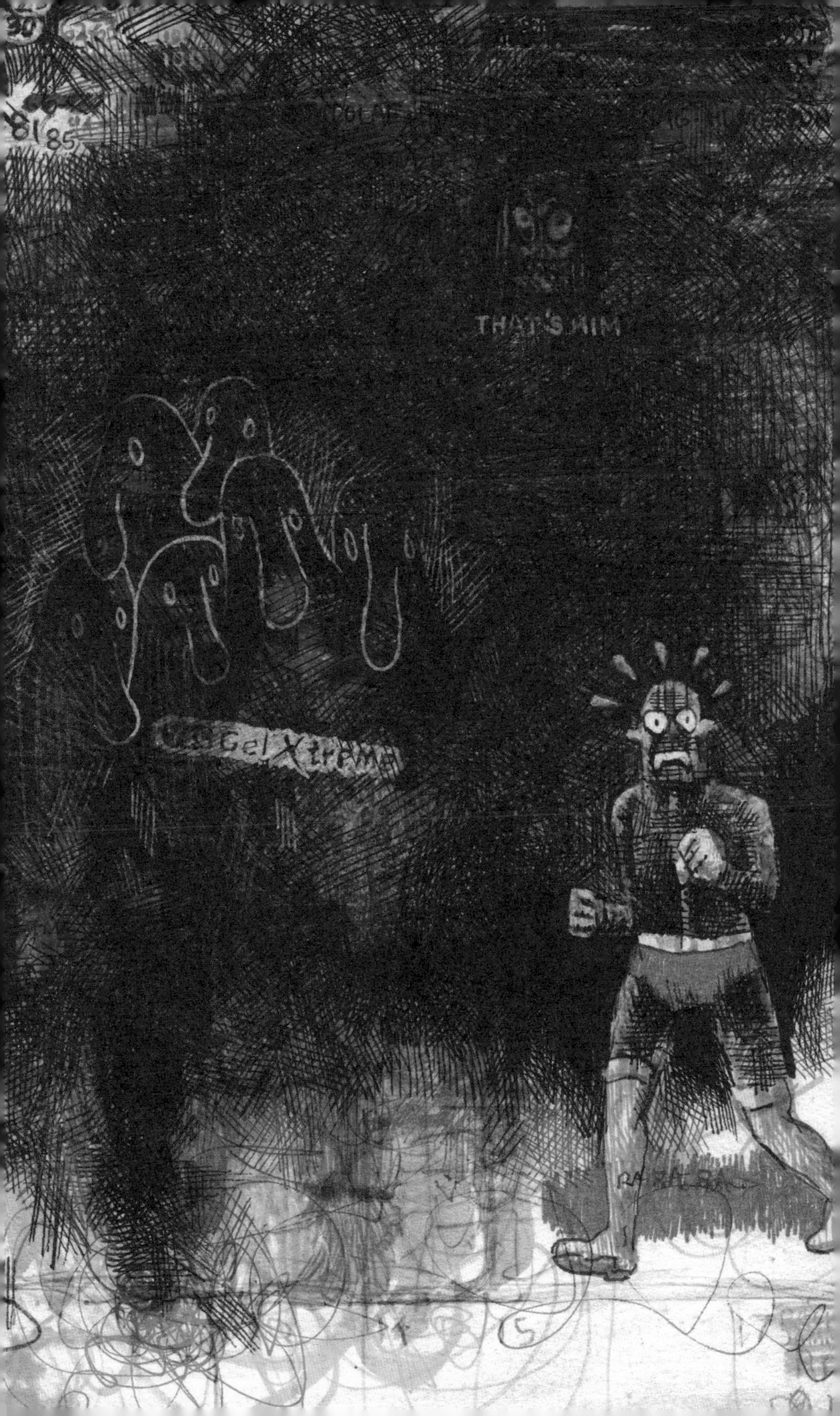
THAT'S HIM

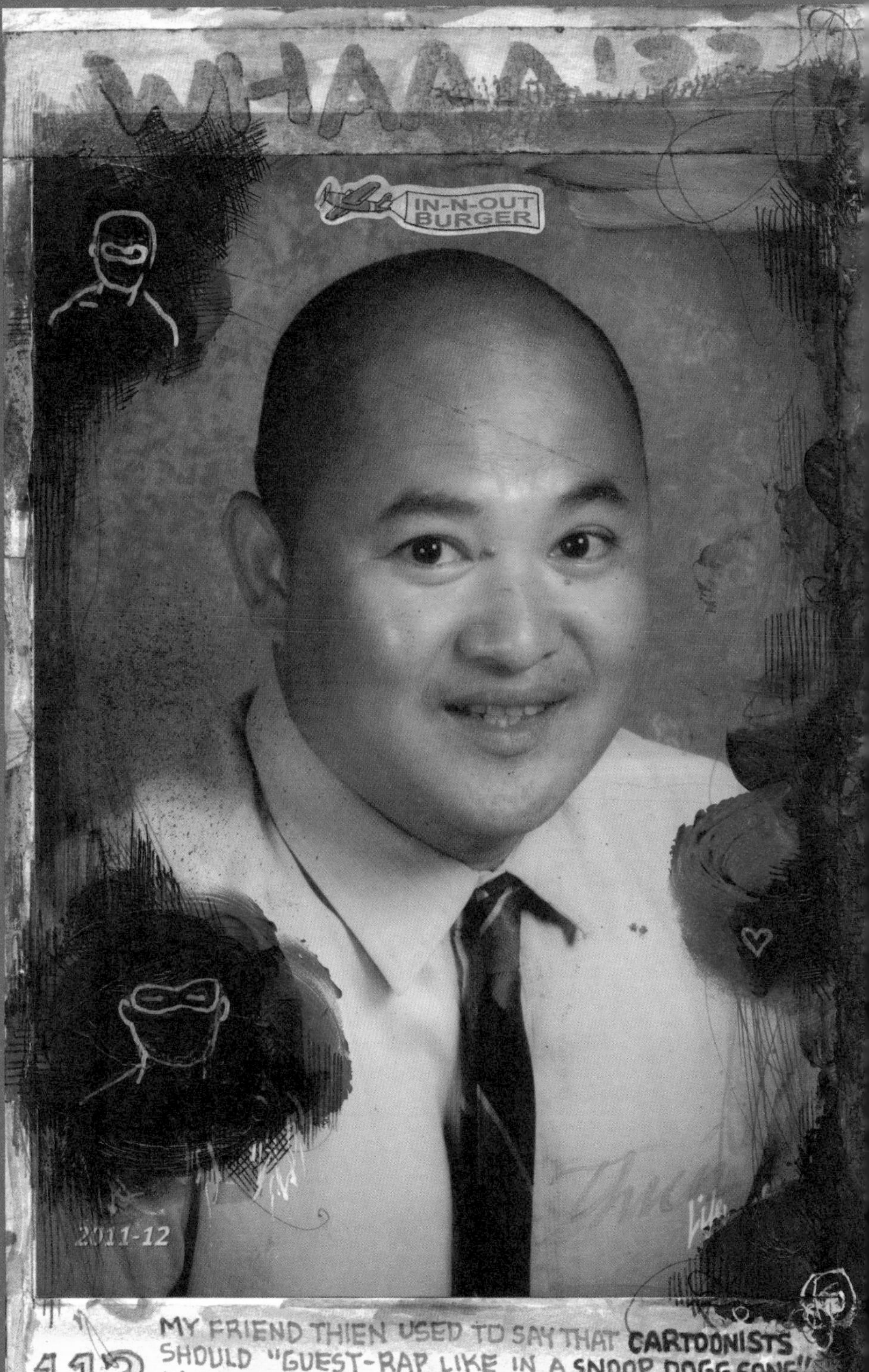
IN-N-OUT BURGER
2011-12
112
MY FRIEND THIEN USED TO SAY THAT CARTOONISTS SHOULD "GUEST-RAP LIKE IN A SNOOP DOGG SONG" IN EACH OTHER'S BOOKS. I ASKED HIM TO DRAW IN MY SKETCHBOOK BUT HE WAS TOO BUSY.

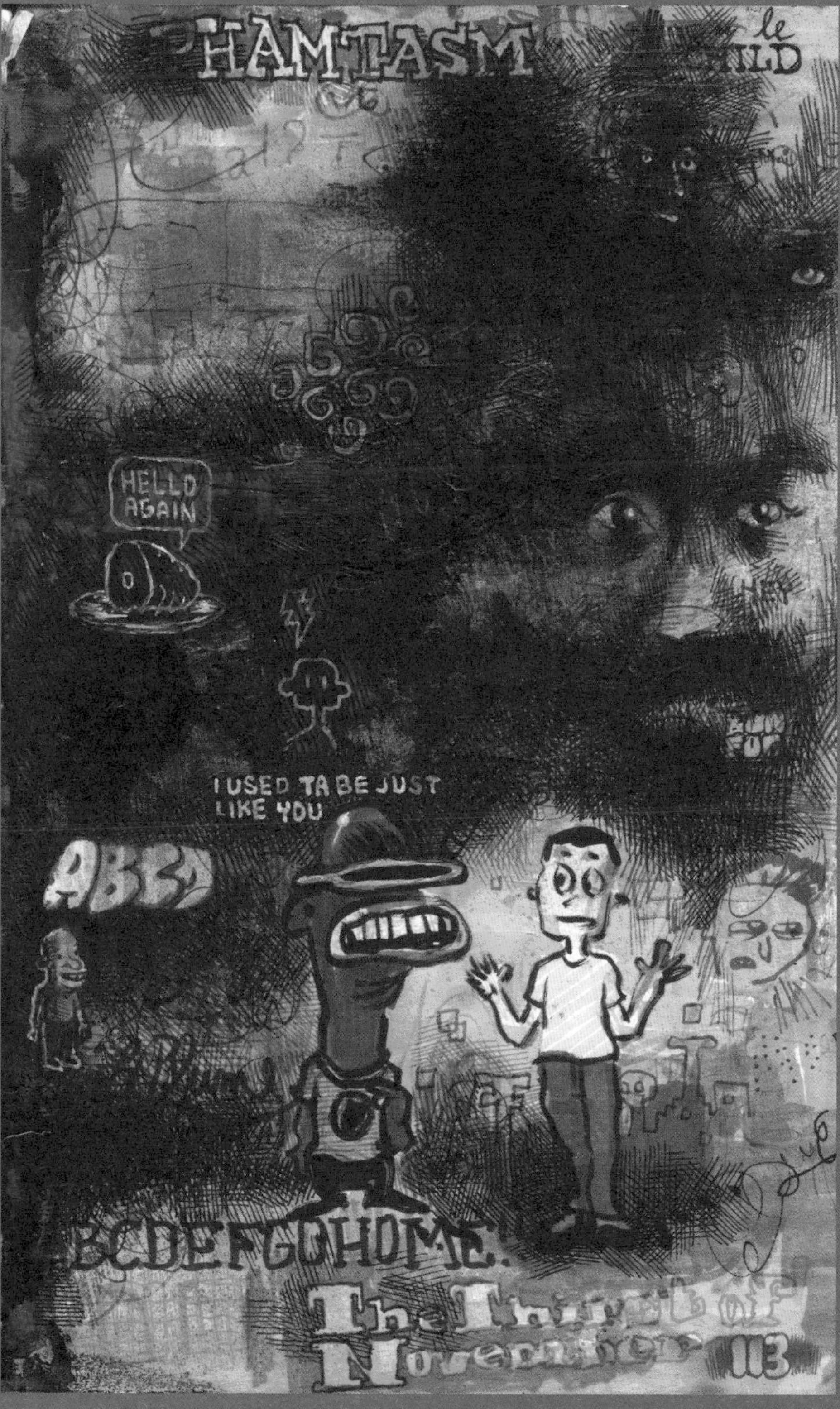
HAMTASM
HELLO AGAIN
I USED TA BE JUST LIKE YOU
BCDEFGOHOME.
113

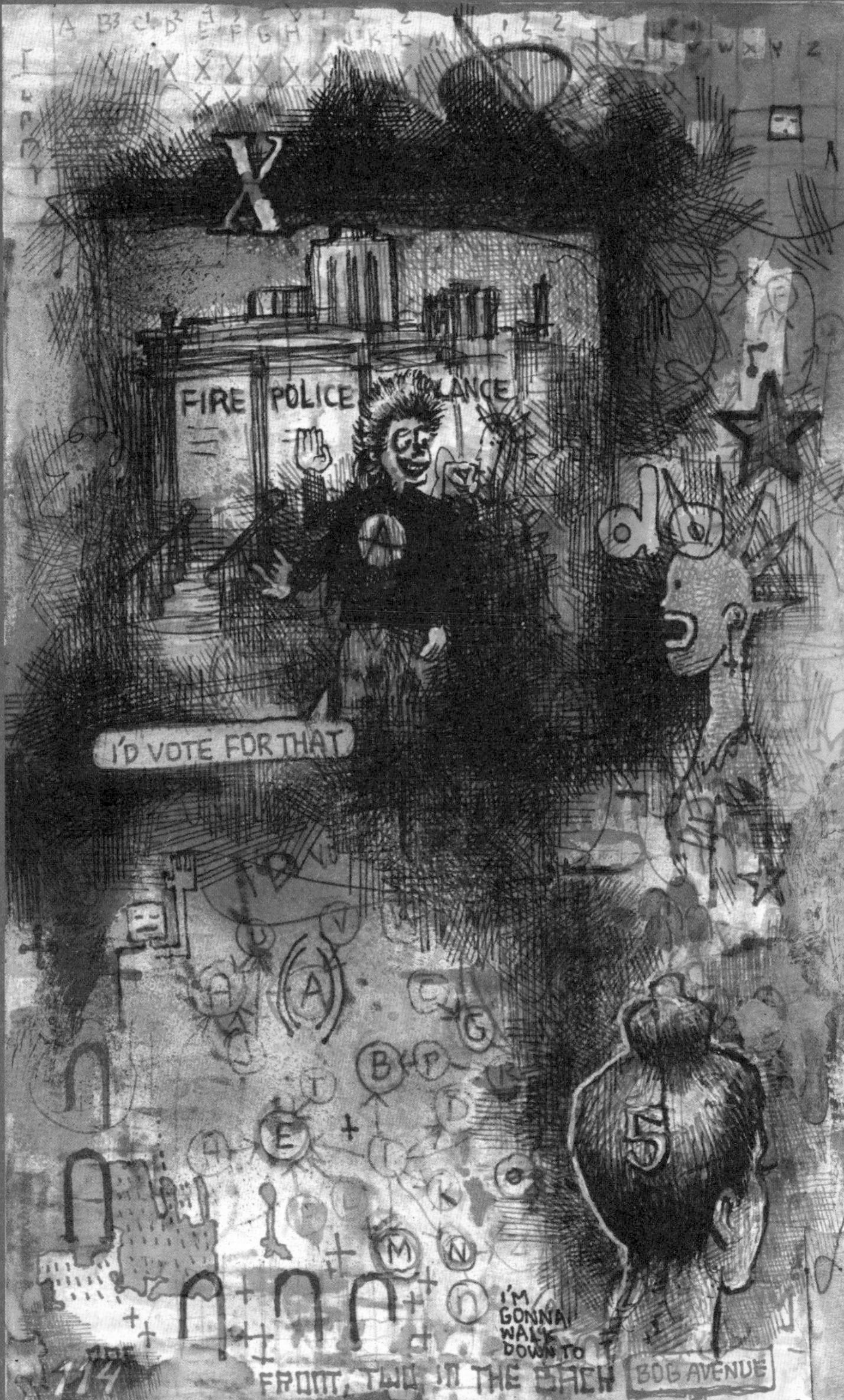
X
FIRE
POLICE
LANCE
I'D VOTE FOR THAT
I'M GONNA WALK DOWN TO
BOG AVENUE
FROM, TWO IN THE BACH
114

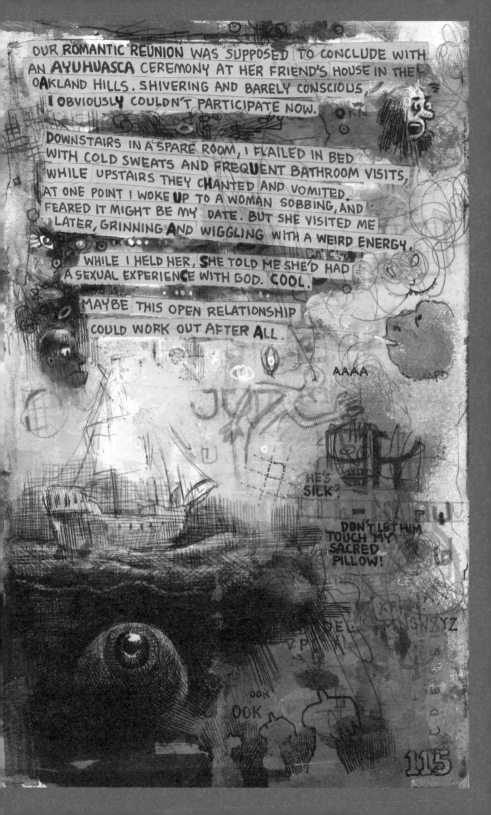

OUR ROMANTIC REUNION WAS SUPPOSED TO CONCLUDE WITH AN **AYUHUASCA** CEREMONY AT HER FRIEND'S HOUSE IN THE OAKLAND HILLS. SHIVERING AND BARELY CONSCIOUS, I OBVIOUSLY COULDN'T PARTICIPATE NOW.

DOWNSTAIRS IN A SPARE ROOM, I FLAILED IN BED WITH COLD SWEATS AND FREQUENT BATHROOM VISITS, WHILE UPSTAIRS THEY CHANTED AND VOMITED. AT ONE POINT I WOKE UP TO A WOMAN SOBBING, AND FEARED IT MIGHT BE MY DATE. BUT SHE VISITED ME LATER, GRINNING AND WIGGLING WITH A WEIRD ENERGY.

WHILE I HELD HER, SHE TOLD ME SHE'D HAD A SEXUAL EXPERIENCE WITH GOD. **COOL.**

MAYBE THIS OPEN RELATIONSHIP COULD WORK OUT AFTER ALL.

AAAA

HE'S SICK?

DON'T LET HIM TOUCH MY SACRED PILLOW!

OOK

OOK

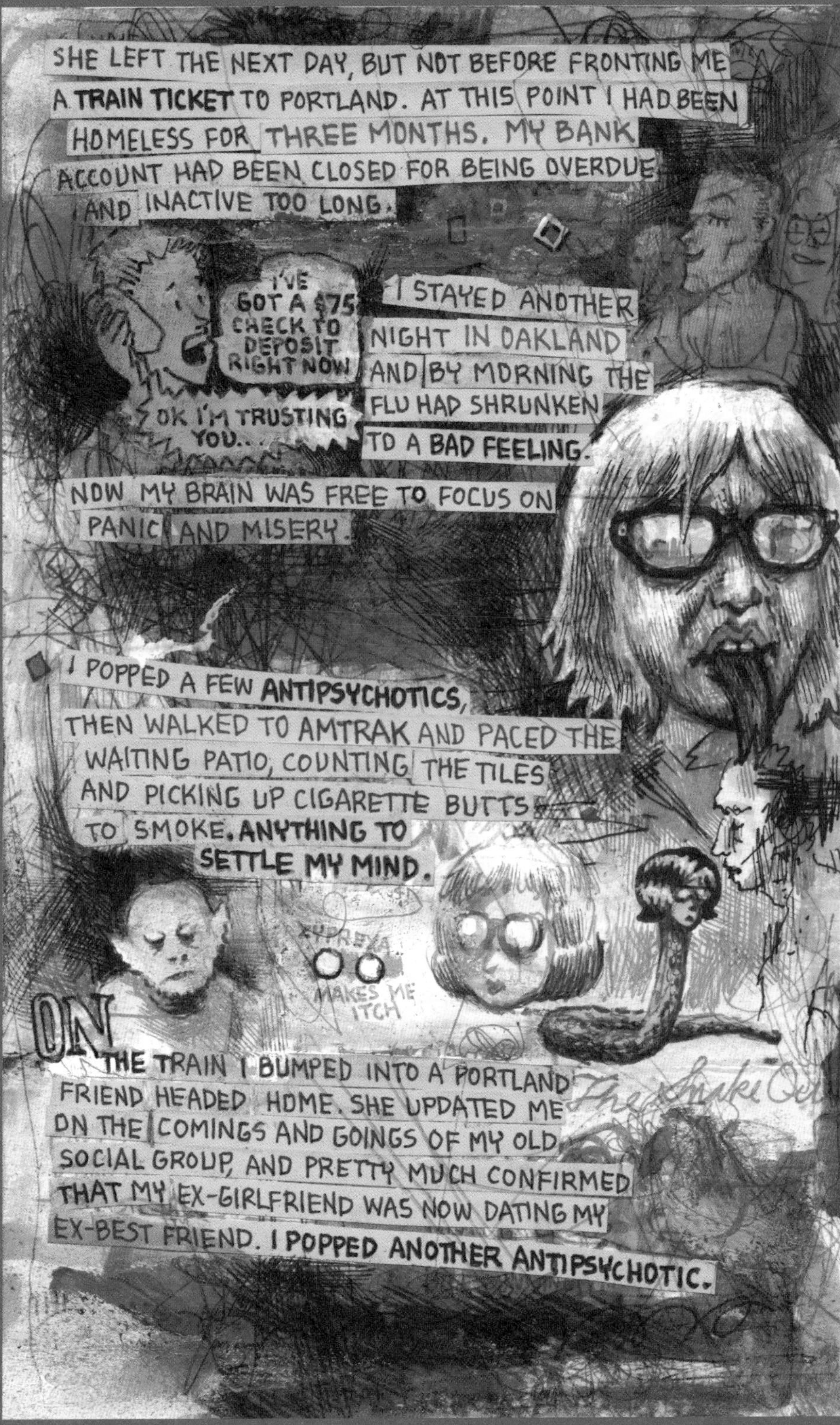
SHE LEFT THE NEXT DAY, BUT NOT BEFORE FRONTING ME A **TRAIN TICKET** TO PORTLAND. AT THIS POINT I HAD BEEN HOMELESS FOR THREE MONTHS. MY BANK ACCOUNT HAD BEEN CLOSED FOR BEING OVERDUE AND INACTIVE TOO LONG.
I'VE GOT A $75 CHECK TO DEPOSIT RIGHT NOW
OK I'M TRUSTING YOU...
I STAYED ANOTHER NIGHT IN OAKLAND AND BY MORNING THE FLU HAD SHRUNKEN TO A **BAD FEELING.**
NOW MY BRAIN WAS FREE TO FOCUS ON PANIC AND MISERY.
I POPPED A FEW **ANTIPSYCHOTICS,** THEN WALKED TO AMTRAK AND PACED THE WAITING PATIO, COUNTING THE TILES AND PICKING UP CIGARETTE BUTTS TO SMOKE. **ANYTHING TO SETTLE MY MIND.**
ZYPREXA
MAKES ME ITCH
ON THE TRAIN I BUMPED INTO A PORTLAND FRIEND HEADED HOME. SHE UPDATED ME ON THE COMINGS AND GOINGS OF MY OLD SOCIAL GROUP, AND PRETTY MUCH CONFIRMED THAT MY EX-GIRLFRIEND WAS NOW DATING MY EX-BEST FRIEND. **I POPPED ANOTHER ANTIPSYCHOTIC.**

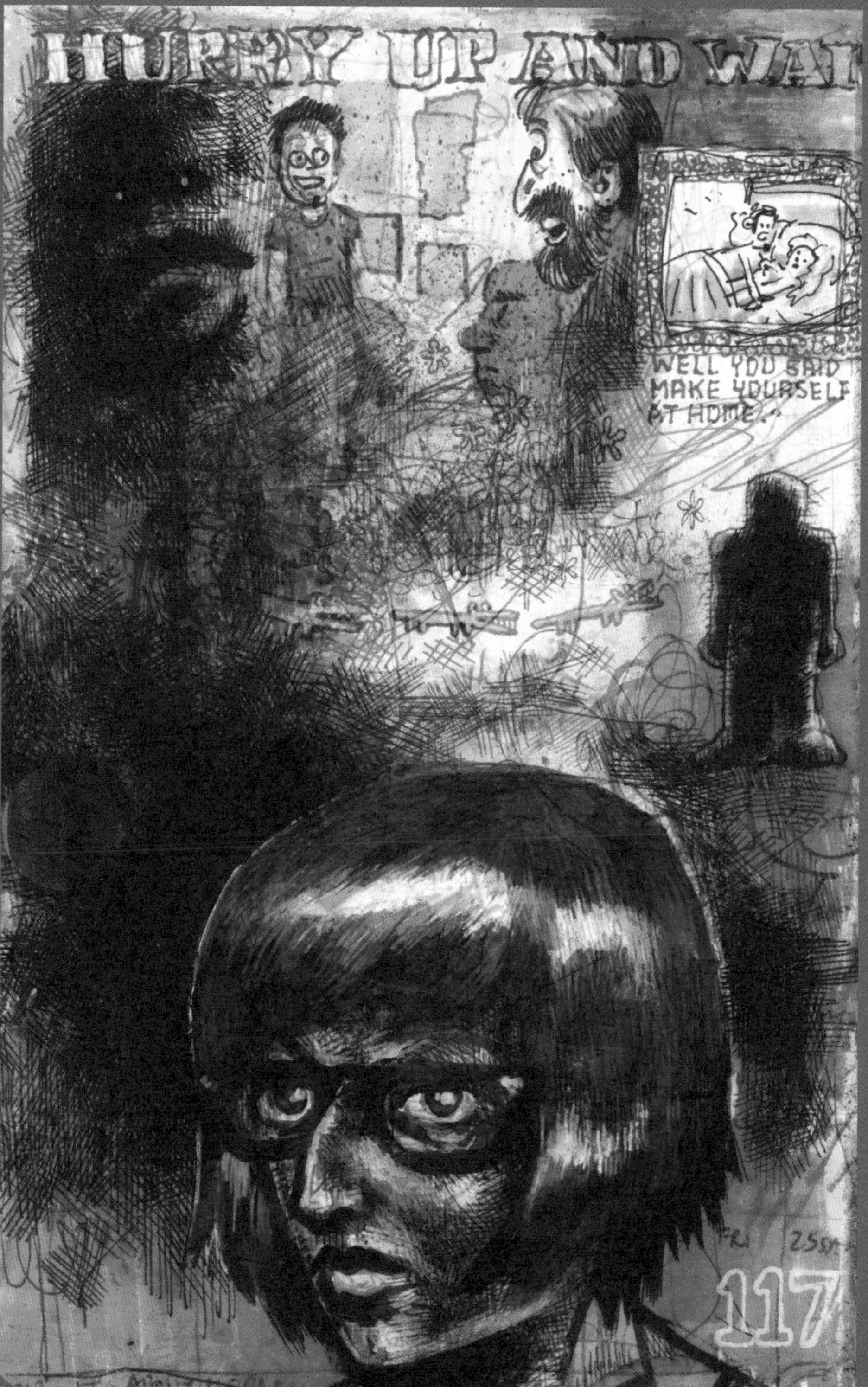
HURRY UP AND WAI
WELL YOU SAID MAKE YOURSELF AT HOME.
117

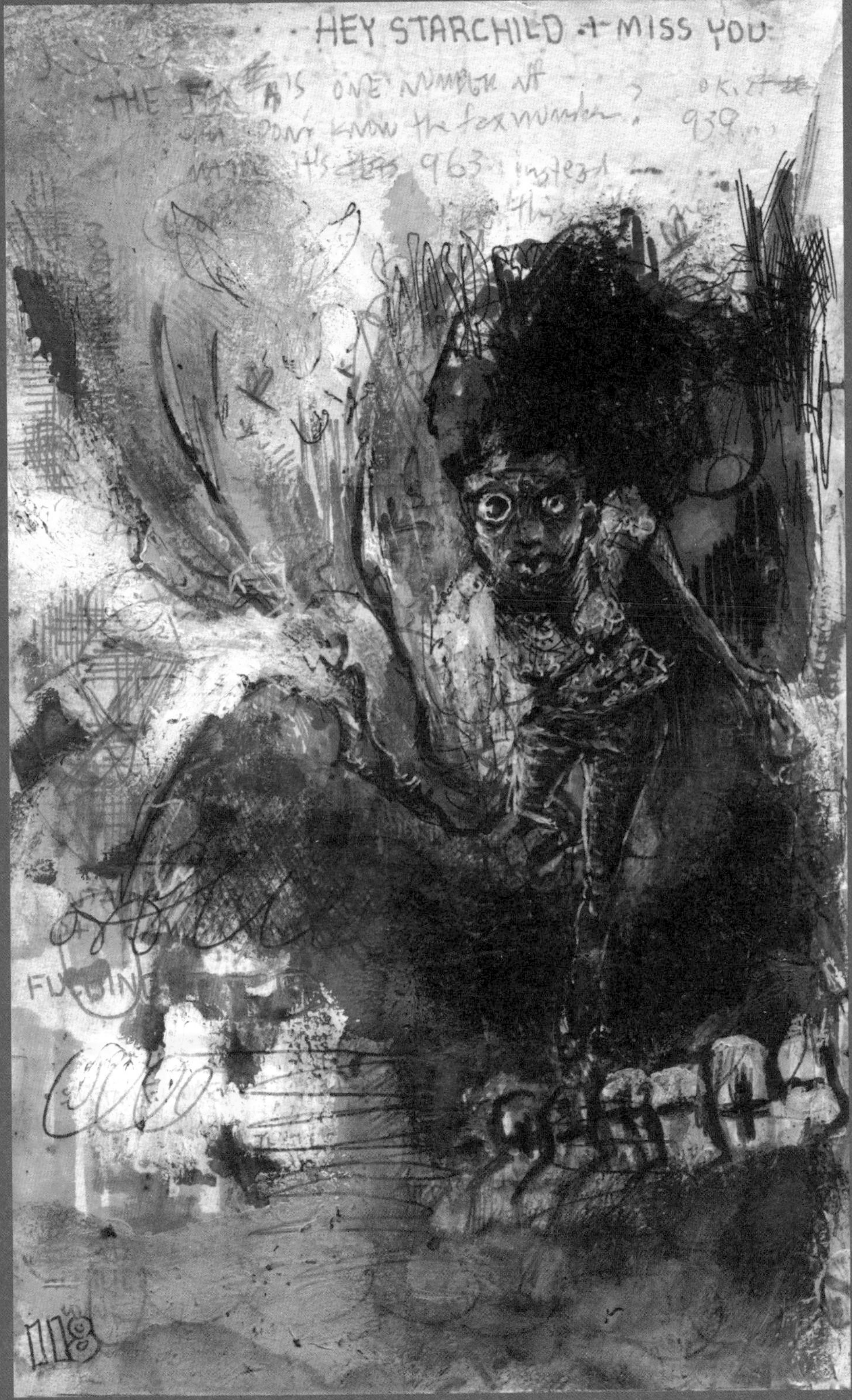
HEY STARCHILD I MISS YOU
it's 963 instead

Lil Red
PRESENT
HOT ROCKS
29 AUG THU NY
LA TUE 24 SEP
SF 10/11 PDX 10/13
LiFE SHiFT
SAND
SORE SNOT

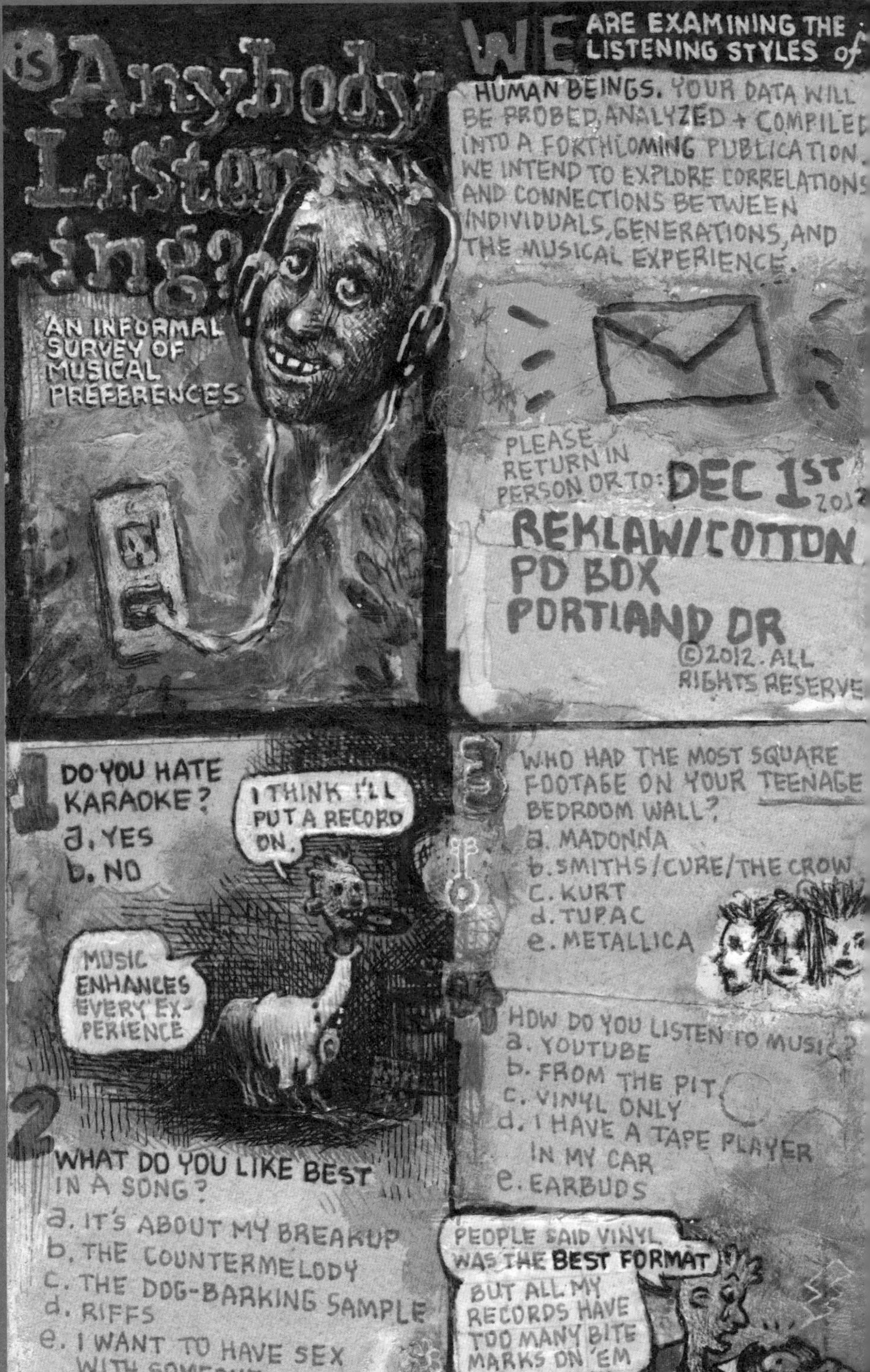
is Anybody Listen-ing?
AN INFORMAL SURVEY OF MUSICAL PREFERENCES
WE ARE EXAMINING THE LISTENING STYLES of HUMAN BEINGS. YOUR DATA WILL BE PROBED, ANALYZED + COMPILED INTO A FORTHCOMING PUBLICATION. WE INTEND TO EXPLORE CORRELATIONS AND CONNECTIONS BETWEEN INDIVIDUALS, GENERATIONS, AND THE MUSICAL EXPERIENCE.
PLEASE RETURN IN PERSON OR TO: DEC 1ST 2012
REKLAW/COTTON
PO BOX
PORTLAND OR
©2012. ALL RIGHTS RESERVE
1 DO YOU HATE KARAOKE?
a. YES
b. NO
I THINK I'LL PUT A RECORD ON.
MUSIC ENHANCES EVERY EX-PERIENCE
2 WHAT DO YOU LIKE BEST IN A SONG?
a. IT'S ABOUT MY BREAKUP
b. THE COUNTERMELODY
c. THE DOG-BARKING SAMPLE
d. RIFFS
e. I WANT TO HAVE SEX WITH SOMEONE IN THE BAND
3 WHO HAD THE MOST SQUARE FOOTAGE ON YOUR TEENAGE BEDROOM WALL?
a. MADONNA
b. SMITHS/CURE/THE CROW
c. KURT
d. TUPAC
e. METALLICA
4 HOW DO YOU LISTEN TO MUSIC?
a. YOUTUBE
b. FROM THE PIT
c. VINYL ONLY
d. I HAVE A TAPE PLAYER IN MY CAR
e. EARBUDS
PEOPLE SAID VINYL WAS THE BEST FORMAT
BUT ALL MY RECORDS HAVE TOO MANY BITE MARKS ON 'EM NOW TO PLAY.

5 HOW OLD ARE YOU?
a. I KNOW ALL THE WORDS TO **BABY GOT BACK**
b. **RUBBER SOUL CHANGED THE WAY I THOUGHT ABOUT THE BEATLES**
c. I'VE NEVER PAID FOR MUSIC
d. MOZART HAD A LIMP HANDSHAKE

6 WHAT'S THE BEST DECADE FOR MUSIC?
a. 1980s
b. 1960s
c. 1560s
d. MUSIC NOW SUCKS
e. TIME IS JUST A **NUMBER**

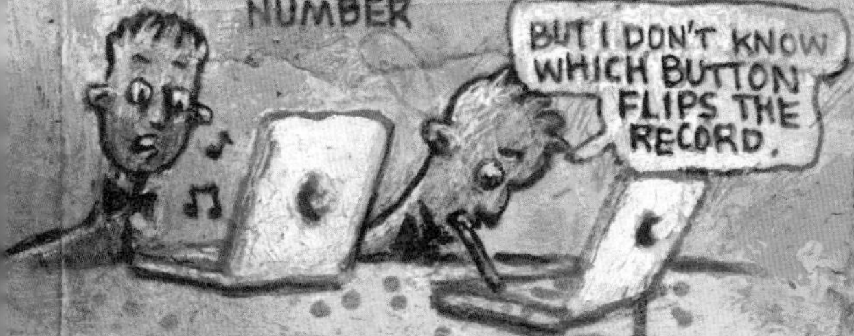
NOW I GOT THIS ITUNE...
BUT I DON'T KNOW WHICH BUTTON FLIPS THE RECORD.

7 WHAT GENRES OF MUSIC DO YOU LIKE?
a. EVERYTHING BUT RAP AND COUNTRY
b. ANYTHING I CAN DOWNLOAD
c. PITCHFORK ROCK
d. JAZZ
e. YOU'VE PROBABLY NEVER HEARD OF IT

8 BEST MALE VOCALIST:
a. CALVIN JOHNSON
b. LEONARD COHEN
c. DANZIG
d. MORRISSEY
e. AUTOTUNE

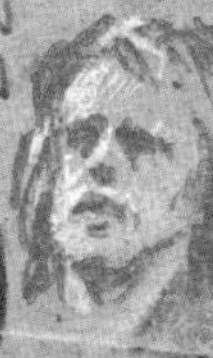

9 WHICH TRAIN?
a. NIGHT TRAIN
b. CRAZY TRAIN
c. COLTRANE
d. HIGH ON COCAINE
e. SOUL TRAIN

10 HOW CAN PEOPLE TELL YOU LIKE A BAND?
a. THESE TATTOOS
b. THIS IS LAST YEAR'S TOUR SHIRT
c. WE RE-FINANCED THE HOUSE TO FOLLOW THEM ON TOUR
d. YOU CAN'T

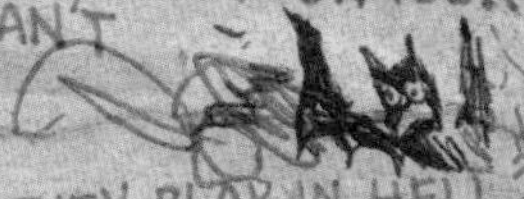

11 WHAT DO THEY PLAY IN HELL?
a. SABBATH
b. DUBSTEP
c. DIMINISHED INTERVALS ON FRENCH HORN
d. ______

(FILL IN THE BLANK. THIS IS WHERE IT GETS INTERACTIVE)

12 WHAT WAS THE FIRST ALBUM YOU BOUGHT WITH YOUR OWN MONEY? ______

13 WHAT WAS THE FIRST BAND YOU WERE OBSESSED WITH? ______

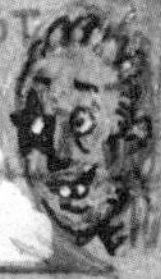

DRAW YOUR FAVORITE BAND LOGOS:

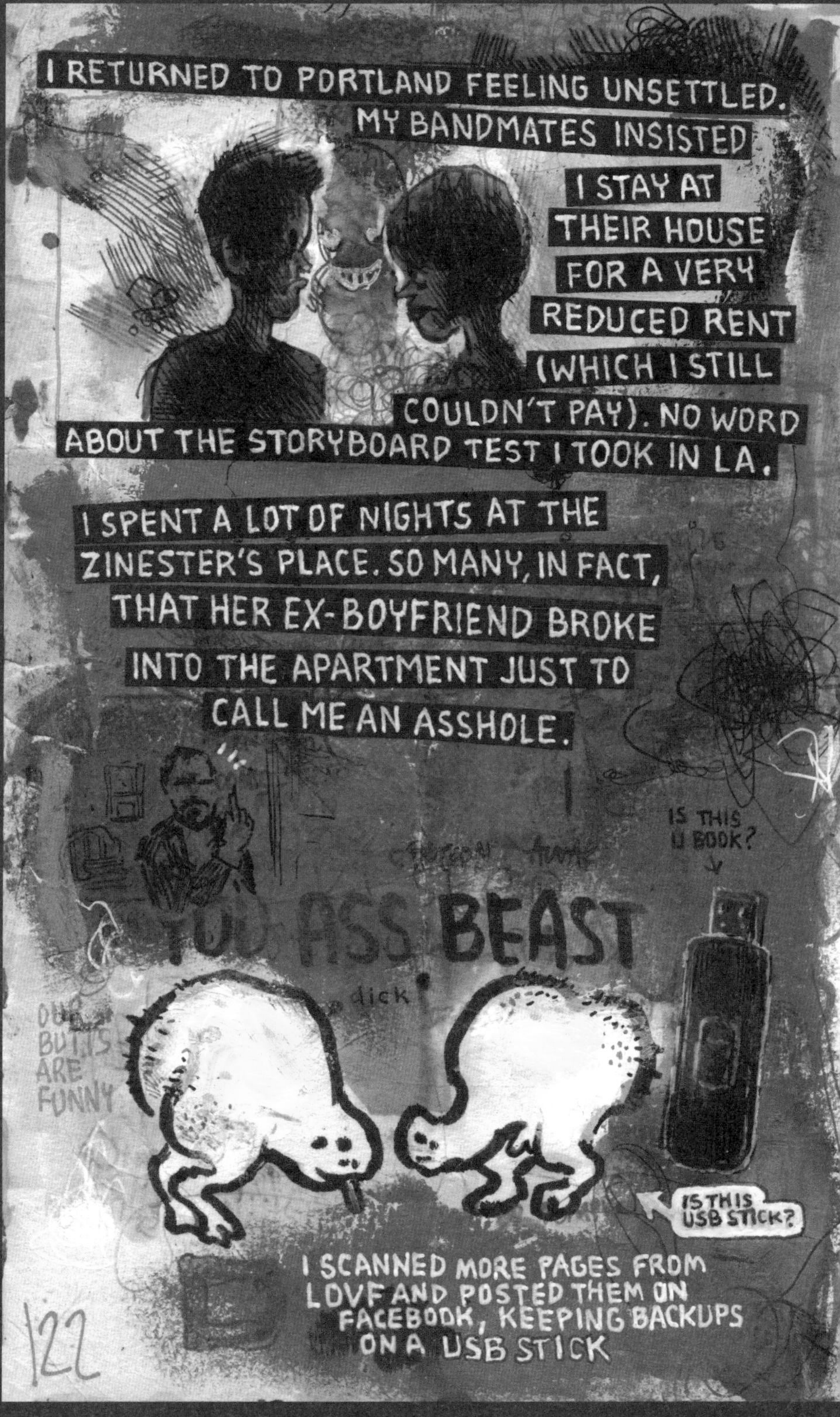
I RETURNED TO PORTLAND FEELING UNSETTLED.
MY BANDMATES INSISTED I STAY AT THEIR HOUSE FOR A VERY REDUCED RENT (WHICH I STILL COULDN'T PAY). NO WORD ABOUT THE STORYBOARD TEST I TOOK IN LA.
I SPENT A LOT OF NIGHTS AT THE ZINESTER'S PLACE. SO MANY, IN FACT, THAT HER EX-BOYFRIEND BROKE INTO THE APARTMENT JUST TO CALL ME AN ASSHOLE.
IS THIS U BOOK?
TOO ASS BEAST
dick
OUR BUTTS ARE FUNNY
IS THIS USB STICK?
I SCANNED MORE PAGES FROM LOVE AND POSTED THEM ON FACEBOOK, KEEPING BACKUPS ON A USB STICK

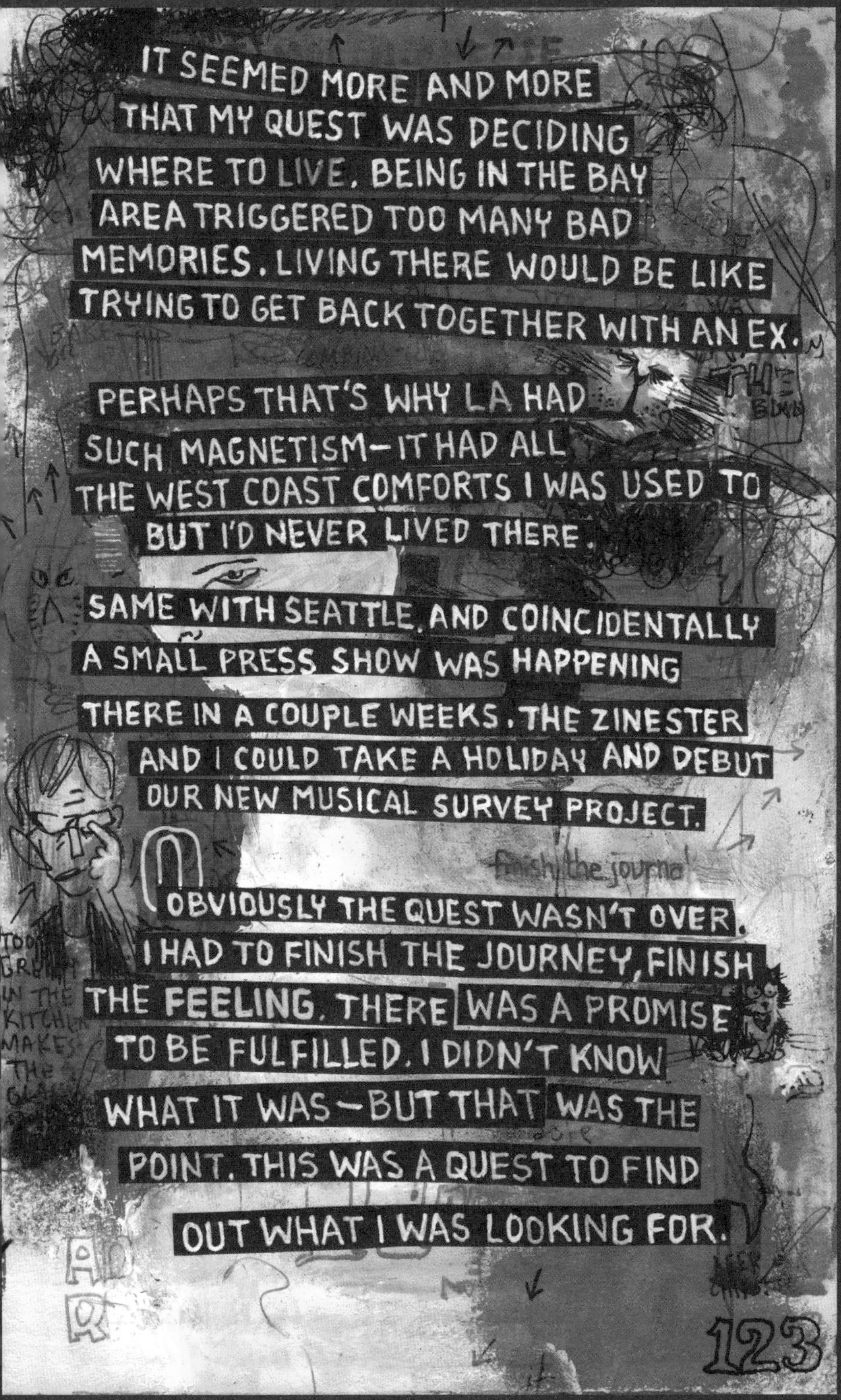
IT SEEMED MORE AND MORE THAT MY QUEST WAS DECIDING WHERE TO LIVE. BEING IN THE BAY AREA TRIGGERED TOO MANY BAD MEMORIES. LIVING THERE WOULD BE LIKE TRYING TO GET BACK TOGETHER WITH AN EX.
PERHAPS THAT'S WHY LA HAD SUCH MAGNETISM—IT HAD ALL THE WEST COAST COMFORTS I WAS USED TO BUT I'D NEVER LIVED THERE.
SAME WITH SEATTLE. AND COINCIDENTALLY A SMALL PRESS SHOW WAS HAPPENING THERE IN A COUPLE WEEKS. THE ZINESTER AND I COULD TAKE A HOLIDAY AND DEBUT OUR NEW MUSICAL SURVEY PROJECT.
OBVIOUSLY THE QUEST WASN'T OVER. I HAD TO FINISH THE JOURNEY, FINISH THE FEELING. THERE WAS A PROMISE TO BE FULFILLED. I DIDN'T KNOW WHAT IT WAS—BUT THAT WAS THE POINT. THIS WAS A QUEST TO FIND OUT WHAT I WAS LOOKING FOR.

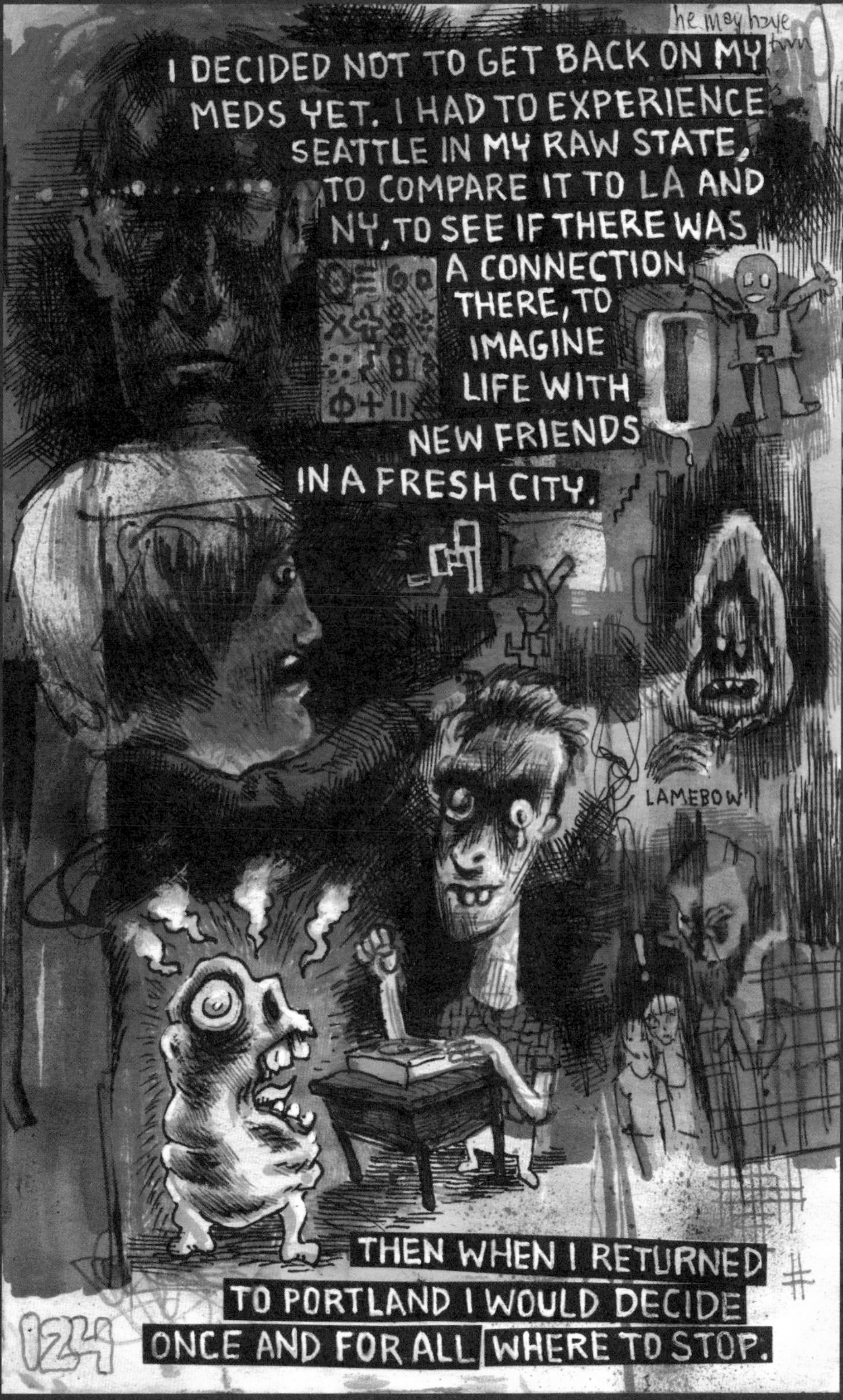
he may have
I DECIDED NOT TO GET BACK ON MY MEDS YET. I HAD TO EXPERIENCE SEATTLE IN MY RAW STATE, TO COMPARE IT TO LA AND NY, TO SEE IF THERE WAS A CONNECTION THERE, TO IMAGINE LIFE WITH NEW FRIENDS IN A FRESH CITY.
LAMEBOW
THEN WHEN I RETURNED TO PORTLAND I WOULD DECIDE ONCE AND FOR ALL WHERE TO STOP.

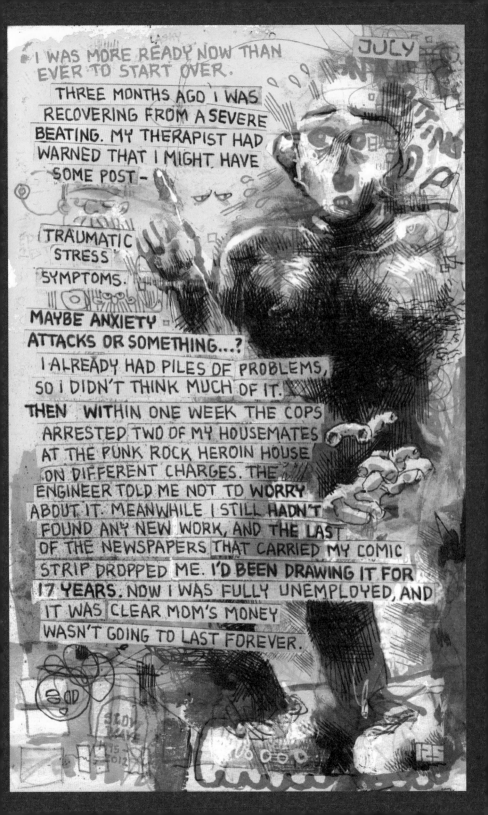

I WAS MORE READY NOW THAN EVER TO START OVER.

JULY

THREE MONTHS AGO I WAS RECOVERING FROM A SEVERE BEATING. MY THERAPIST HAD WARNED THAT I MIGHT HAVE SOME POST—

TRAUMATIC STRESS SYMPTOMS.

MAYBE ANXIETY ATTACKS OR SOMETHING...? I ALREADY HAD PILES OF PROBLEMS, SO I DIDN'T THINK MUCH OF IT.

THEN WITHIN ONE WEEK THE COPS ARRESTED TWO OF MY HOUSEMATES AT THE PUNK ROCK HEROIN HOUSE ON DIFFERENT CHARGES. THE ENGINEER TOLD ME NOT TO WORRY ABOUT IT. MEANWHILE I STILL HADN'T FOUND ANY NEW WORK, AND THE LAST OF THE NEWSPAPERS THAT CARRIED MY COMIC STRIP DROPPED ME. I'D BEEN DRAWING IT FOR 17 YEARS. NOW I WAS FULLY UNEMPLOYED, AND IT WAS CLEAR MOM'S MONEY WASN'T GOING TO LAST FOREVER.

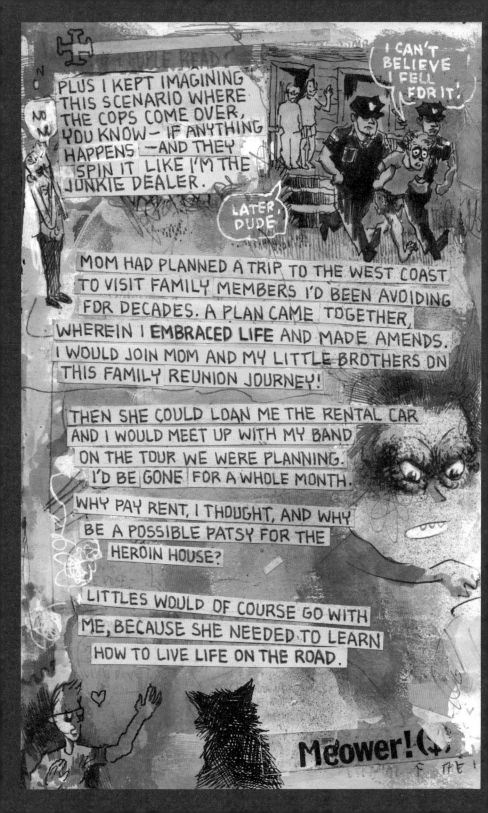

PLUS I KEPT IMAGINING THIS SCENARIO WHERE THE COPS COME OVER, YOU KNOW — IF ANYTHING HAPPENS — AND THEY SPIN IT LIKE I'M THE JUNKIE DEALER.

I CAN'T BELIEVE I FELL FOR IT!

LATER, DUDE

MOM HAD PLANNED A TRIP TO THE WEST COAST TO VISIT FAMILY MEMBERS I'D BEEN AVOIDING FOR DECADES. A PLAN CAME TOGETHER, WHEREIN I **EMBRACED LIFE** AND MADE AMENDS. I WOULD JOIN MOM AND MY LITTLE BROTHERS ON THIS FAMILY REUNION JOURNEY!

THEN SHE COULD LOAN ME THE RENTAL CAR AND I WOULD MEET UP WITH MY BAND ON THE TOUR WE WERE PLANNING. I'D BE GONE FOR A WHOLE MONTH.

WHY PAY RENT, I THOUGHT, AND WHY BE A POSSIBLE PATSY FOR THE HEROIN HOUSE?

LITTLES WOULD OF COURSE GO WITH ME, BECAUSE SHE NEEDED TO LEARN HOW TO LIVE LIFE ON THE ROAD.

Meower!

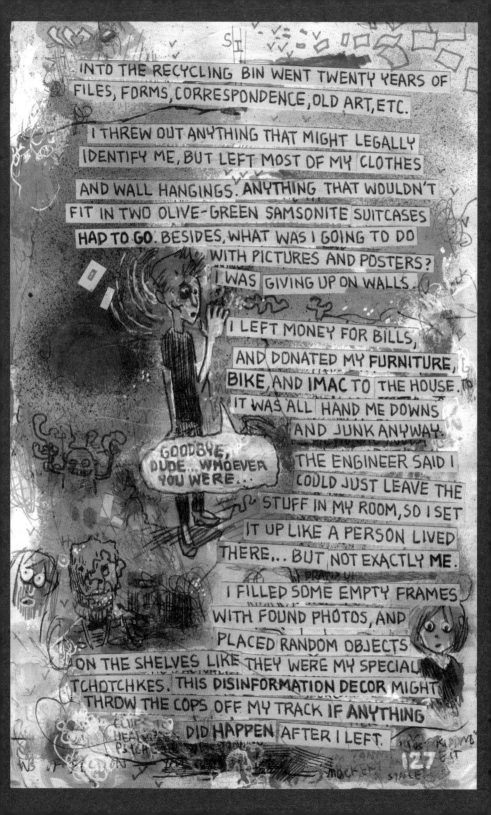

INTO THE RECYCLING BIN WENT TWENTY YEARS OF FILES, FORMS, CORRESPONDENCE, OLD ART, ETC.

I THREW OUT ANYTHING THAT MIGHT LEGALLY IDENTIFY ME, BUT LEFT MOST OF MY CLOTHES AND WALL HANGINGS. ANYTHING THAT WOULDN'T FIT IN TWO OLIVE-GREEN SAMSONITE SUITCASES HAD TO GO. BESIDES, WHAT WAS I GOING TO DO WITH PICTURES AND POSTERS? I WAS GIVING UP ON WALLS.

I LEFT MONEY FOR BILLS, AND DONATED MY FURNITURE, BIKE, AND IMAC TO THE HOUSE. IT WAS ALL HAND ME DOWNS AND JUNK ANYWAY.

GOODBYE, DUDE... WHOEVER YOU WERE...

THE ENGINEER SAID I COULD JUST LEAVE THE STUFF IN MY ROOM, SO I SET IT UP LIKE A PERSON LIVED THERE... BUT NOT EXACTLY ME.

I FILLED SOME EMPTY FRAMES WITH FOUND PHOTOS, AND PLACED RANDOM OBJECTS ON THE SHELVES LIKE THEY WERE MY SPECIAL TCHOTCHKES. THIS DISINFORMATION DECOR MIGHT THROW THE COPS OFF MY TRACK IF ANYTHING DID HAPPEN AFTER I LEFT.

127

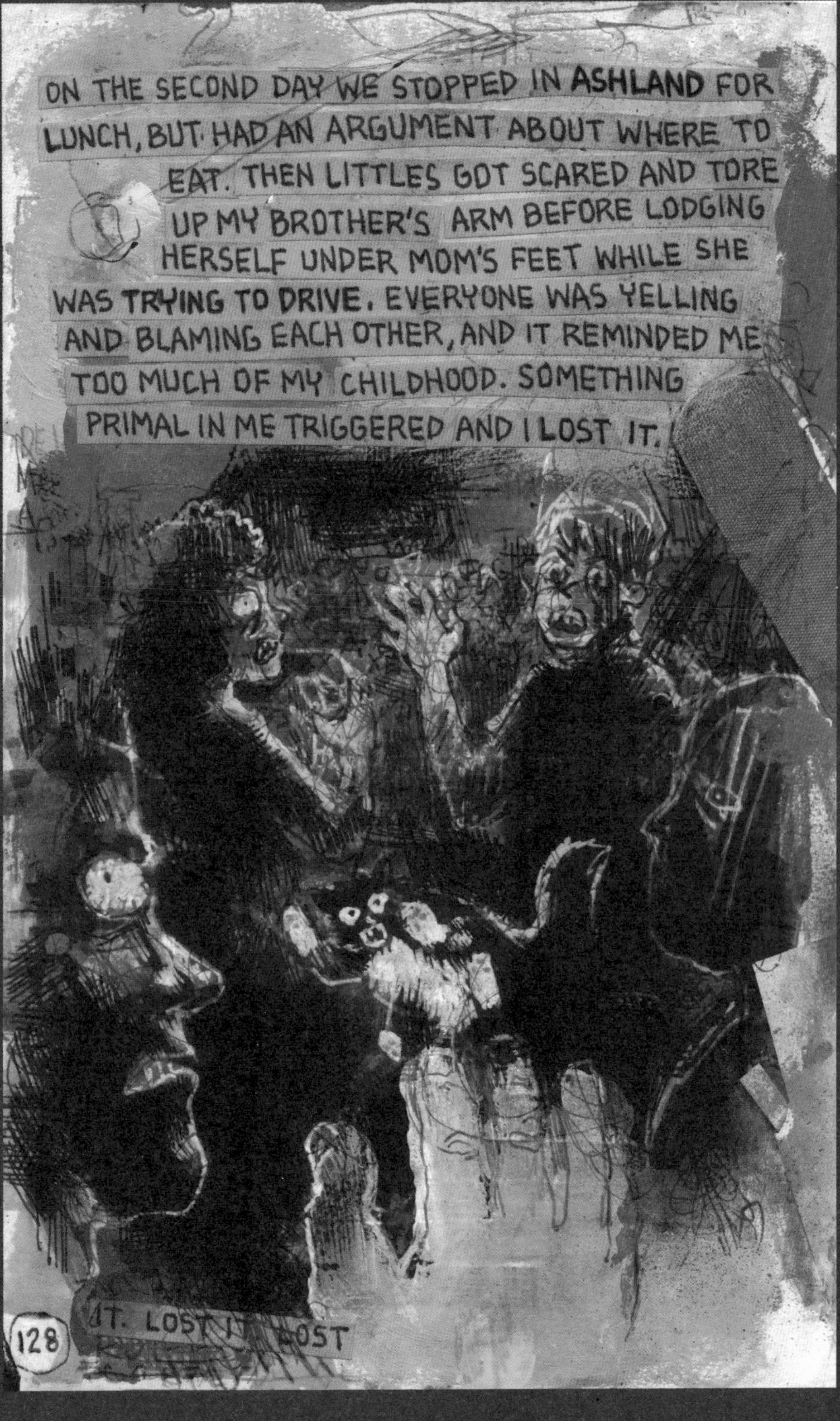
ON THE SECOND DAY WE STOPPED IN ASHLAND FOR LUNCH, BUT HAD AN ARGUMENT ABOUT WHERE TO EAT. THEN LITTLES GOT SCARED AND TORE UP MY BROTHER'S ARM BEFORE LODGING HERSELF UNDER MOM'S FEET WHILE SHE WAS TRYING TO DRIVE. EVERYONE WAS YELLING AND BLAMING EACH OTHER, AND IT REMINDED ME TOO MUCH OF MY CHILDHOOD. SOMETHING PRIMAL IN ME TRIGGERED AND I LOST IT.
IT. LOST IT. LOST

WE SLOWED DOWN AND PARKED WITHOUT
INCIDENT. MY BRAIN WAS
MOLTEN ANXIETY.
I STUFFED LITTLES IN HER
CARRIER, RANTED AT EVERYONE UNINTELLIGIBLY,
AND STORMED OFF, HEADED TOWARD SOME SORT
OF PARK. AS I CROSSED A PEDESTRIAN BRIDGE
OVER THE FREEWAY I THOUGHT A BETTER IDEA
WOULD BE TO JUMP OFF

BOOM

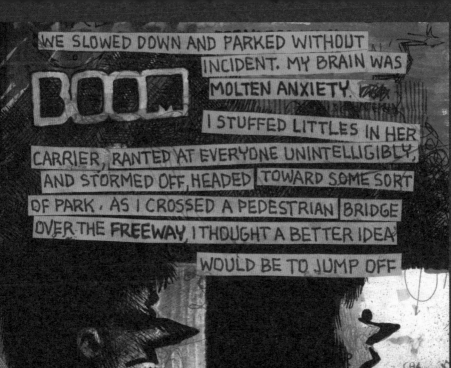

WOW

MOM

AS A TEENAGER I
WAS

A. POPULAR

B. ANGSTY

C. NERDY

D. REPRESSED

E. A JERK

129

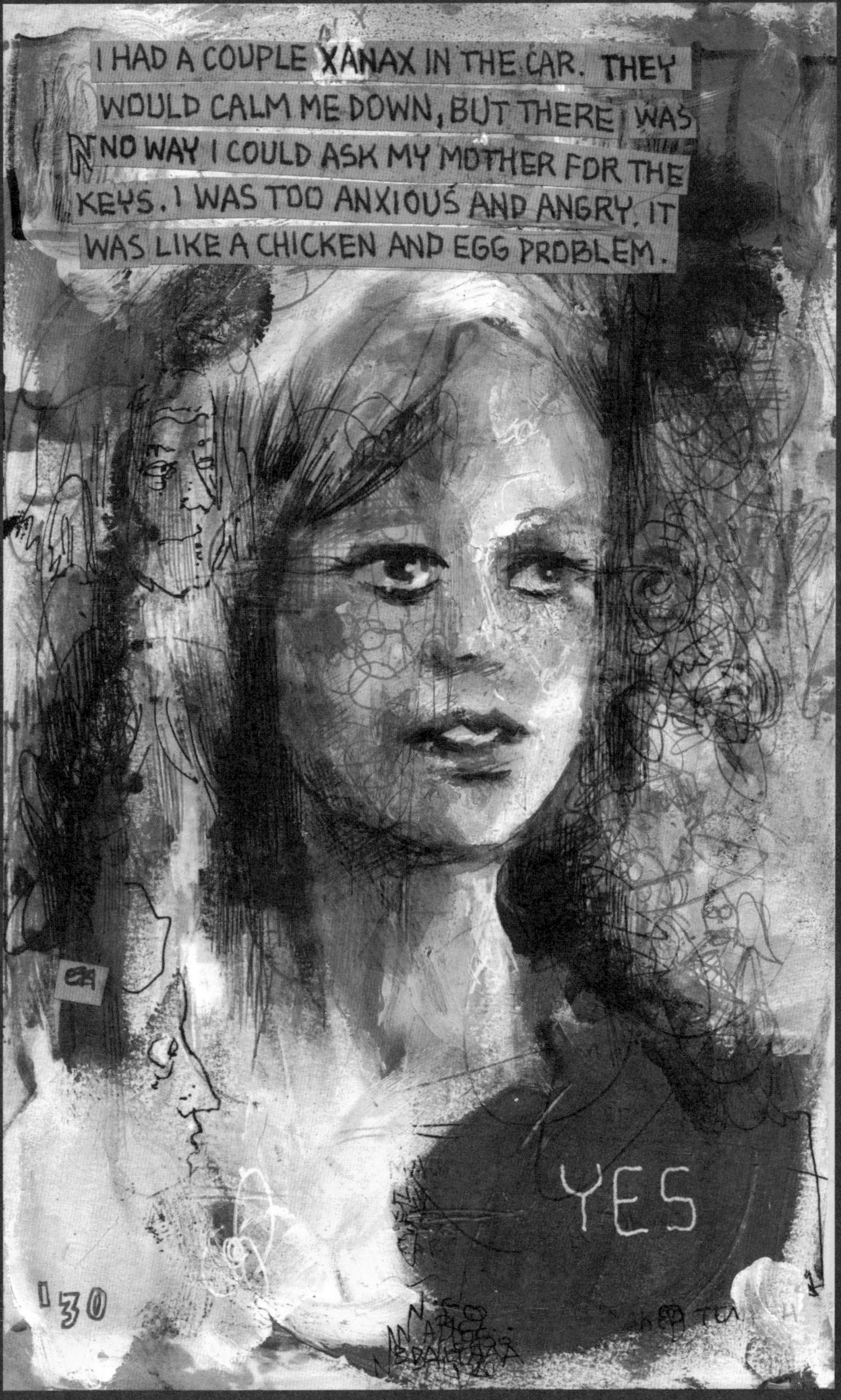
I HAD A COUPLE XANAX IN THE CAR. THEY WOULD CALM ME DOWN, BUT THERE WAS NO WAY I COULD ASK MY MOTHER FOR THE KEYS. I WAS TOO ANXIOUS AND ANGRY. IT WAS LIKE A CHICKEN AND EGG PROBLEM.
YES

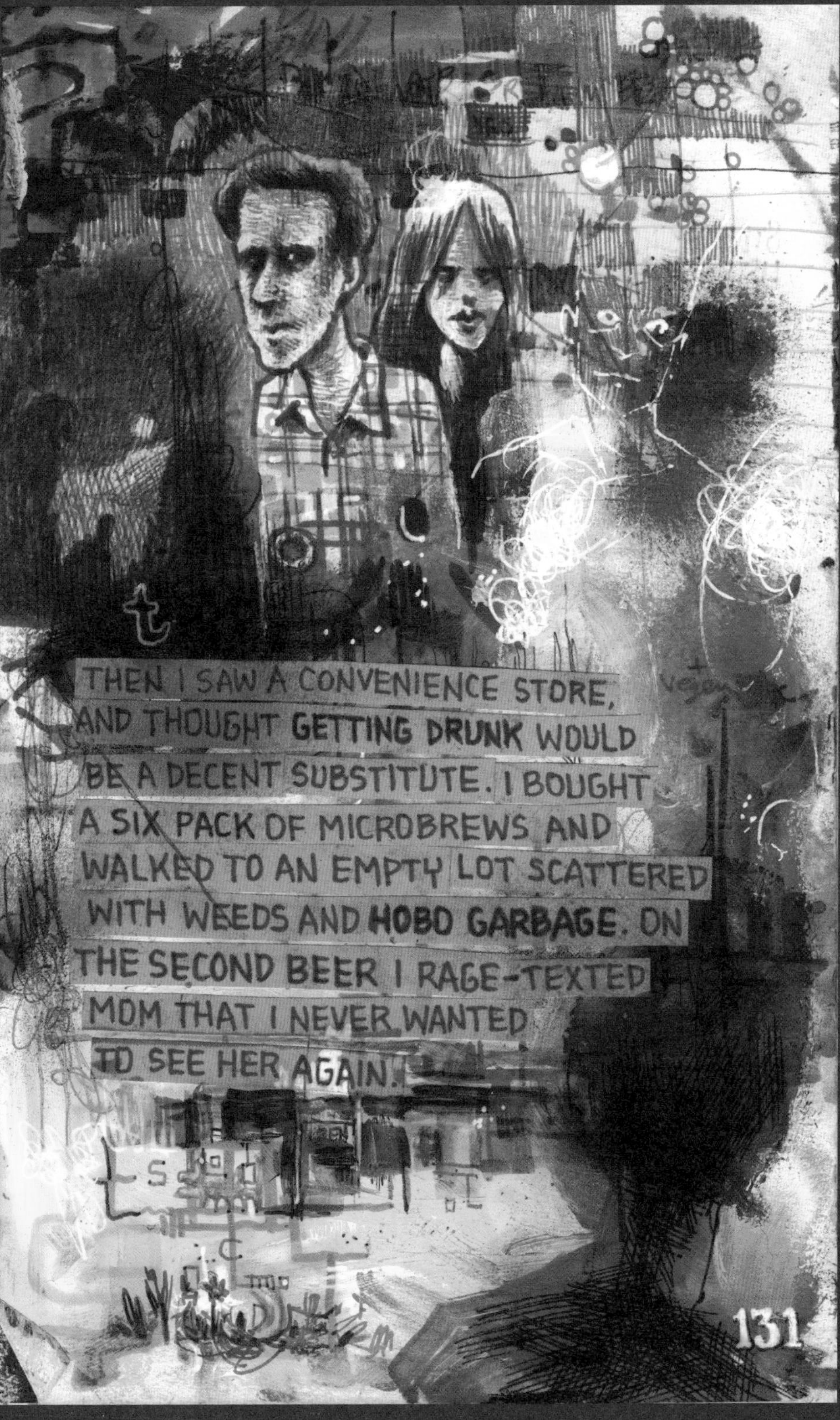
THEN I SAW A CONVENIENCE STORE,
AND THOUGHT GETTING DRUNK WOULD
BE A DECENT SUBSTITUTE. I BOUGHT
A SIX PACK OF MICROBREWS AND
WALKED TO AN EMPTY LOT SCATTERED
WITH WEEDS AND HOBO GARBAGE. ON
THE SECOND BEER I RAGE-TEXTED
MOM THAT I NEVER WANTED
TO SEE HER AGAIN.

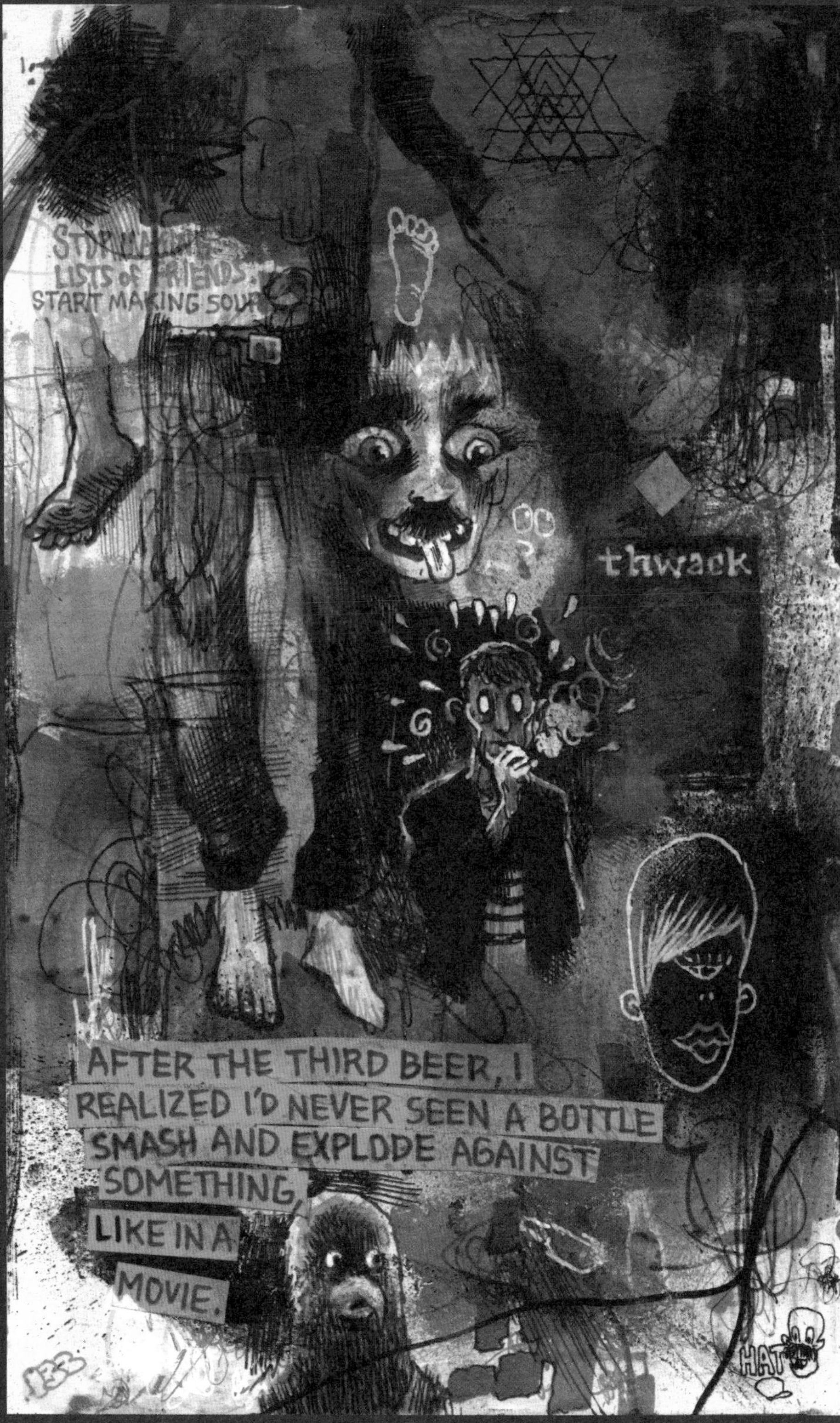
LISTS of FRIENDS.
START MAKING SOU
thwack
AFTER THE THIRD BEER, I
REALIZED I'D NEVER SEEN A BOTTLE
SMASH AND EXPLODE AGAINST
SOMETHING,
LIKE IN A
MOVIE.
HAT

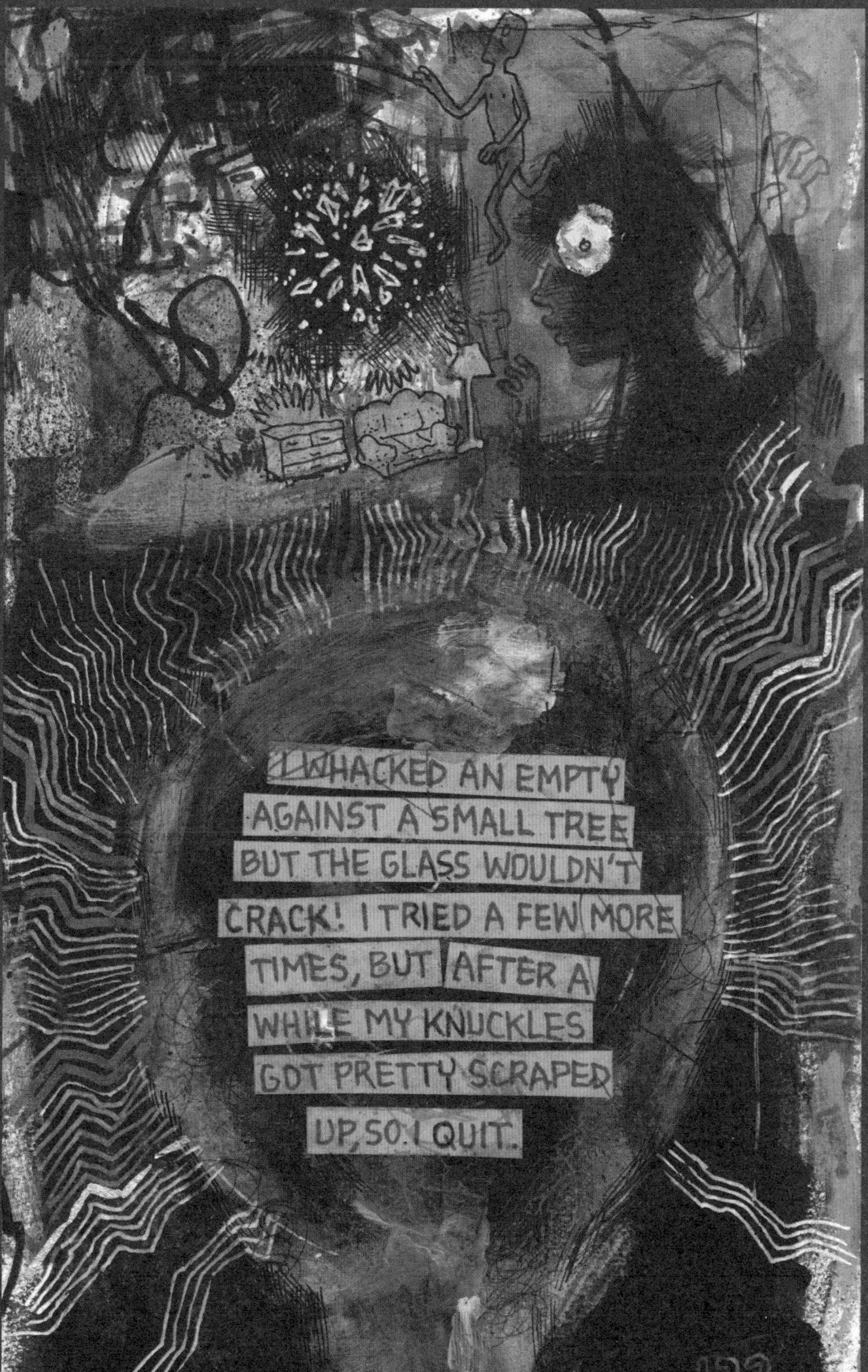
I WHACKED AN EMPTY
AGAINST A SMALL TREE
BUT THE GLASS WOULDN'T
CRACK! I TRIED A FEW MORE
TIMES, BUT AFTER A
WHILE MY KNUCKLES
GOT PRETTY SCRAPED
UP, SO I QUIT.

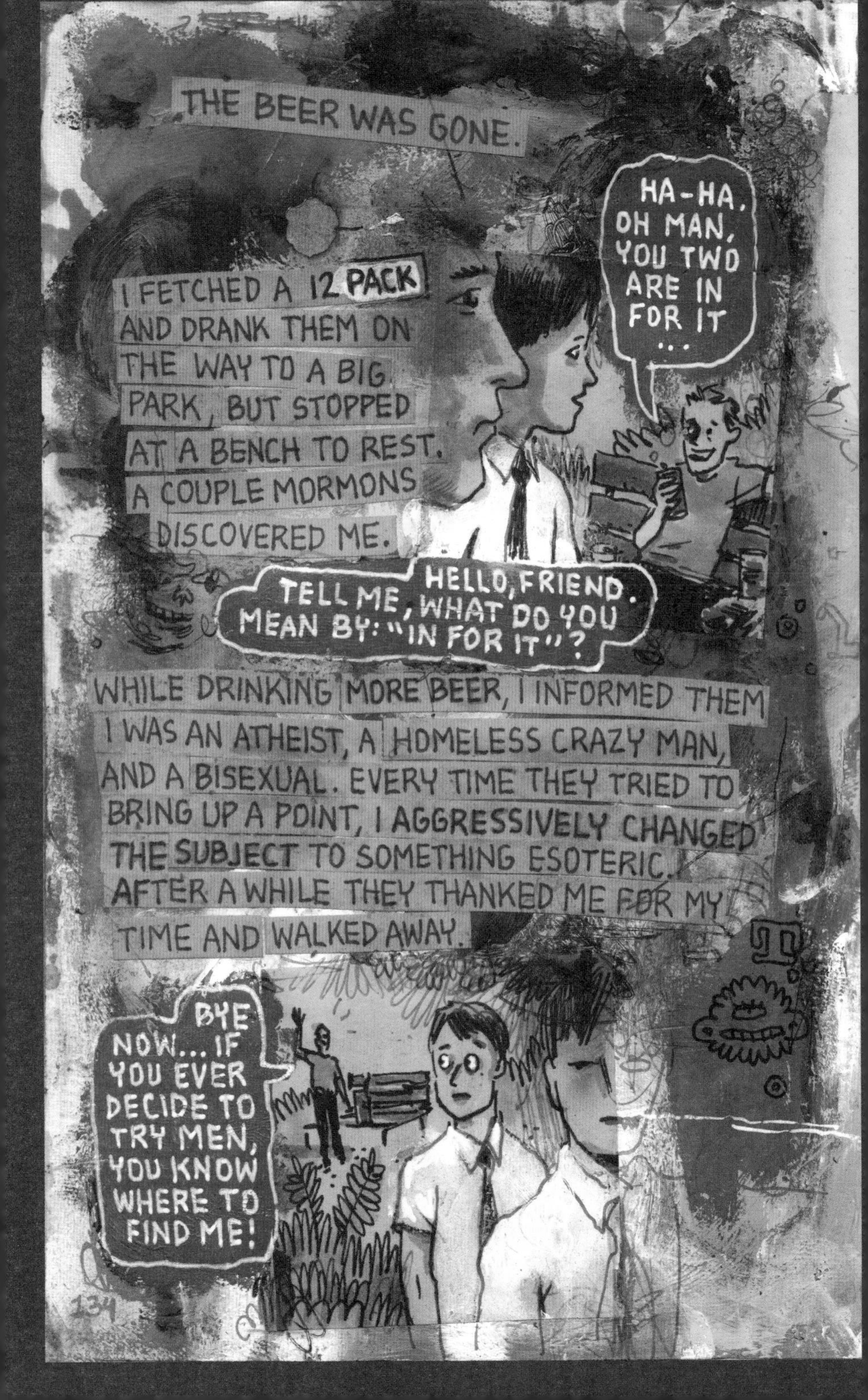
THE BEER WAS GONE.
HA-HA. OH MAN, YOU TWO ARE IN FOR IT ...
I FETCHED A 12 PACK AND DRANK THEM ON THE WAY TO A BIG PARK, BUT STOPPED AT A BENCH TO REST. A COUPLE MORMONS DISCOVERED ME.
HELLO, FRIEND. TELL ME, WHAT DO YOU MEAN BY: "IN FOR IT"?
WHILE DRINKING MORE BEER, I INFORMED THEM I WAS AN ATHEIST, A HOMELESS CRAZY MAN, AND A BISEXUAL. EVERY TIME THEY TRIED TO BRING UP A POINT, I AGGRESSIVELY CHANGED THE SUBJECT TO SOMETHING ESOTERIC. AFTER A WHILE THEY THANKED ME FOR MY TIME AND WALKED AWAY.
BYE NOW... IF YOU EVER DECIDE TO TRY MEN, YOU KNOW WHERE TO FIND ME!

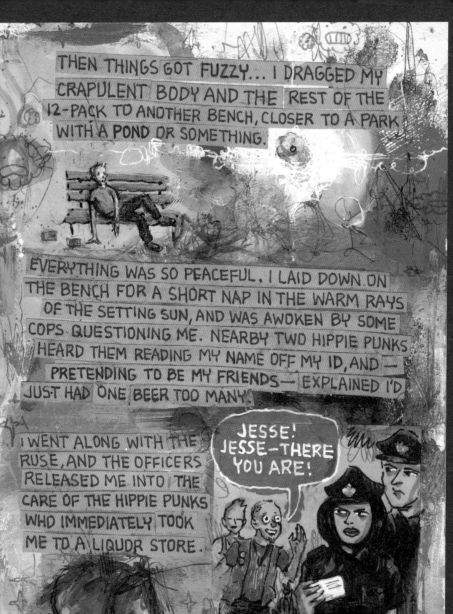

THEN THINGS GOT FUZZY... I DRAGGED MY CRAPULENT BODY AND THE REST OF THE 12-PACK TO ANOTHER BENCH, CLOSER TO A PARK WITH A POND OR SOMETHING.

EVERYTHING WAS SO PEACEFUL. I LAID DOWN ON THE BENCH FOR A SHORT NAP IN THE WARM RAYS OF THE SETTING SUN, AND WAS AWOKEN BY SOME COPS QUESTIONING ME. NEARBY TWO HIPPIE PUNKS HEARD THEM READING MY NAME OFF MY ID, AND — PRETENDING TO BE MY FRIENDS— EXPLAINED I'D JUST HAD ONE BEER TOO MANY.

I WENT ALONG WITH THE RUSE, AND THE OFFICERS RELEASED ME INTO THE CARE OF THE HIPPIE PUNKS WHO IMMEDIATELY TOOK ME TO A LIQUOR STORE.

JESSE! JESSE—THERE YOU ARE!

STROPBURG, QC
"QUEASY"
can I stop you for a moment so I can ORK some measurements?
ORK?
NO ORK!
Fanks!
SEVEN!
FOOLBLAST
U R big
THE DAYS OF THE WEEK WILL BE LIKE YEARS TO HIM, SO THAT BY WEEK-END, HE WILL BE 7 YEARS DIFFERENT...
←7 ORK
ya! It's not so dangerous!
A NEW MAN.

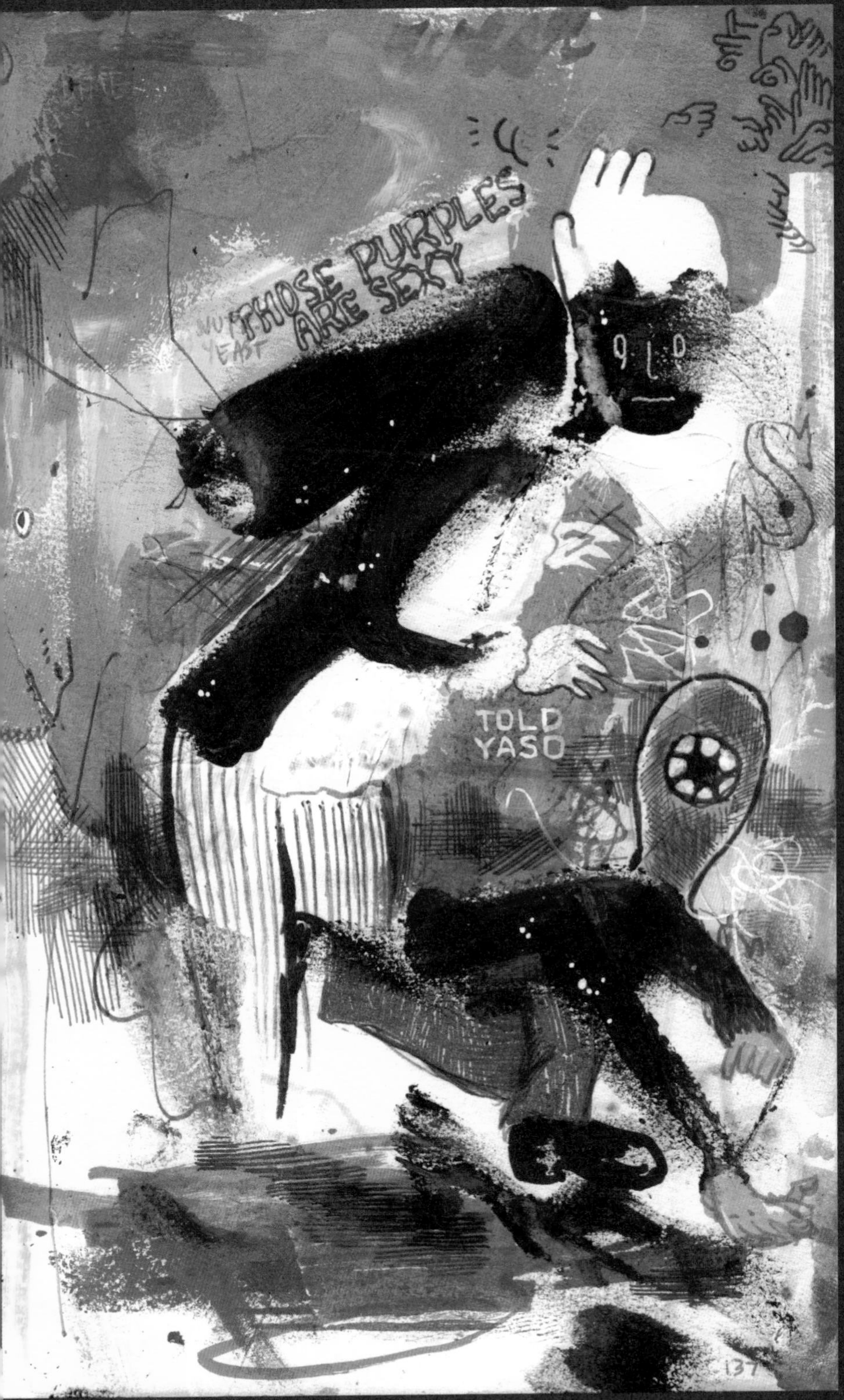
THOSE PURPLES
ARE SEXY
TOLD
YASO

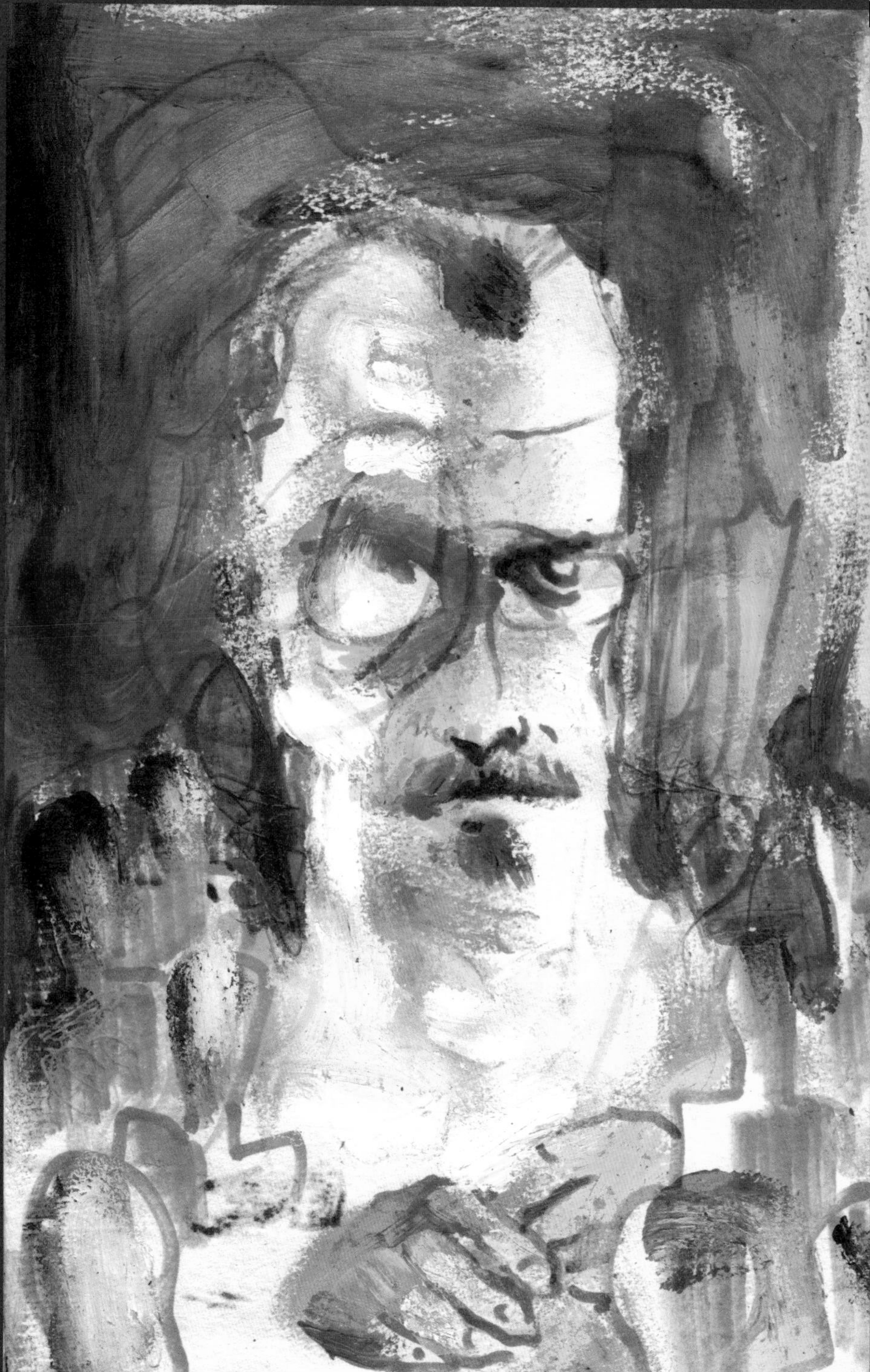

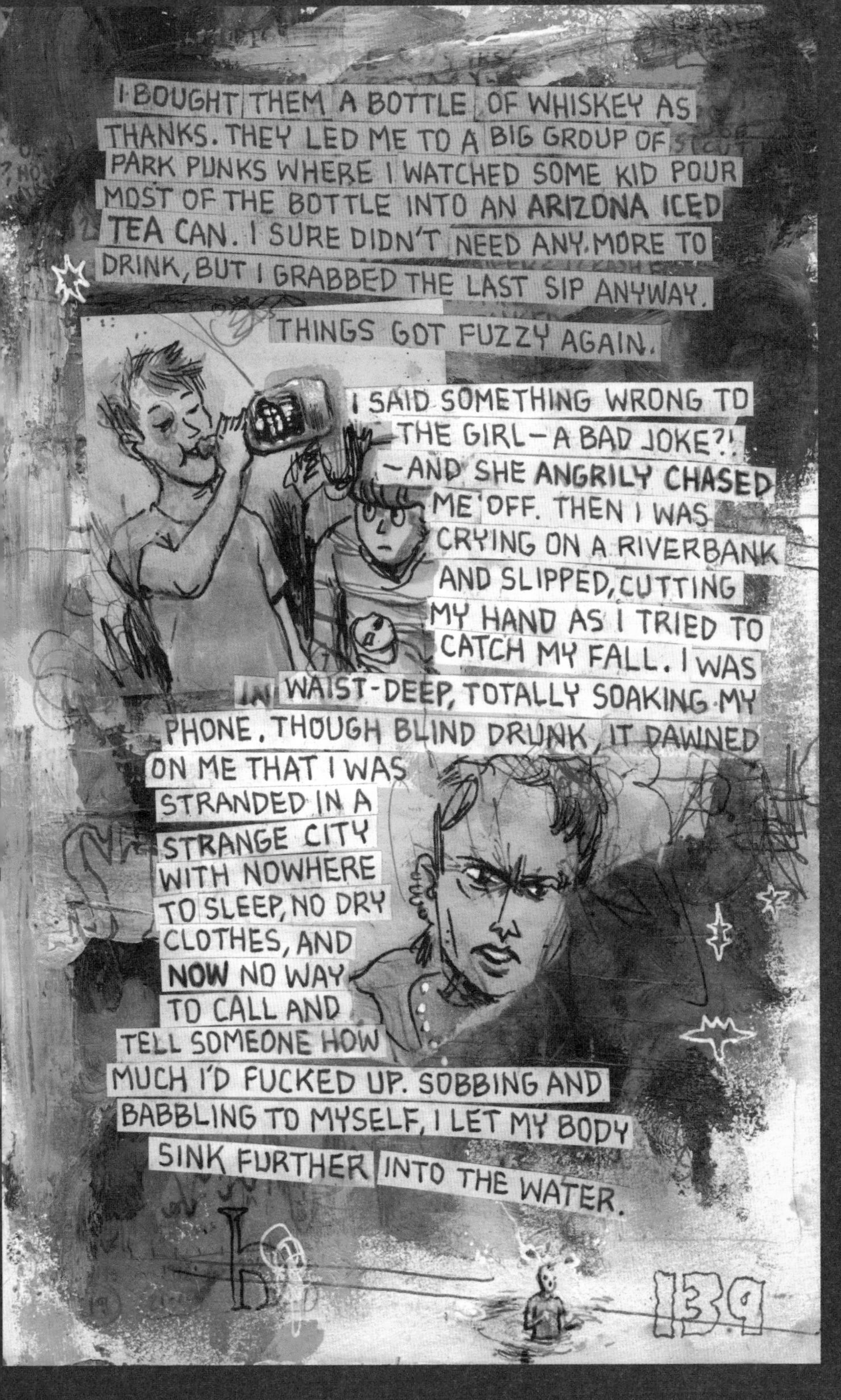

I BOUGHT THEM A BOTTLE OF WHISKEY AS THANKS. THEY LED ME TO A BIG GROUP OF PARK PUNKS WHERE I WATCHED SOME KID POUR MOST OF THE BOTTLE INTO AN **ARIZONA ICED TEA** CAN. I SURE DIDN'T NEED ANY MORE TO DRINK, BUT I GRABBED THE LAST SIP ANYWAY.

THINGS GOT FUZZY AGAIN.

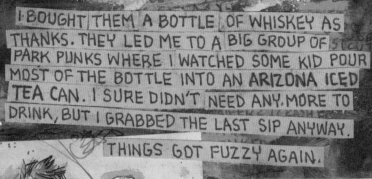

I SAID SOMETHING WRONG TO THE GIRL — A BAD JOKE?! — AND SHE ANGRILY CHASED ME OFF. THEN I WAS CRYING ON A RIVERBANK AND SLIPPED, CUTTING MY HAND AS I TRIED TO CATCH MY FALL. I WAS IN WAIST-DEEP, TOTALLY SOAKING MY PHONE. THOUGH BLIND DRUNK, IT DAWNED ON ME THAT I WAS STRANDED IN A STRANGE CITY WITH NOWHERE TO SLEEP, NO DRY CLOTHES, AND **NOW** NO WAY TO CALL AND TELL SOMEONE HOW MUCH I'D FUCKED UP. SOBBING AND BABBLING TO MYSELF, I LET MY BODY SINK FURTHER INTO THE WATER.

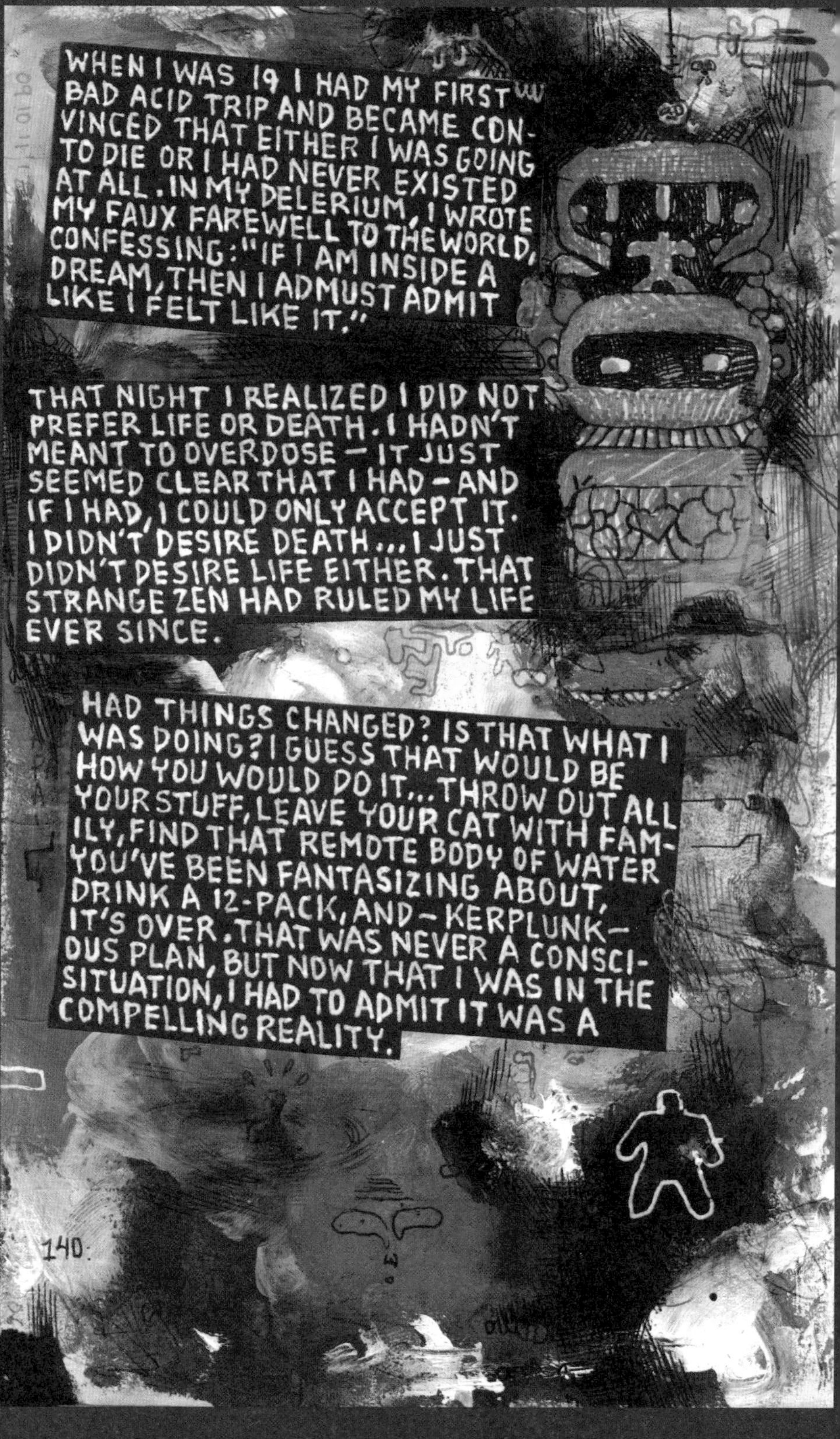
WHEN I WAS 19 I HAD MY FIRST
BAD ACID TRIP AND BECAME CON-
VINCED THAT EITHER I WAS GOING
TO DIE OR I HAD NEVER EXISTED
AT ALL. IN MY DELERIUM, I WROTE
MY FAUX FAREWELL TO THE WORLD,
CONFESSING: "IF I AM INSIDE A
DREAM, THEN I ADMUST ADMIT
LIKE I FELT LIKE IT."
THAT NIGHT I REALIZED I DID NOT
PREFER LIFE OR DEATH. I HADN'T
MEANT TO OVERDOSE — IT JUST
SEEMED CLEAR THAT I HAD — AND
IF I HAD, I COULD ONLY ACCEPT IT.
I DIDN'T DESIRE DEATH... I JUST
DIDN'T DESIRE LIFE EITHER. THAT
STRANGE ZEN HAD RULED MY LIFE
EVER SINCE.
HAD THINGS CHANGED? IS THAT WHAT I
WAS DOING? I GUESS THAT WOULD BE
HOW YOU WOULD DO IT... THROW OUT ALL
YOUR STUFF, LEAVE YOUR CAT WITH FAM-
ILY, FIND THAT REMOTE BODY OF WATER
YOU'VE BEEN FANTASIZING ABOUT,
DRINK A 12-PACK, AND — KERPLUNK —
IT'S OVER. THAT WAS NEVER A CONSCI-
OUS PLAN, BUT NOW THAT I WAS IN THE
SITUATION, I HAD TO ADMIT IT WAS A
COMPELLING REALITY.
140.

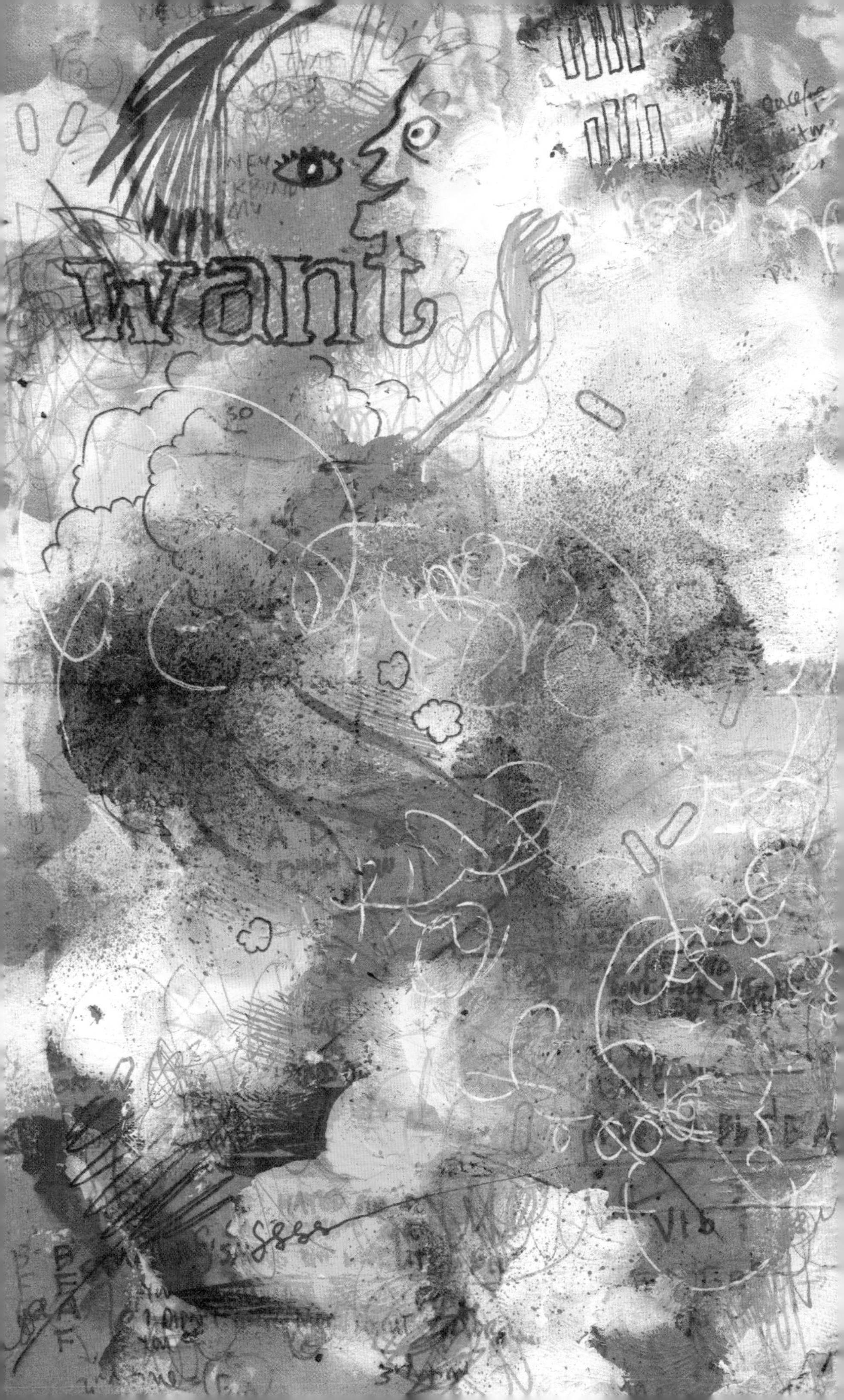
want

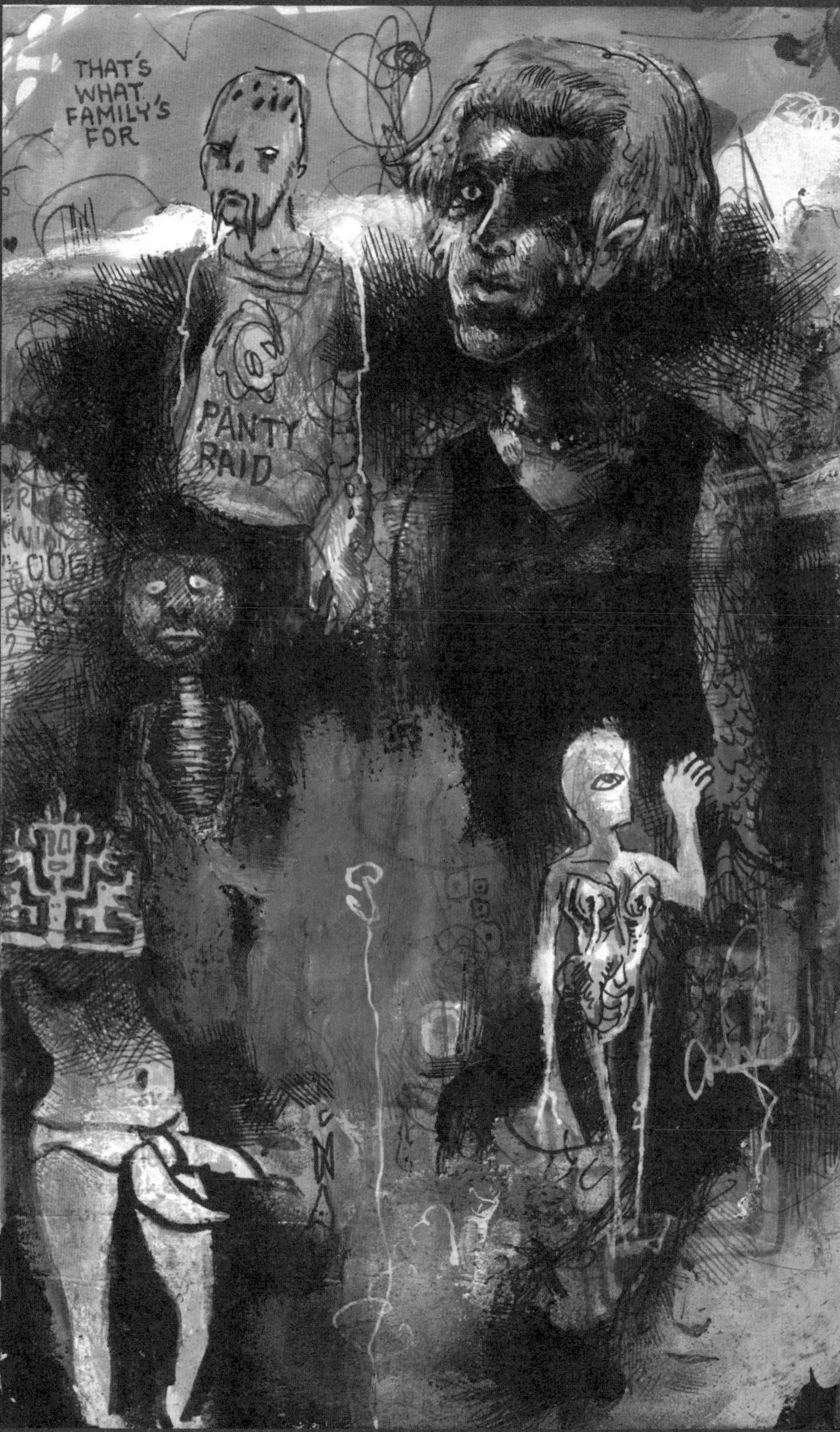
THAT'S WHAT FAMILY'S FOR
PANTY RAID

HO
i'm the one who has to clean up thesparkles.
SAD SLOW BROS INC

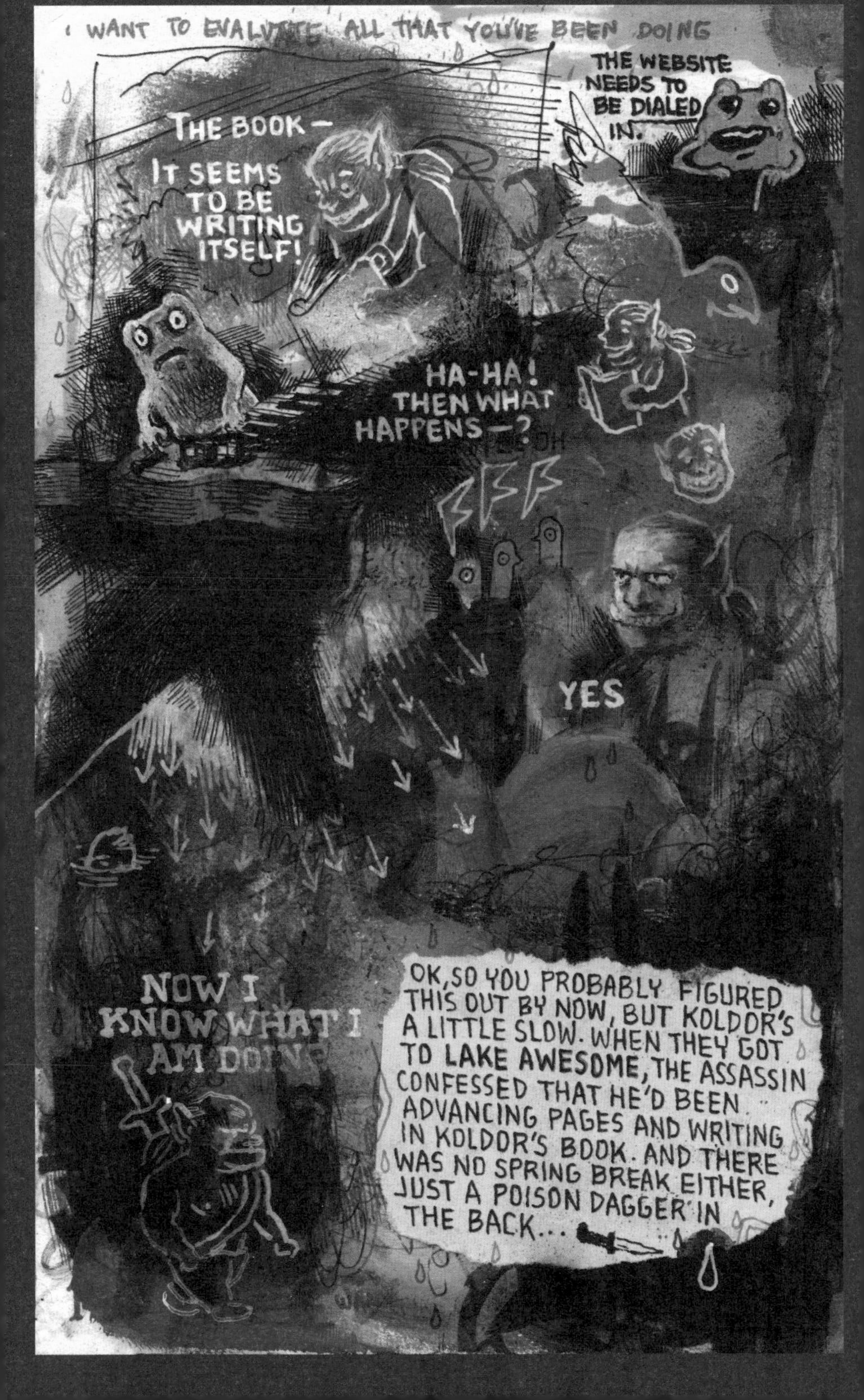
I WANT TO EVALUATE ALL THAT YOU'VE BEEN DOING
THE WEBSITE NEEDS TO BE DIALED IN.
THE BOOK— IT SEEMS TO BE WRITING ITSELF!
HA-HA! THEN WHAT HAPPENS—?
YES
NOW I KNOW WHAT I AM DOIN
OK, SO YOU PROBABLY FIGURED THIS OUT BY NOW, BUT KOLDOR'S A LITTLE SLOW. WHEN THEY GOT TO LAKE AWESOME, THE ASSASSIN CONFESSED THAT HE'D BEEN ADVANCING PAGES AND WRITING IN KOLDOR'S BOOK. AND THERE WAS NO SPRING BREAK EITHER, JUST A POISON DAGGER IN THE BACK...

YOU SEE, IT WAS TOO DAN-
GEROUS FOR HIM TO TRAVEL
ALONE IN THE NORTH WITH
SNILBIN'S RACIST ANTI-
KOBOLD LAWS. GARLTH'S
OBSESSION WAS TO VISIT ALL
THE LAKES IN THE VALLEY AND
COLLECT THE COMMEMORA-
TIVE MUG FROM
EACH ONE.

145

SUDDENLY STRONG ARMS YANKED ME OUT OF THE WATER, THEN GRASPED AND RESTRAINED ME. "MY GLASSES!" I SHOUTED. I'D TAKEN THEM OFF WHEN I STARTED CRYING, BEFORE I FELL IN. "I LEFT MY GLASSES THERE!" I TRIED TO TWIST TO POINT THEM OUT, BUT THE HARD ARMS ONLY GRIPPED ME TIGHTER. NO ONE LISTENED AS THEY HOISTED ME THROUGH THE BRUSH AND INTO A PARKING LOT WHERE I WAS SURPRISED TO SEE A LOT OF COP CARS AND PEOPLE. HAD I BEEN BOBBING IN THE WATER LONG ENOUGH TO DRAW A CROWD?

AT SOME POINT THEY BOUND MY WRISTS AND SHOVED ME INTO THE HARD PLASTIC BACK SEAT OF A POLICE CAR. I COMPLAINED ABOUT MY ARTHRITIS, AND REPEATED

"I LEFT MY GLASSES BY THE RIVER"

UNTIL EVENTUALLY SOMEONE WENT BACK TO LOOK. I WAITED FOR A WHILE, STRETCHED ACROSS THE RIGID BUCKET SEATS, BUT THE COPS RETURNED WITH

NOTHING.

GNOMES AREN'T ELVES
tsk!
NO mes
NO MORE THAN THREE

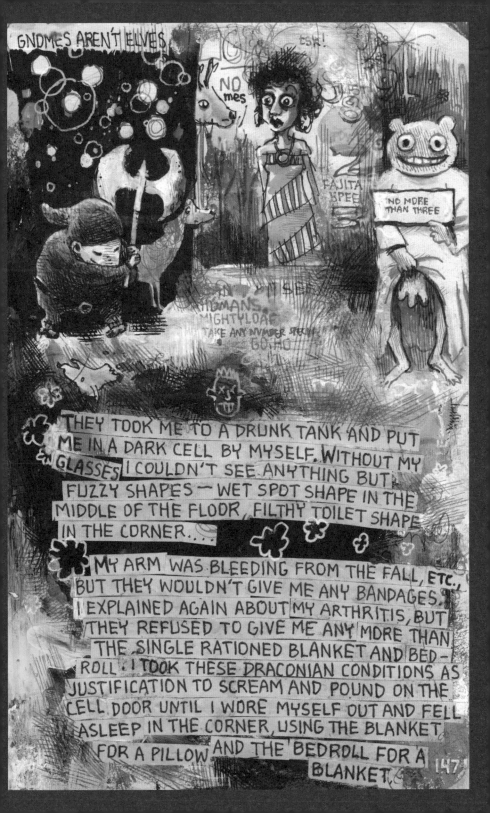

THEY TOOK ME TO A DRUNK TANK AND PUT ME IN A DARK CELL BY MYSELF. WITHOUT MY GLASSES I COULDN'T SEE ANYTHING BUT FUZZY SHAPES — WET SPOT SHAPE IN THE MIDDLE OF THE FLOOR, FILTHY TOILET SHAPE IN THE CORNER....

MY ARM WAS BLEEDING FROM THE FALL, ETC., BUT THEY WOULDN'T GIVE ME ANY BANDAGES. I EXPLAINED AGAIN ABOUT MY ARTHRITIS, BUT THEY REFUSED TO GIVE ME ANY MORE THAN THE SINGLE RATIONED BLANKET AND BED-ROLL. I TOOK THESE DRACONIAN CONDITIONS AS JUSTIFICATION TO SCREAM AND POUND ON THE CELL DOOR UNTIL I WORE MYSELF OUT AND FELL ASLEEP IN THE CORNER, USING THE BLANKET FOR A PILLOW AND THE BEDROLL FOR A BLANKET.

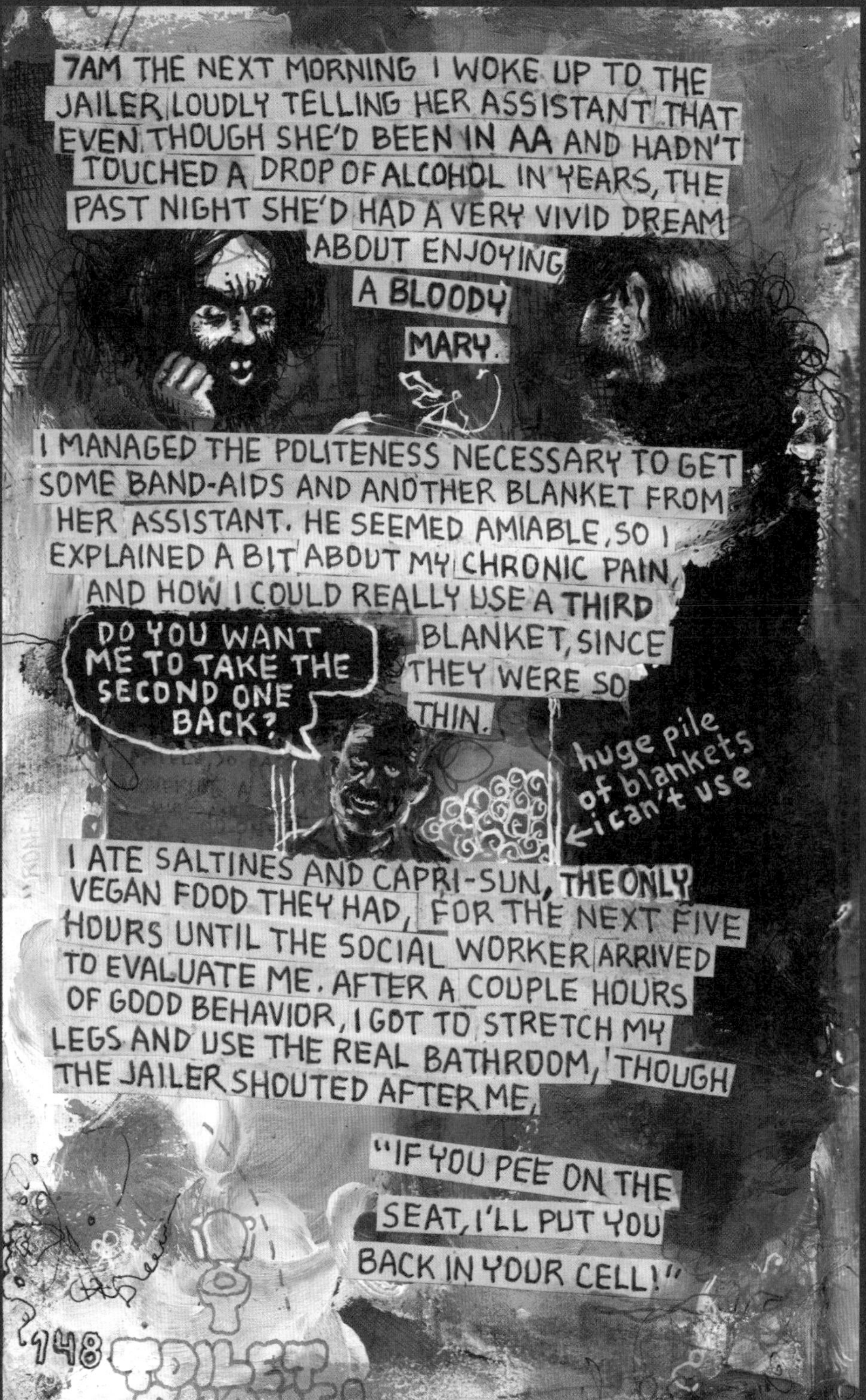
7AM THE NEXT MORNING I WOKE UP TO THE JAILER LOUDLY TELLING HER ASSISTANT THAT EVEN THOUGH SHE'D BEEN IN AA AND HADN'T TOUCHED A DROP OF ALCOHOL IN YEARS, THE PAST NIGHT SHE'D HAD A VERY VIVID DREAM ABOUT ENJOYING A BLOODY MARY.
I MANAGED THE POLITENESS NECESSARY TO GET SOME BAND-AIDS AND ANOTHER BLANKET FROM HER ASSISTANT. HE SEEMED AMIABLE, SO I EXPLAINED A BIT ABOUT MY CHRONIC PAIN, AND HOW I COULD REALLY USE A THIRD BLANKET, SINCE THEY WERE SO THIN.
DO YOU WANT ME TO TAKE THE SECOND ONE BACK?
huge pile of blankets ←i can't use
I ATE SALTINES AND CAPRI-SUN, THE ONLY VEGAN FOOD THEY HAD, FOR THE NEXT FIVE HOURS UNTIL THE SOCIAL WORKER ARRIVED TO EVALUATE ME. AFTER A COUPLE HOURS OF GOOD BEHAVIOR, I GOT TO STRETCH MY LEGS AND USE THE REAL BATHROOM, THOUGH THE JAILER SHOUTED AFTER ME,
"IF YOU PEE ON THE SEAT, I'LL PUT YOU BACK IN YOUR CELL!"
TOILET SHAME!

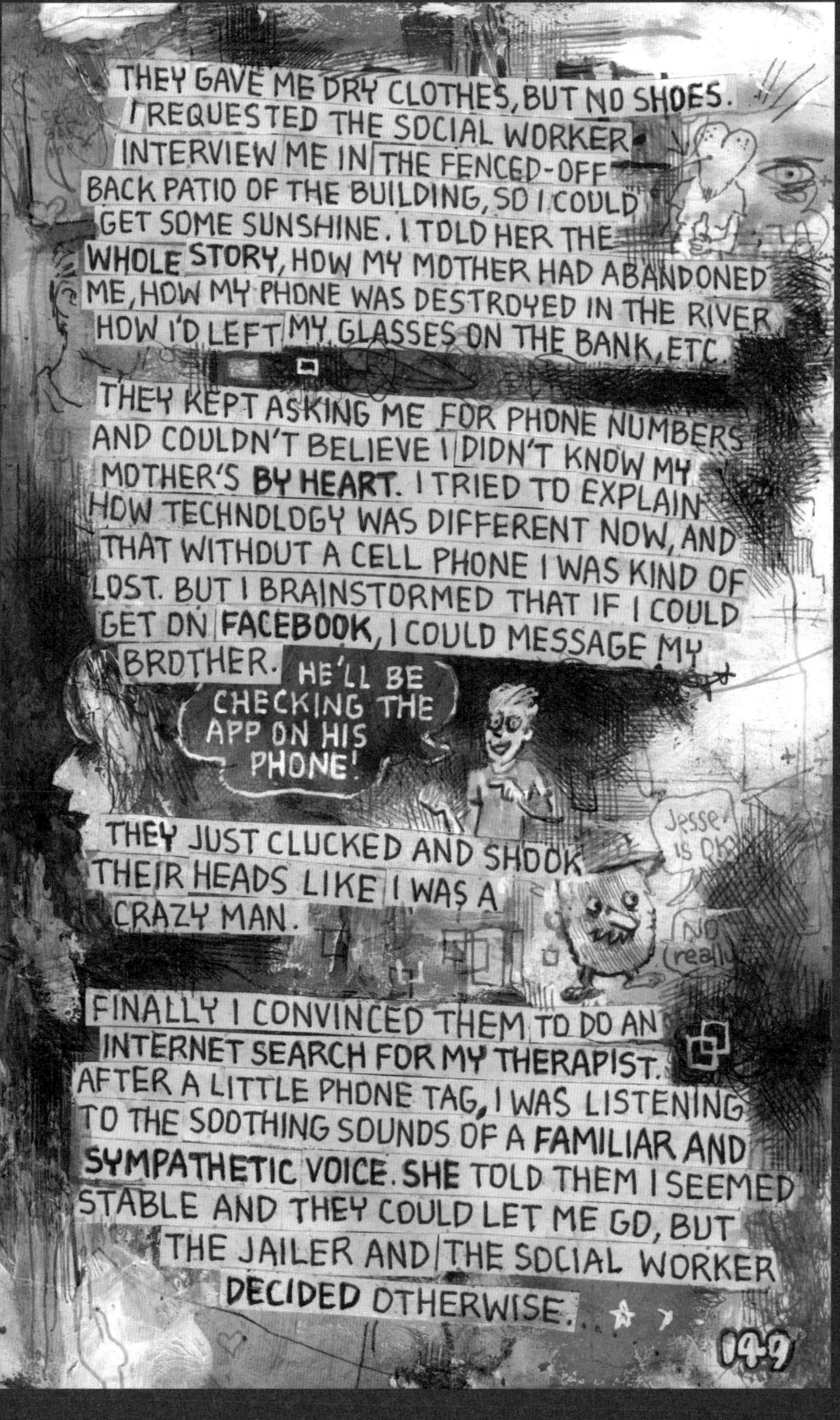
THEY GAVE ME DRY CLOTHES, BUT NO SHOES. I REQUESTED THE SOCIAL WORKER INTERVIEW ME IN THE FENCED-OFF BACK PATIO OF THE BUILDING, SO I COULD GET SOME SUNSHINE. I TOLD HER THE WHOLE STORY, HOW MY MOTHER HAD ABANDONED ME, HOW MY PHONE WAS DESTROYED IN THE RIVER HOW I'D LEFT MY GLASSES ON THE BANK, ETC.
THEY KEPT ASKING ME FOR PHONE NUMBERS AND COULDN'T BELIEVE I DIDN'T KNOW MY MOTHER'S BY HEART. I TRIED TO EXPLAIN HOW TECHNOLOGY WAS DIFFERENT NOW, AND THAT WITHOUT A CELL PHONE I WAS KIND OF LOST. BUT I BRAINSTORMED THAT IF I COULD GET ON FACEBOOK, I COULD MESSAGE MY BROTHER.
HE'LL BE CHECKING THE APP ON HIS PHONE!
THEY JUST CLUCKED AND SHOOK THEIR HEADS LIKE I WAS A CRAZY MAN.
Jesse is OK
NO
FINALLY I CONVINCED THEM TO DO AN INTERNET SEARCH FOR MY THERAPIST. AFTER A LITTLE PHONE TAG, I WAS LISTENING TO THE SOOTHING SOUNDS OF A FAMILIAR AND SYMPATHETIC VOICE. SHE TOLD THEM I SEEMED STABLE AND THEY COULD LET ME GO, BUT THE JAILER AND THE SOCIAL WORKER DECIDED OTHERWISE.

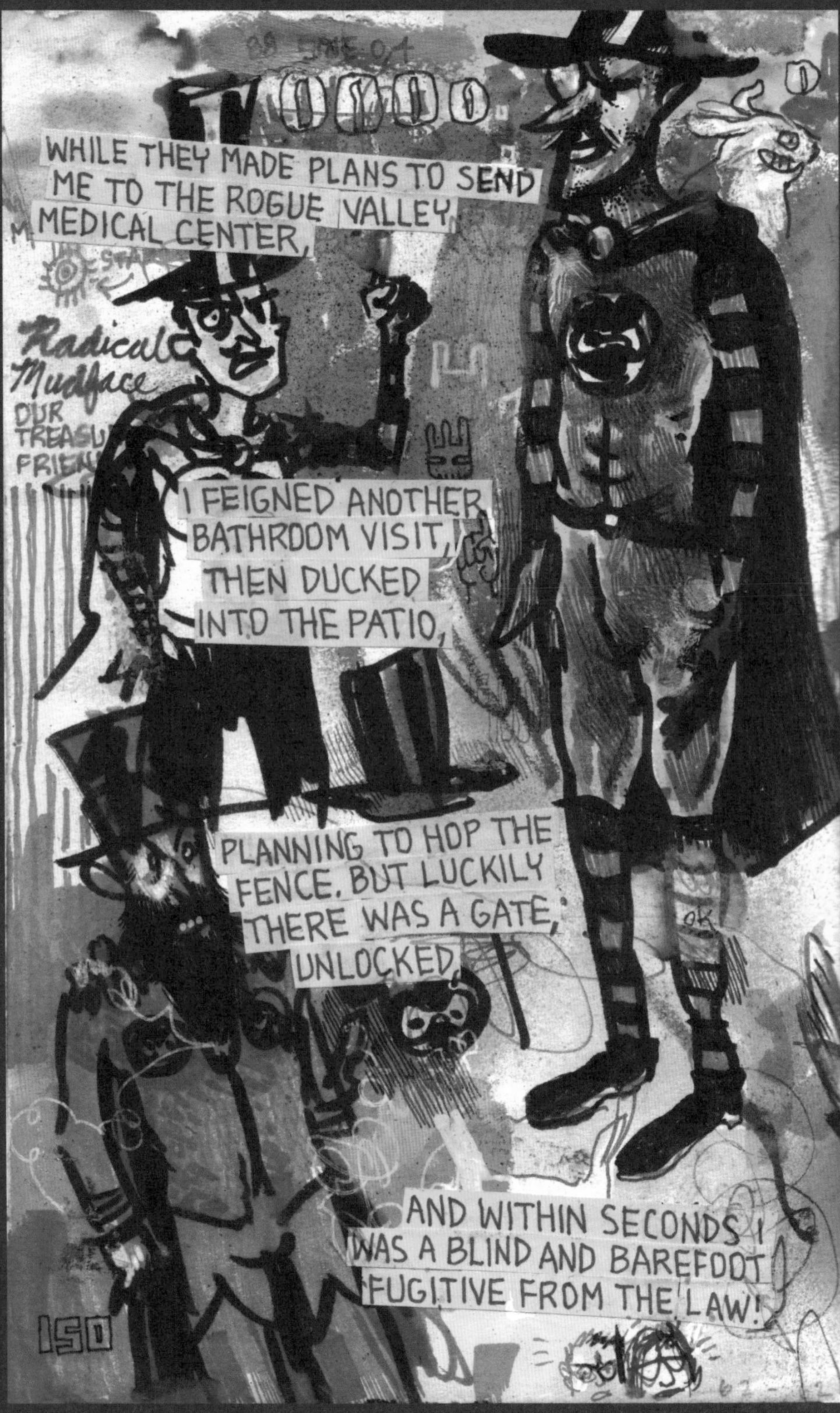

WHILE THEY MADE PLANS TO SEND ME TO THE ROGUE VALLEY MEDICAL CENTER,
Radical Mudface
I FEIGNED ANOTHER BATHROOM VISIT, THEN DUCKED INTO THE PATIO,
PLANNING TO HOP THE FENCE. BUT LUCKILY THERE WAS A GATE, UNLOCKED,
AND WITHIN SECONDS I WAS A BLIND AND BAREFOOT FUGITIVE FROM THE LAW!

NUTRIAMAN
i love the crippling self-doubt... it keeps me going
WITCH BEARD
BEARS WITH BEARDS

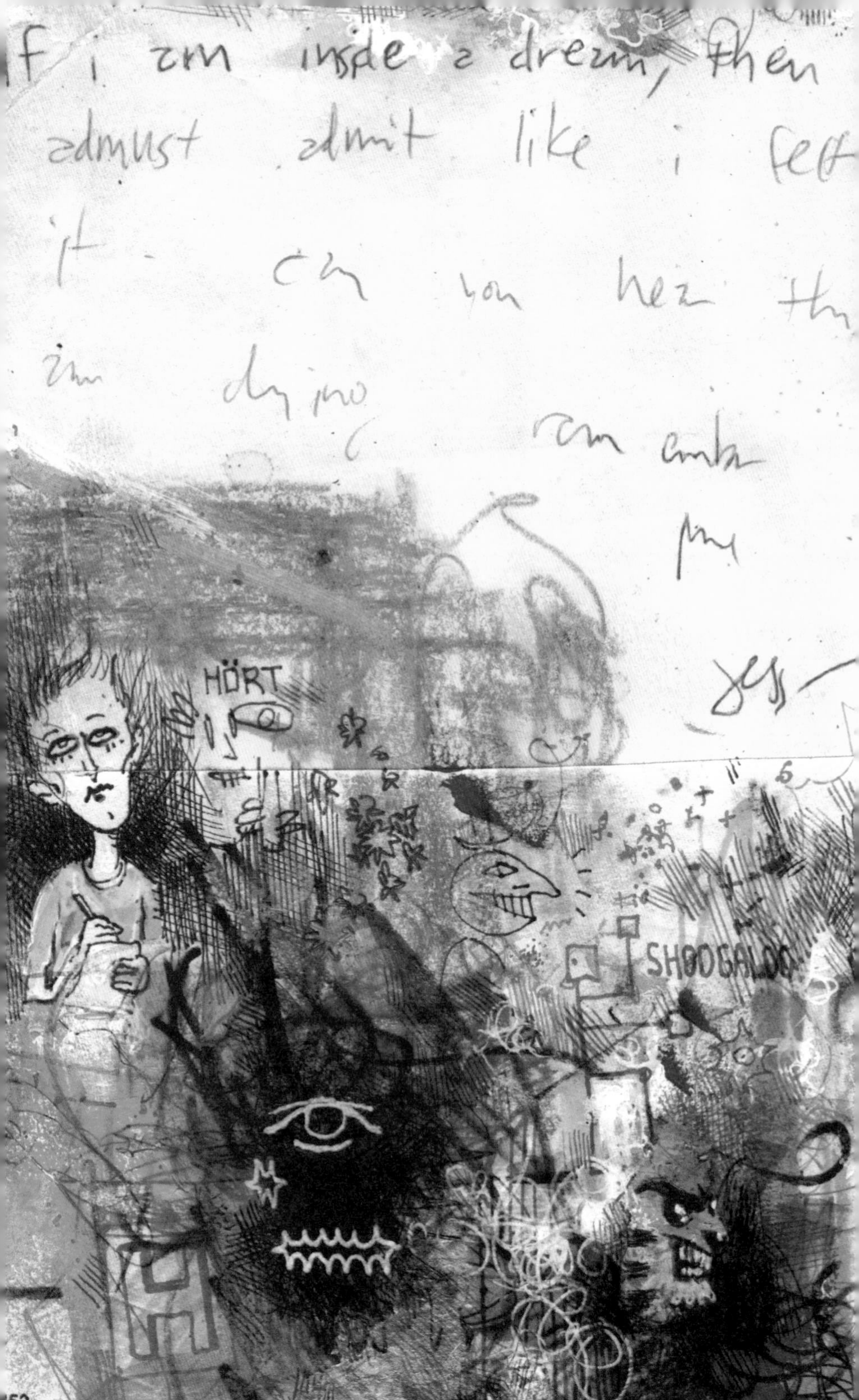
f i am inside a dream, then
admust admit like i feel
it
HÖRT

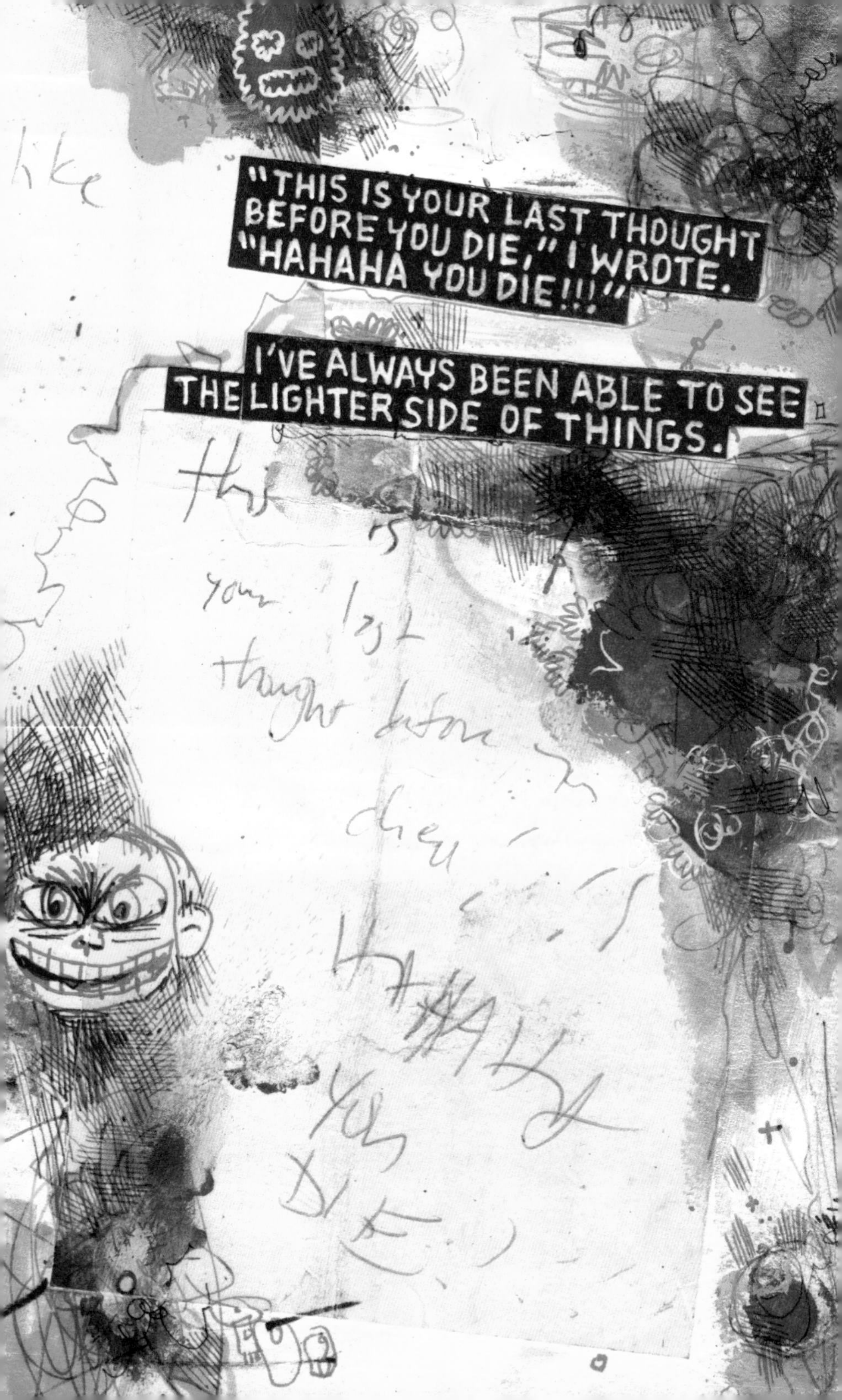
"THIS IS YOUR LAST THOUGHT BEFORE YOU DIE," I WROTE. "HAHAHA YOU DIE!!!"
I'VE ALWAYS BEEN ABLE TO SEE THE LIGHTER SIDE OF THINGS.

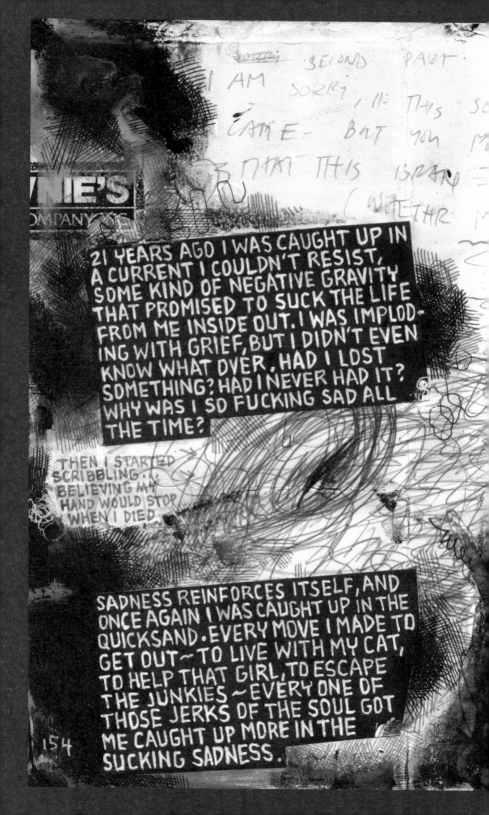

SORRY SECOND PART.
I AM SORRY, IF THIS SO
CAME - BUT YOU M
THAT THIS BRAN
(WHETHR

WINIE'S
COMPANY IN

21 YEARS AGO I WAS CAUGHT UP IN A CURRENT I COULDN'T RESIST, SOME KIND OF NEGATIVE GRAVITY THAT PROMISED TO SUCK THE LIFE FROM ME INSIDE OUT. I WAS IMPLODING WITH GRIEF, BUT I DIDN'T EVEN KNOW WHAT OVER. HAD I LOST SOMETHING? HAD I NEVER HAD IT? WHY WAS I SO FUCKING SAD ALL THE TIME?

THEN I STARTED SCRIBBLING, BELIEVING MY HAND WOULD STOP WHEN I DIED.

154

SADNESS REINFORCES ITSELF, AND ONCE AGAIN I WAS CAUGHT UP IN THE QUICKSAND. EVERY MOVE I MADE TO GET OUT ~ TO LIVE WITH MY CAT, TO HELP THAT GIRL, TO ESCAPE THE JUNKIES ~ EVERY ONE OF THOSE JERKS OF THE SOUL GOT ME CAUGHT UP MORE IN THE SUCKING SADNESS.

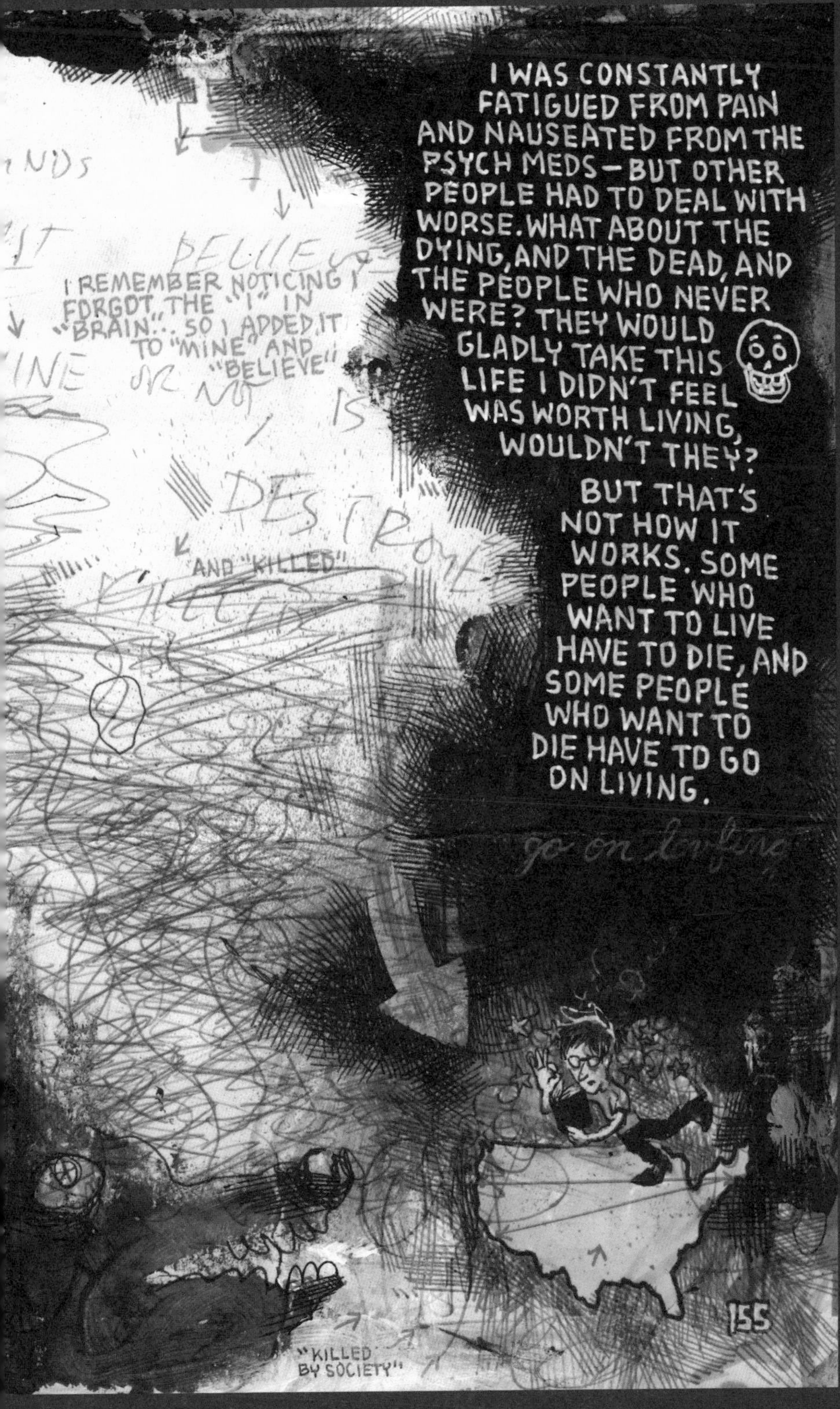
I WAS CONSTANTLY FATIGUED FROM PAIN AND NAUSEATED FROM THE PSYCH MEDS—BUT OTHER PEOPLE HAD TO DEAL WITH WORSE. WHAT ABOUT THE DYING, AND THE DEAD, AND THE PEOPLE WHO NEVER WERE? THEY WOULD GLADLY TAKE THIS LIFE I DIDN'T FEEL WAS WORTH LIVING, WOULDN'T THEY?
BUT THAT'S NOT HOW IT WORKS. SOME PEOPLE WHO WANT TO LIVE HAVE TO DIE, AND SOME PEOPLE WHO WANT TO DIE HAVE TO GO ON LIVING.
I REMEMBER NOTICING I FORGOT THE "I" IN "BRAIN"... SO I ADDED IT TO "MINE" AND "BELIEVE"
AND "KILLED"
go on loving
"KILLED BY SOCIETY"

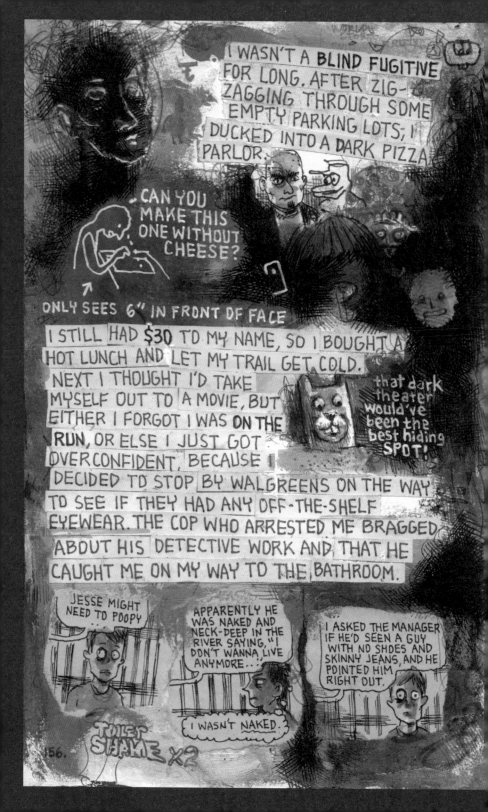

I WASN'T A **BLIND FUGITIVE** FOR LONG. AFTER ZIG-ZAGGING THROUGH SOME EMPTY PARKING LOTS, I DUCKED INTO A DARK PIZZA PARLOR.

CAN YOU MAKE THIS ONE WITHOUT CHEESE?

ONLY SEES 6" IN FRONT OF FACE

I STILL HAD $30 TO MY NAME, SO I BOUGHT A HOT LUNCH AND LET MY TRAIL GET COLD. NEXT I THOUGHT I'D TAKE MYSELF OUT TO A MOVIE, BUT EITHER I FORGOT I WAS **ON THE RUN**, OR ELSE I JUST GOT OVERCONFIDENT, BECAUSE I DECIDED TO STOP BY WALGREENS ON THE WAY TO SEE IF THEY HAD ANY OFF-THE-SHELF EYEWEAR. THE COP WHO ARRESTED ME BRAGGED ABOUT HIS DETECTIVE WORK AND THAT HE CAUGHT ME ON MY WAY TO THE BATHROOM.

that dark theater would've been the best hiding SPOT!

JESSE MIGHT NEED TO POOPY...

APPARENTLY HE WAS NAKED AND NECK-DEEP IN THE RIVER SAYING, "I DON'T WANNA LIVE ANYMORE..."

I WASN'T NAKED.

I ASKED THE MANAGER IF HE'D SEEN A GUY WITH NO SHOES AND SKINNY JEANS, AND HE POINTED HIM RIGHT OUT.

TOILET SHAKE x2

156.

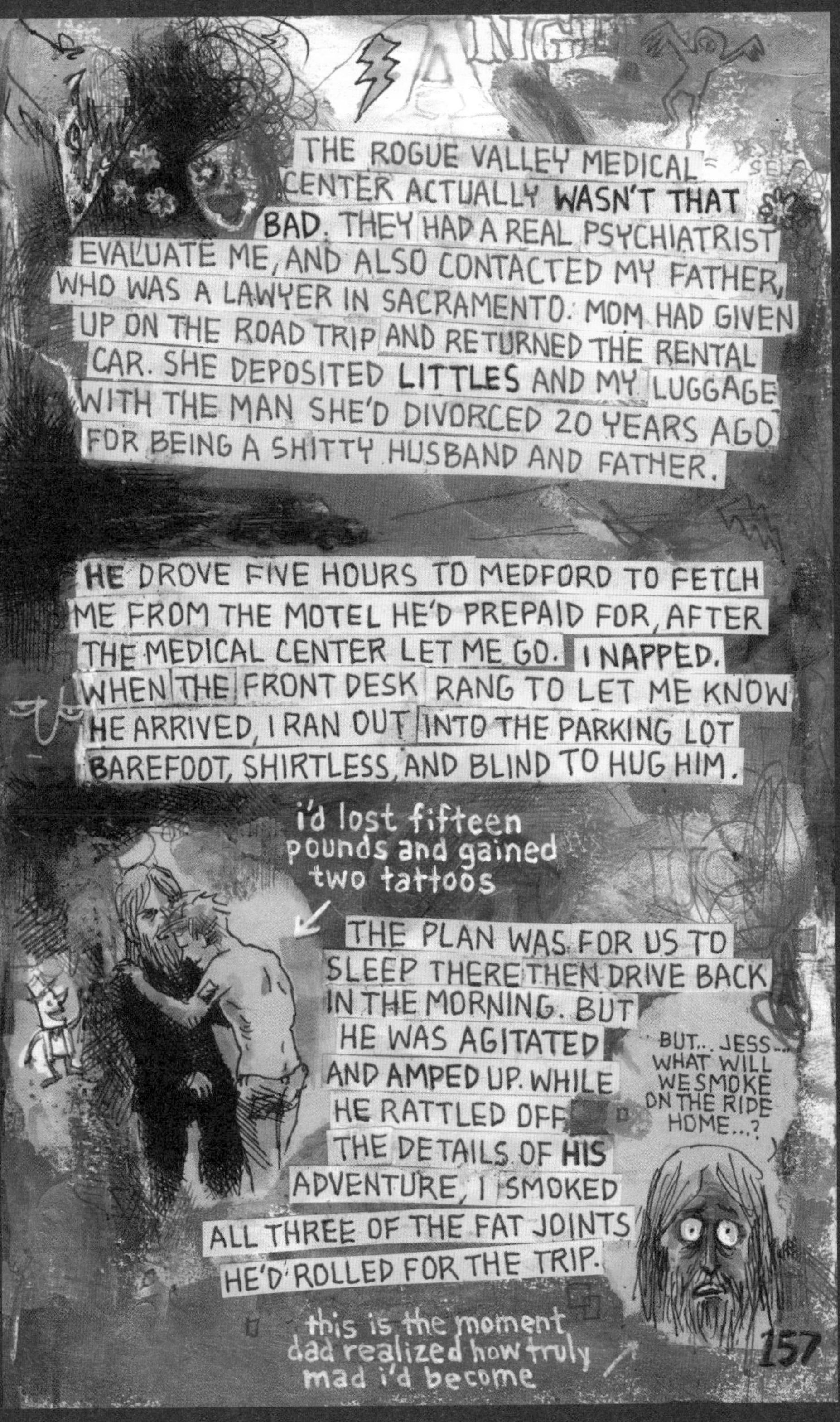
THE ROGUE VALLEY MEDICAL CENTER ACTUALLY WASN'T THAT BAD. THEY HAD A REAL PSYCHIATRIST EVALUATE ME, AND ALSO CONTACTED MY FATHER, WHO WAS A LAWYER IN SACRAMENTO. MOM HAD GIVEN UP ON THE ROAD TRIP AND RETURNED THE RENTAL CAR. SHE DEPOSITED LITTLES AND MY LUGGAGE WITH THE MAN SHE'D DIVORCED 20 YEARS AGO FOR BEING A SHITTY HUSBAND AND FATHER.
HE DROVE FIVE HOURS TO MEDFORD TO FETCH ME FROM THE MOTEL HE'D PREPAID FOR, AFTER THE MEDICAL CENTER LET ME GO. I NAPPED. WHEN THE FRONT DESK RANG TO LET ME KNOW HE ARRIVED, I RAN OUT INTO THE PARKING LOT BAREFOOT, SHIRTLESS, AND BLIND TO HUG HIM.
i'd lost fifteen pounds and gained two tattoos
THE PLAN WAS FOR US TO SLEEP THERE THEN DRIVE BACK IN THE MORNING. BUT HE WAS AGITATED AND AMPED UP. WHILE HE RATTLED OFF THE DETAILS OF HIS ADVENTURE, I SMOKED ALL THREE OF THE FAT JOINTS HE'D ROLLED FOR THE TRIP.
BUT... JESS... WHAT WILL WE SMOKE ON THE RIDE HOME...?
this is the moment dad realized how truly mad i'd become

WITHIN AN HOUR WE WERE IN THE CAR. WE GOT TO HIS "CAVE" AT DAWN. HE LAID DOWN ON THE COUCH AND DIRECTED ME TO THE BED, WHERE I CURLED UP WITH LITTLES..I WANTED TO SLEEP FOREVER, BUT WOKE UP TO DAD SCREAMING AT SOME NEIGHBORS.

LATER WE WENT TO SAFEWAY FOR GROCERIES AND BEER. A MAN BACKING OUT OF HIS PARKING SPOT WAS HEADED FOR DAD, SO I TUGGED HIM ALONG. WHEN HE REALIZED WHAT WAS HAPPENING, DAD LET THE DRIVER KNOW TOO.

"CONSCI...

2 E G3

I AM AN ELEMENT OF THE REAL"

YOU DUMB FUCKER!

HE IMMEDIATELY PUT ON A HAPPY FACE AND FOLLOWED UP WITH SOME FATHERLY WISDOM..

KICK

SEE, SON... THAT'S HOW YOU TREAT PEOPLE.

I THOUGHT IT WAS IRONIC THAT DAD DIDN'T THANK ME, BUT LATER CHRIS POINTED OUT THAT I SHOULD HAVE LET HIM GET HIT SO HE COULD SUE THE GUY.

MORAL RELATIVITY!!!

158

I COULDN'T TAKE ALL THE YELLING AND KICKING. MY BAND WAS PICKING ME UP AT 5 PM THE NEXT DAY, SO I ONLY HAD TO SURVIVE 24 MORE HOURS WITH DAD. I TOLD HIM I NEEDED TO GO OUT FOR SOME AIR.

I'M WORRIED ABOUT YOU.

I'M OK.

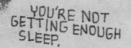

YOU'RE NOT GETTING ENOUGH SLEEP.

ACTUALLY, ACCORDING TO MY CHART, I'M AVERAGING 9 HRS/DAY!

MAYBE YOU COULD USE SOME MORE SLEEP...

YOU'RE NOT LISTENING.

A FEW BLOCKS DOWN THE STREET, I HEARD SOMEONE CALL OUT.

HEY!

WHAT'S UP

YOU SEEM COOL

WANT TO SMOKE DMT WITH US?

OF COURSE.

SMOKING DRUGS WITH HIPSTER KIDS SOUNDED WAY MORE FUN THAN GETTING LIFE LESSONS FROM DAD. BUT THERE WASN'T MUCH DMT~ BARELY ENOUGH TO GET ONE PERSON HIGH. THE GIRL WHO OWNED THE APARTMENT, AND THE DRUGS, DECIDED TO SPLIT IT EVENLY BETWEEN THE SIX PEOPLE AT HER PARTY. THEN SHE SMOKED FIRST.

WHOA THE COLORS!

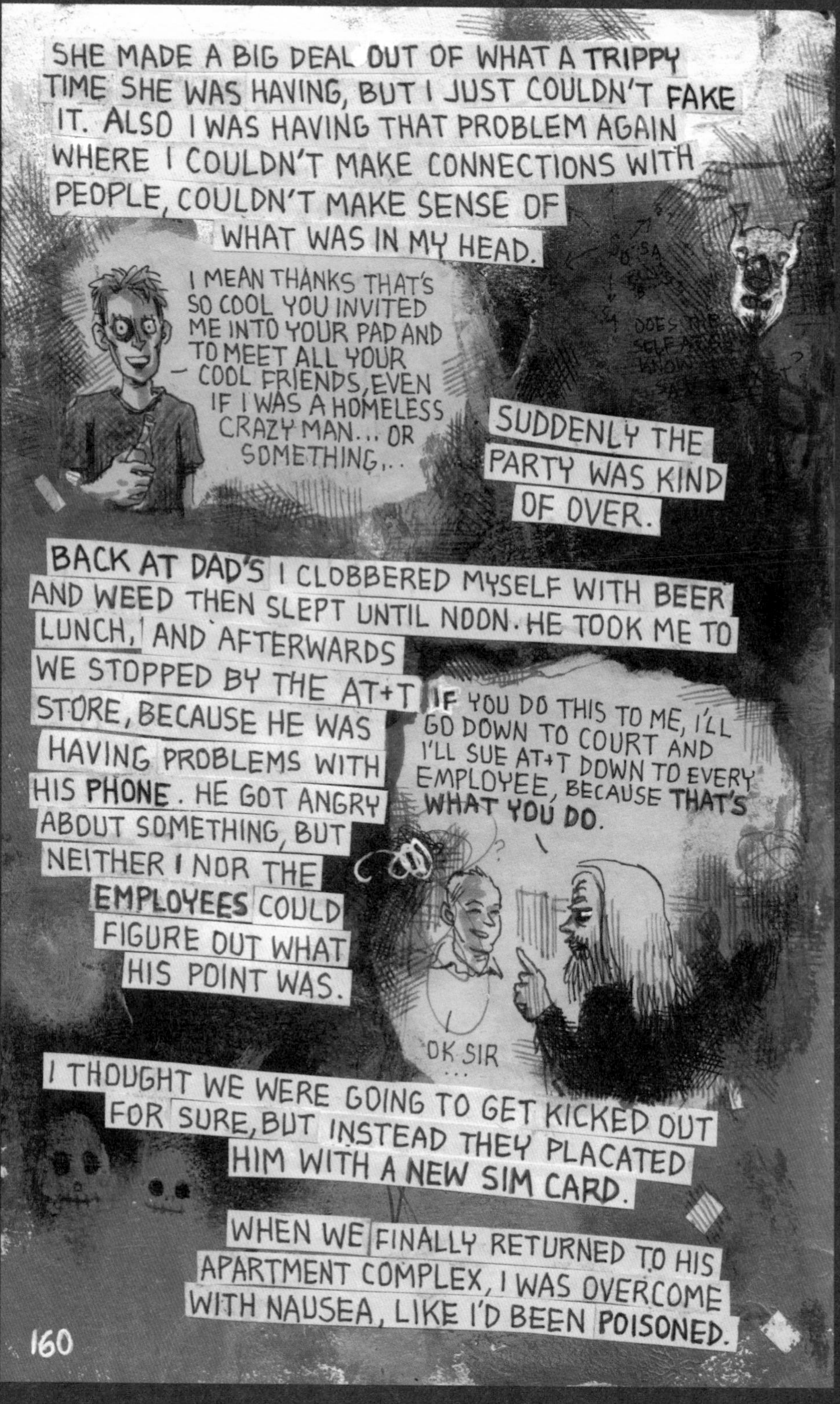
SHE MADE A BIG DEAL OUT OF WHAT A TRIPPY TIME SHE WAS HAVING, BUT I JUST COULDN'T FAKE IT. ALSO I WAS HAVING THAT PROBLEM AGAIN WHERE I COULDN'T MAKE CONNECTIONS WITH PEOPLE, COULDN'T MAKE SENSE OF WHAT WAS IN MY HEAD.
I MEAN THANKS THAT'S SO COOL YOU INVITED ME INTO YOUR PAD AND TO MEET ALL YOUR COOL FRIENDS, EVEN IF I WAS A HOMELESS CRAZY MAN... OR SOMETHING...
SUDDENLY THE PARTY WAS KIND OF OVER.
BACK AT DAD'S I CLOBBERED MYSELF WITH BEER AND WEED THEN SLEPT UNTIL NOON. HE TOOK ME TO LUNCH, AND AFTERWARDS WE STOPPED BY THE AT+T STORE, BECAUSE HE WAS HAVING PROBLEMS WITH HIS PHONE. HE GOT ANGRY ABOUT SOMETHING, BUT NEITHER I NOR THE EMPLOYEES COULD FIGURE OUT WHAT HIS POINT WAS.
IF YOU DO THIS TO ME, I'LL GO DOWN TO COURT AND I'LL SUE AT+T DOWN TO EVERY EMPLOYEE, BECAUSE THAT'S WHAT YOU DO.
OK SIR ...
I THOUGHT WE WERE GOING TO GET KICKED OUT FOR SURE, BUT INSTEAD THEY PLACATED HIM WITH A NEW SIM CARD.
WHEN WE FINALLY RETURNED TO HIS APARTMENT COMPLEX, I WAS OVERCOME WITH NAUSEA, LIKE I'D BEEN POISONED.

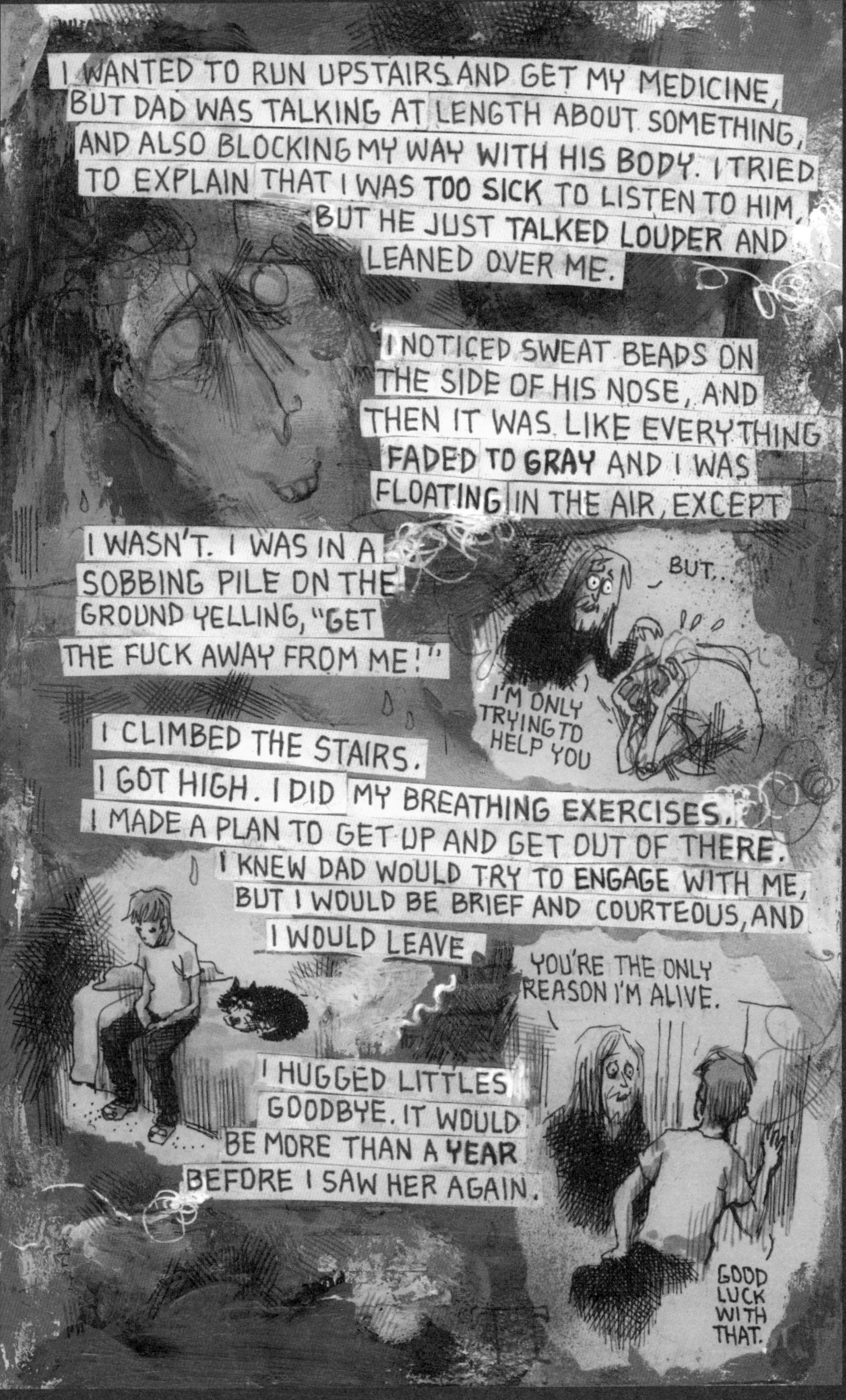
I WANTED TO RUN UPSTAIRS AND GET MY MEDICINE, BUT DAD WAS TALKING AT LENGTH ABOUT SOMETHING, AND ALSO BLOCKING MY WAY WITH HIS BODY. I TRIED TO EXPLAIN THAT I WAS TOO SICK TO LISTEN TO HIM, BUT HE JUST TALKED LOUDER AND LEANED OVER ME.
I NOTICED SWEAT BEADS ON THE SIDE OF HIS NOSE, AND THEN IT WAS LIKE EVERYTHING FADED TO GRAY AND I WAS FLOATING IN THE AIR, EXCEPT
I WASN'T. I WAS IN A SOBBING PILE ON THE GROUND YELLING, "GET THE FUCK AWAY FROM ME!"
BUT...
I'M ONLY TRYING TO HELP YOU
I CLIMBED THE STAIRS. I GOT HIGH. I DID MY BREATHING EXERCISES. I MADE A PLAN TO GET UP AND GET OUT OF THERE. I KNEW DAD WOULD TRY TO ENGAGE WITH ME, BUT I WOULD BE BRIEF AND COURTEOUS, AND I WOULD LEAVE.
YOU'RE THE ONLY REASON I'M ALIVE.
I HUGGED LITTLES GOODBYE. IT WOULD BE MORE THAN A YEAR BEFORE I SAW HER AGAIN.
GOOD LUCK WITH THAT.

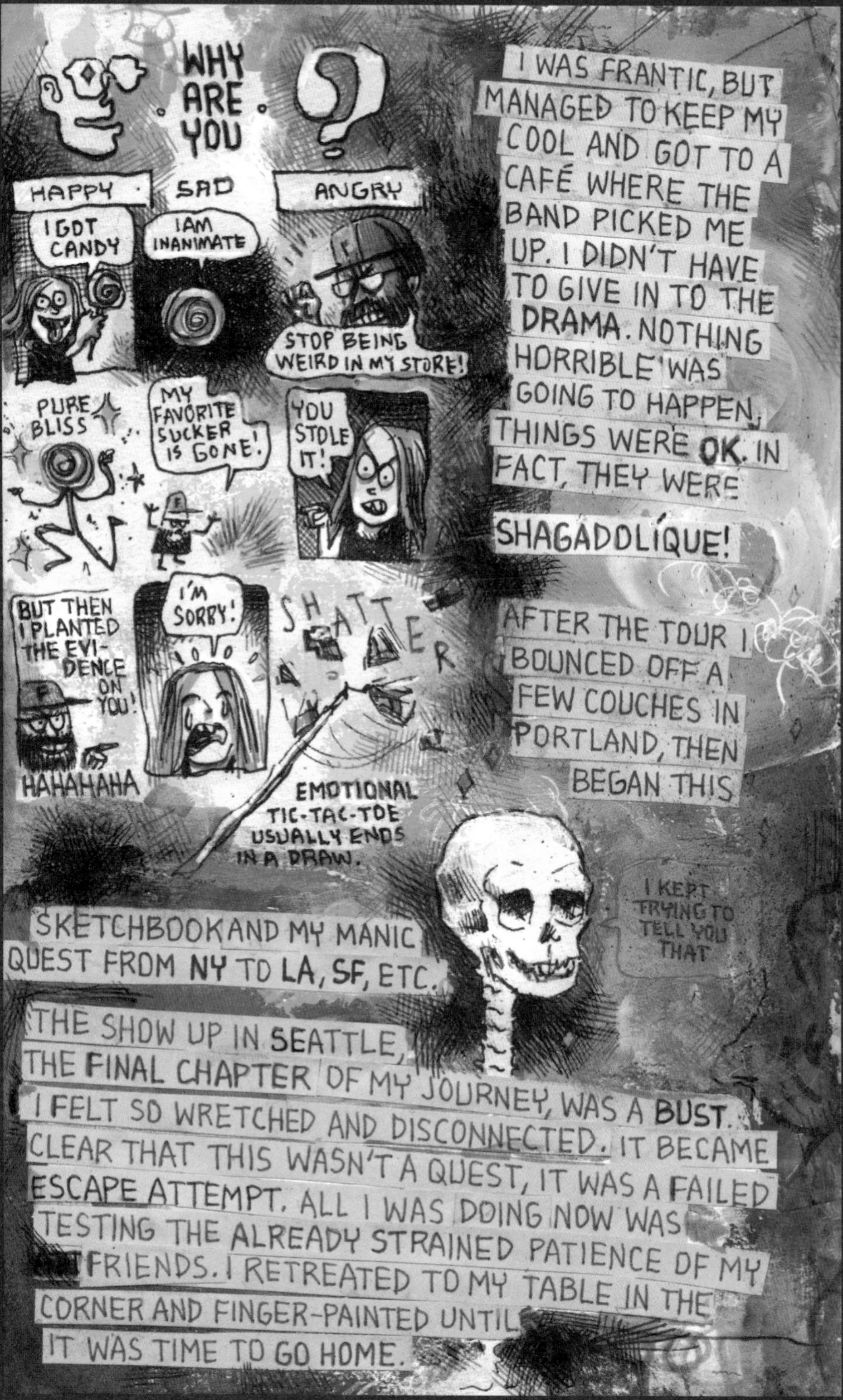
WHY ARE YOU
HAPPY
SAD
ANGRY
I GOT CANDY
I AM INANIMATE
STOP BEING WEIRD IN MY STORE!
PURE BLISS
MY FAVORITE SUCKER IS GONE!
YOU STOLE IT!
BUT THEN I PLANTED THE EVIDENCE ON YOU!
HAHAHAHA
I'M SORRY!
SHATTER
EMOTIONAL TIC-TAC-TOE USUALLY ENDS IN A DRAW.
I WAS FRANTIC, BUT MANAGED TO KEEP MY COOL AND GOT TO A CAFÉ WHERE THE BAND PICKED ME UP. I DIDN'T HAVE TO GIVE IN TO THE DRAMA. NOTHING HORRIBLE WAS GOING TO HAPPEN. THINGS WERE OK. IN FACT, THEY WERE
SHAGADOLIQUE!
AFTER THE TOUR I BOUNCED OFF A FEW COUCHES IN PORTLAND, THEN BEGAN THIS
SKETCHBOOK AND MY MANIC QUEST FROM NY TO LA, SF, ETC.
I KEPT TRYING TO TELL YOU THAT
THE SHOW UP IN SEATTLE, THE FINAL CHAPTER OF MY JOURNEY, WAS A BUST. I FELT SO WRETCHED AND DISCONNECTED. IT BECAME CLEAR THAT THIS WASN'T A QUEST, IT WAS A FAILED ESCAPE ATTEMPT. ALL I WAS DOING NOW WAS TESTING THE ALREADY STRAINED PATIENCE OF MY FRIENDS. I RETREATED TO MY TABLE IN THE CORNER AND FINGER-PAINTED UNTIL IT WAS TIME TO GO HOME.

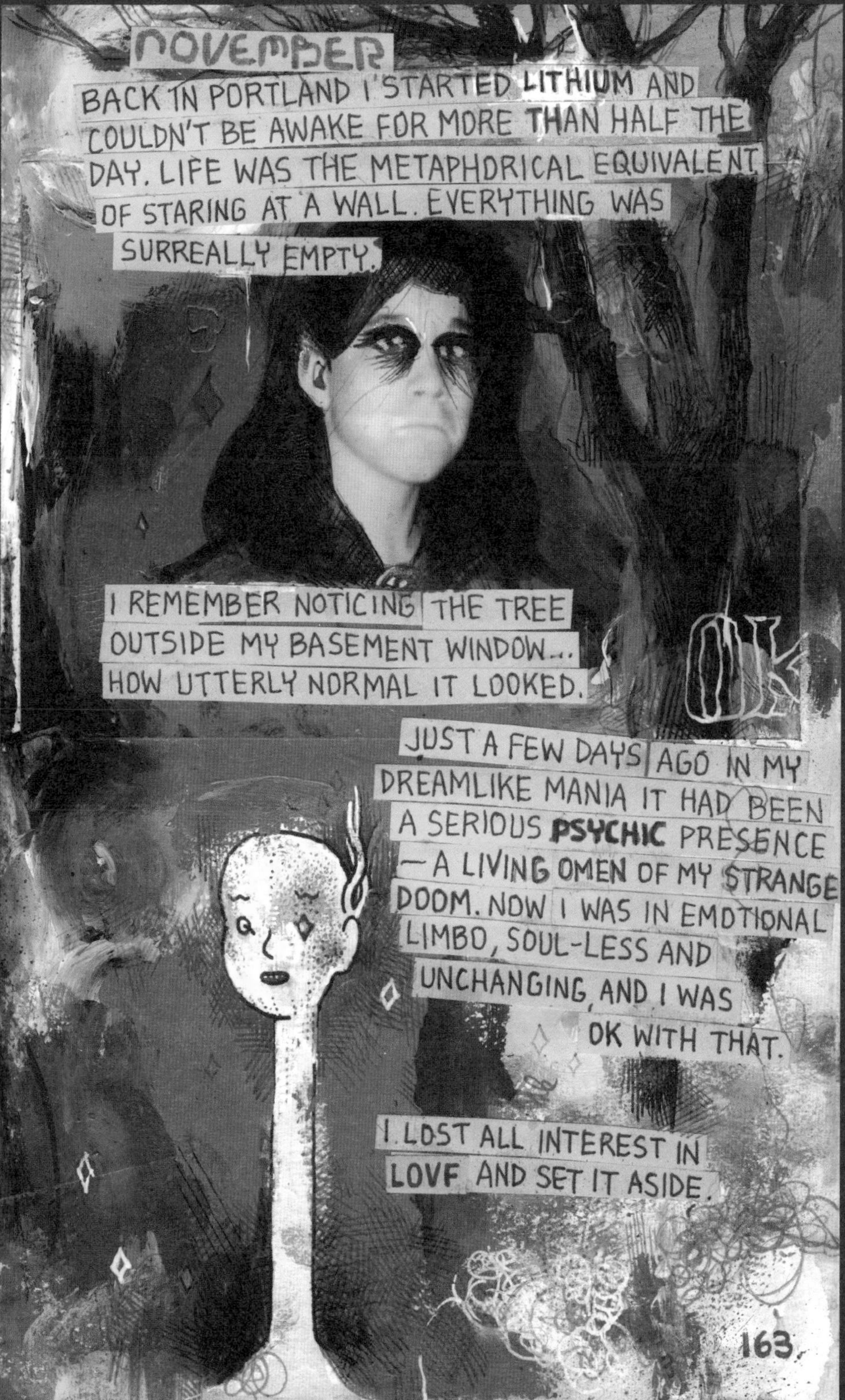
NOVEMBER
BACK IN PORTLAND I STARTED LITHIUM AND COULDN'T BE AWAKE FOR MORE THAN HALF THE DAY. LIFE WAS THE METAPHORICAL EQUIVALENT OF STARING AT A WALL. EVERYTHING WAS SURREALLY EMPTY.
I REMEMBER NOTICING THE TREE OUTSIDE MY BASEMENT WINDOW... HOW UTTERLY NORMAL IT LOOKED.
JUST A FEW DAYS AGO IN MY DREAMLIKE MANIA IT HAD BEEN A SERIOUS PSYCHIC PRESENCE — A LIVING OMEN OF MY STRANGE DOOM. NOW I WAS IN EMOTIONAL LIMBO, SOUL-LESS AND UNCHANGING, AND I WAS OK WITH THAT.
I LOST ALL INTEREST IN LOVE AND SET IT ASIDE.

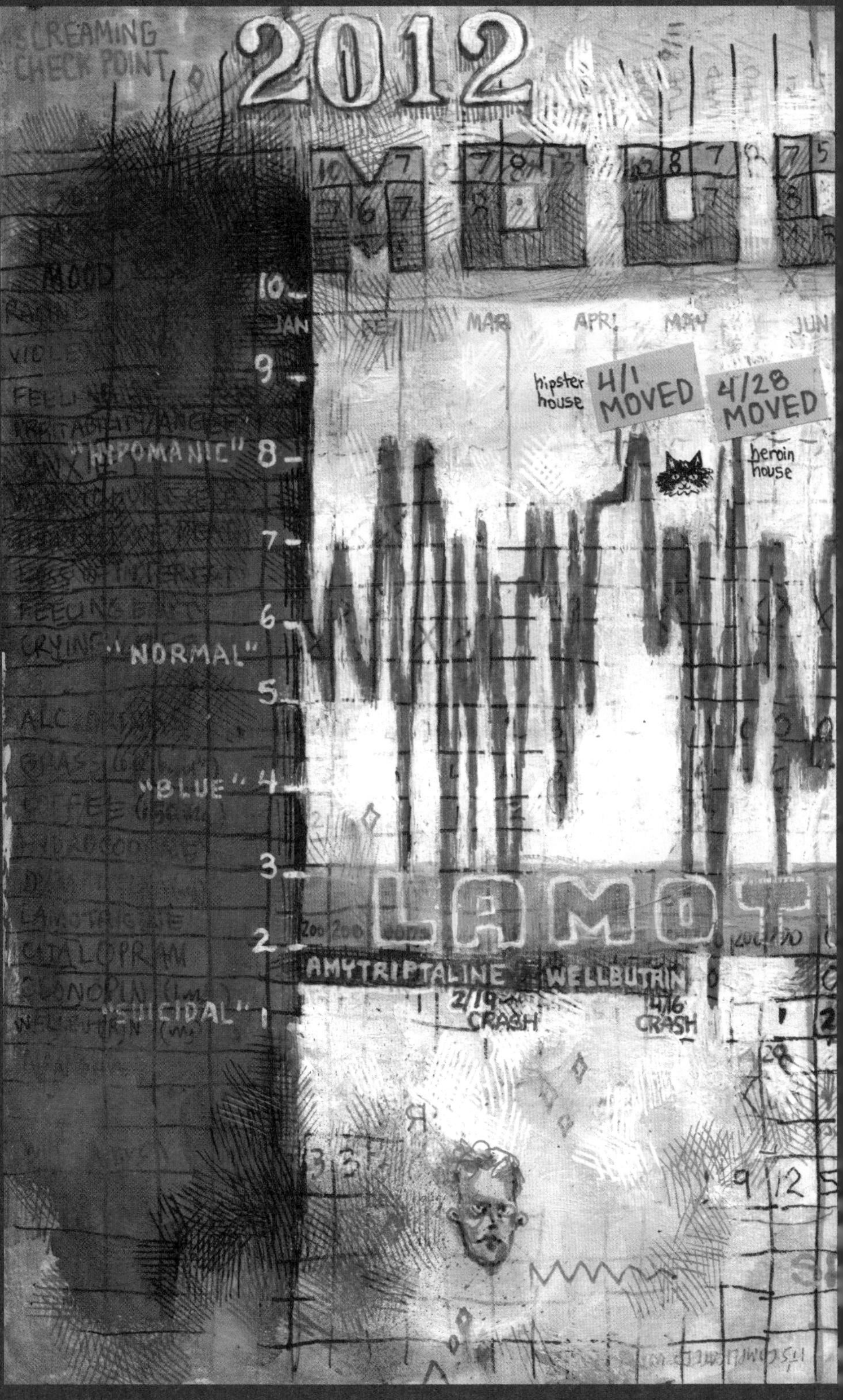
SCREAMING CHECK POINT
2012
MOOD
10
JAN
MAR
APR
MAY
JUN
9
hipster house
4/1 MOVED
4/28 MOVED
heroin house
8
"HYPOMANIC"
7
6
"NORMAL"
5
"BLUE"
4
3
LAMOT
2
AMYTRIPTALINE
WELLBUTRIN
2/19 CRASH
4/16 CRASH
"SUICIDAL"
1

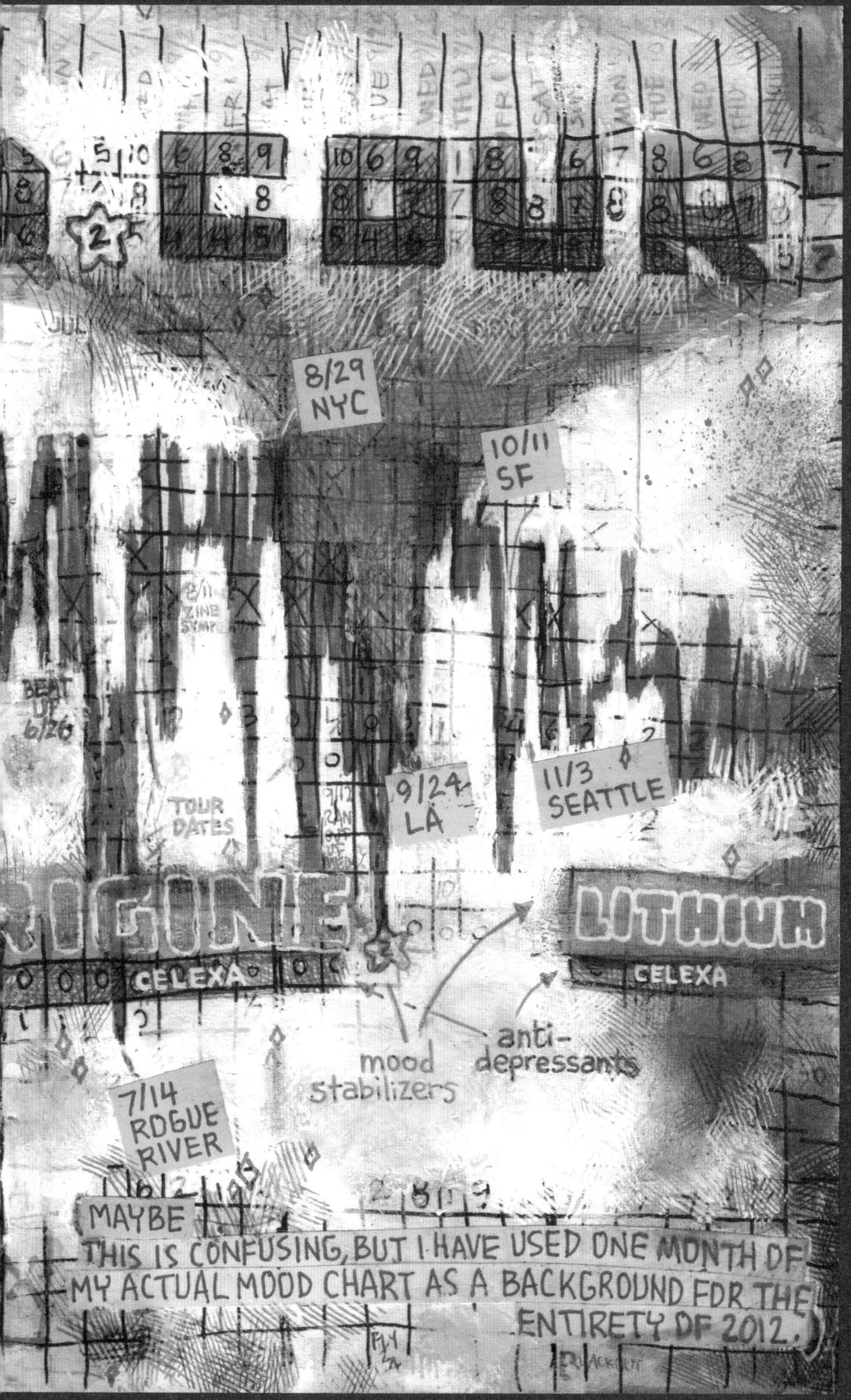
8/29
NYC
10/11
SF
8/11
ZINE
SYMP
BEAT
UP
6/26
TOUR
DATES
9/24
LA
11/3
SEATTLE
LITHIUM
CELEXA
CELEXA
mood
stabilizers
anti-
depressants
7/14
ROGUE
RIVER
MAYBE
THIS IS CONFUSING, BUT I HAVE USED ONE MONTH OF
MY ACTUAL MOOD CHART AS A BACKGROUND FOR THE
ENTIRETY OF 2012.

IN A FEW MONTHS I SETTLED
MY MEDS AND BEGAN TO WORK
AGAIN. I CROSS-HATCHED AND FINGER-
PAINTED LOVF, FLESHED OUT FIGURES,
AND ADDED A HALF-FORGOTTEN DREAM-
NARRATIVE, CORRODED BY MADNESS AND
SHROUDED BY MEDICATION. IT'S LIKE I FOUND
THE SKETCHBOOK OF A HOMELESS CRAZY MAN
AND MADE A STORY OUT OF IT. BUT THIS WAS
ALSO MY DIARY—I WAS THAT HOMELESS
CRAZY MAN.

LOVF WASN'T JUST A GUIDEBOOK, LOVF
BECAME MY MIRROR. I WANTED TO CAPTURE
HOW IT FELT WHILE I WAS HAVING THE
BEST AND WORST EXPERIENCES OF MY
LIFE. I TREATED EVERY DAY AS IF IT WAS
MY LAST—AS IF IT SHOULD BE MY LAST—
TAKING EVERYTHING IN AND EXPRESSING
MYSELF AS HARD AS I COULD. I WAS
PUBLISHING MYSELF.

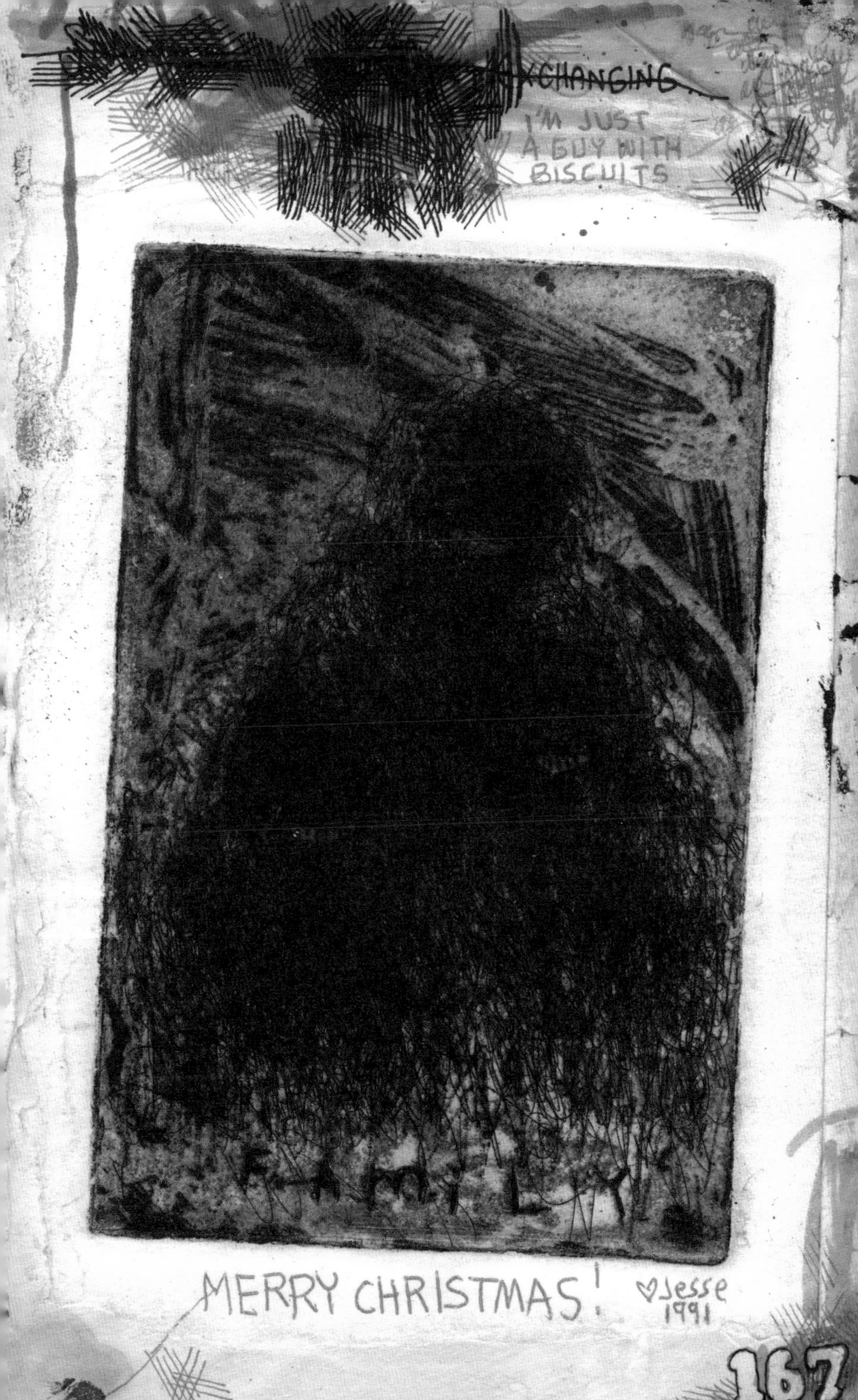

[redacted] CHANGING
I'M JUST A GUY WITH BISCUITS
MERRY CHRISTMAS!
♡Jesse 1991

OF COURSE LOVF IS A LIE—ITS EVENTS DECONSTRUCTED, REVERSE-ENGINEERED, AND DELIBERATELY OBFUSCATED; ITS CHARACTERS COMPROMISES OF REALITY, AESTHETIC EXPEDIENCIES DISGUISED FOR PRIVACY, THEN EXTRUDED INTO THE SYMBOLIC.

I DON'T KNOW WHAT I THINK OF LOVF ANYMORE. IT DOESN'T SEEM LIKE I'M THE PERSON WHO WROTE THIS BOOK, OR RATHER: I CAN'T IDENTIFY WITH A GUY WHO GETS UP EVERY DAY HOPING HE WILL BECOME SOMEONE ELSE, TRYING OUT DIFFERENT PERSONAS LIKE A KID WITH A TRUNK FULL OF COSTUMES... A GUY WHO LABELLED HIS BOOK "LOVE," THEN IMMEDIATELY CRINGED AT THE OSTENTATIOUS EMOTION, AND SMEARED IT INTO A NONSENSICAL WORD (PRONOUNCED "LAWVF"?). IT FEELS LIKE I DISAPPEARED AND SOME CREEP TOOK OVER MY LIFE, MESSED UP MY FINANCES, THREW OUT MY STUFF, ALIENATED MY FRIENDS, AND ULTIMATELY TRIED TO WIPE ME OUT.

AS FOR KOLDOR, HE MADE THE SAVING THROW VS POISON (HALF-OGRES HAVE A HIGH CONSTITUTION) AND RECOVERED AFTER ONE AWFUL NIGHT. THE FOLLOWING SPRING THEY SAW HIM AT A TAVERN IN THREEBURG, GOING ON ABOUT A THUNDER DRAGON...

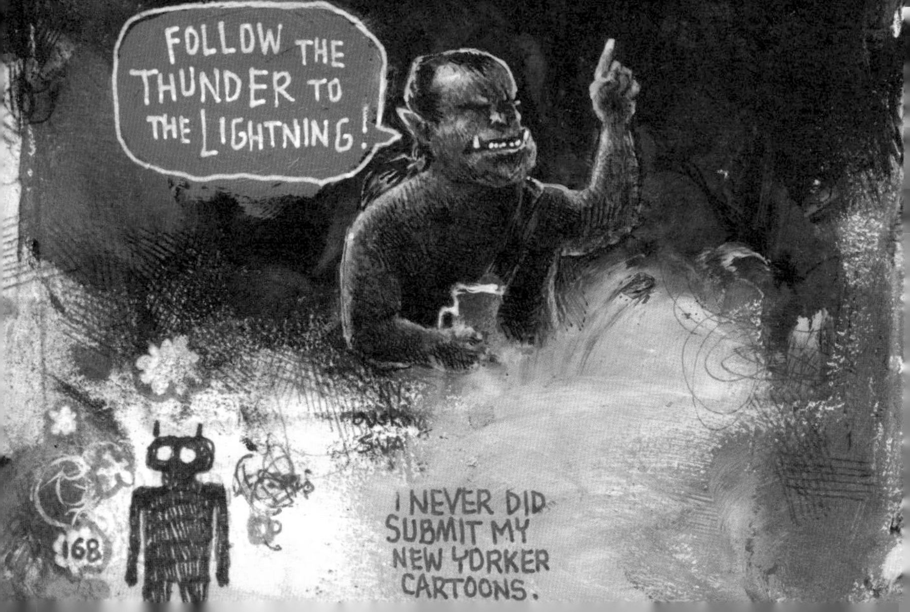

FOLLOW THE THUNDER TO THE LIGHTNING!
I NEVER DID SUBMIT MY NEW YORKER CARTOONS.

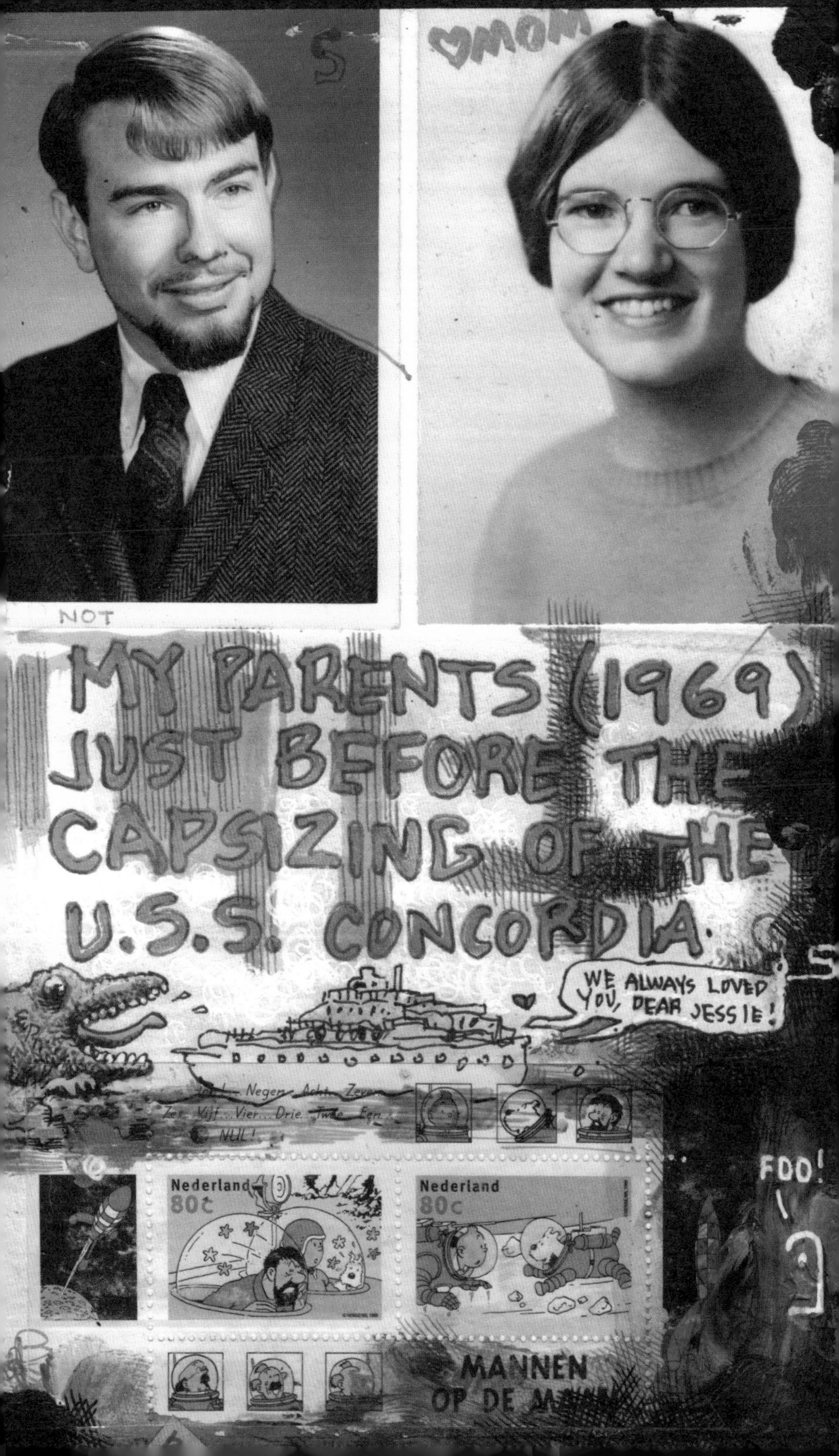
5
MOM
NOT
MY PARENTS (1969) JUST BEFORE THE CAPSIZING OF THE U.S.S. CONCORDIA.
WE ALWAYS LOVED YOU, DEAR JESSIE!
...Negen...Acht...Zeven...
Zes...Vijf...Vier...Drie...Twee...Een...
NUL!
Nederland 80c
Nederland 80c
FDO!
MANNEN
OP DE

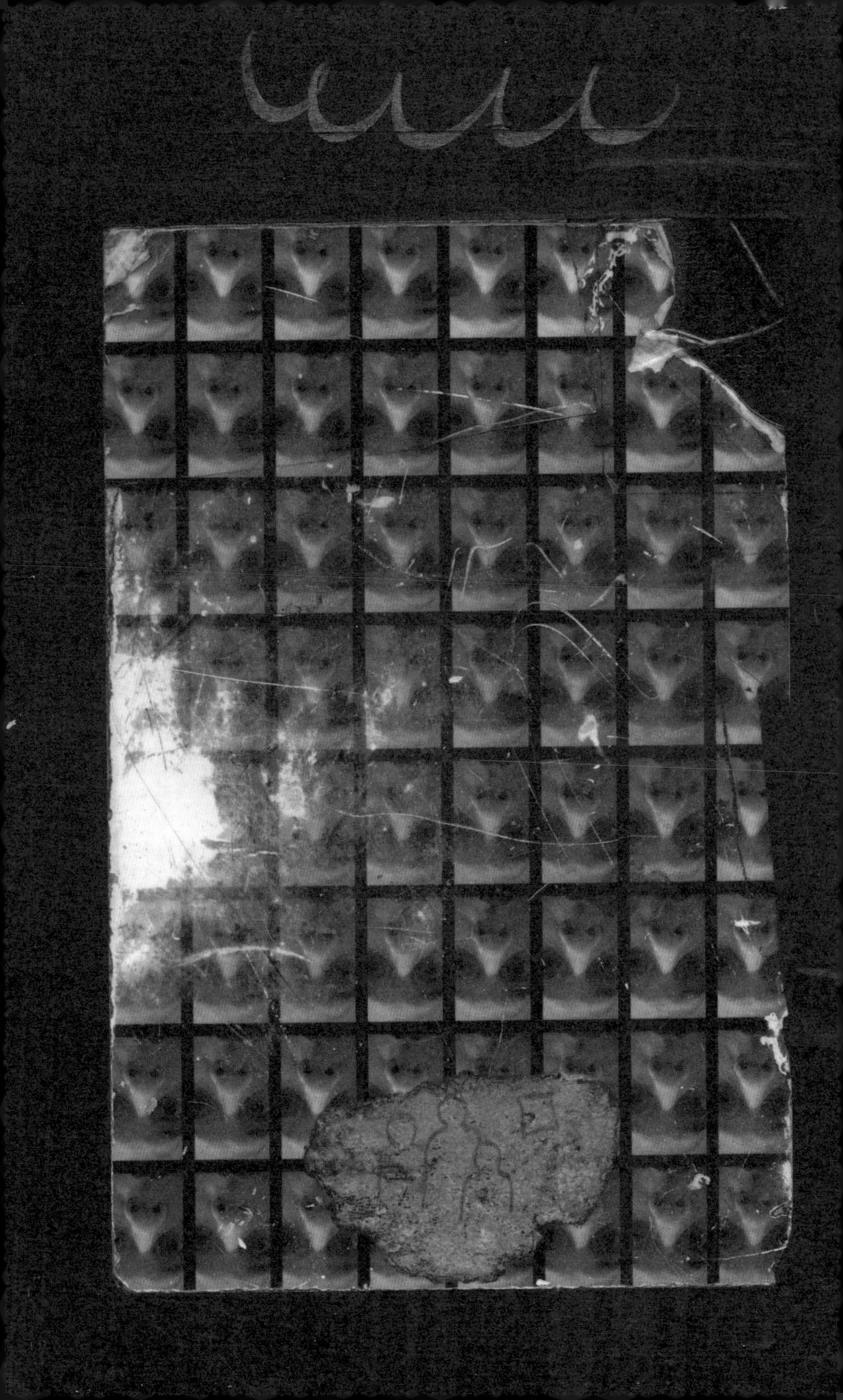

COLLABORATIONS

NICK ABADZIS (PG 53) TREVOR ALIXOPULOS (PG 85), ANDRICE ARP (PG 42-43), CHRIS BRANDT (PG 79,83), MARK CAMPOS (PG 23), BEN CATMULL (PG 115,162), RACHEL COTTON (PG 120-121), VANESSA DAVIS (PG 84), JOSH FRANKEL (PG 143), STEFAN GRUBER (PG 21,136,163), DAMIEN JAY (PG 90), MINTY LEWIS (PG 92), HELLEN JO (PG 93,94-95), NOMI KANE (PG 17), AMY KUTTAB (PG 35), HAZEL NEWLEVANT (PG 14,19,27,29,31,39,40,54,64,69), MARION NEWLEVANT (PG 65), THIEN PHAM (PG 112), JEN VAUGHN (PG 13), SHAWN WACO (PG 76) CALVIN WONG (PG 92), AND MICKEY ZACCHILLI (PG 57,58-59)

THANK YOU

TO ALL OF THE ABOVE FOR YOUR FRIENDSHIP AND TOLERANCE;

TO ROBYN CHAPMAN / PAPER ROCKET, WHO PUBLISHED AN EARLY VERSION OF THE NEW YORK CHAPTER;

TO RACHEL, JOHNNY, NOAM, FANTAGRAPHICS, ERIC, GARY, PJ, KEVIN, CRAIG, AND FAREL FOR HELP IN MAKING THIS A REAL BOOK; TO EVERYONE WHO SUPPORTED THE KICKSTARTER;

TO ALL OF THE PEOPLE WHO HARBORED ME WHILE I WAS IN THE GRIPS OF THIS STRANGENESS;

AND ESPECIALLY TO GARIET AND ORLY "MY BANDMATES," FOR THE SUPPORT, THE MAGIC, AND THE ROCKNROLL.

SE REKLAW LIVES IN PORTLAND, OREGON WITH
CAT LITTLES. HIS OTHER BOOKS INCLUDE
CH TAG, THE NIGHT OF YOUR LIFE, AND APPLICANT.